Budget Concepts
for Economic Analysis

Studies of Government Finance

TITLES PUBLISHED

Budget Concepts

for Economic Analysis

WILFRED LEWIS, Jr. *Editor*

Studies of Government Finance

THE BROOKINGS INSTITUTION

WASHINGTON, D.C.

Foreword

In October 1967, a commission composed of distinguished public officials and private experts delivered recommendations, as requested by the President, on format and definitions to be used in the budget of the United States. The *Report of the President's Commission on Budget Concepts* was favorably received and most of its recommendations were adopted in the budget transmitted by the President to the Congress for fiscal 1969, with an indication that other recommendations, especially those that require more time and effort, will be adopted in later years.

In the course of its deliberations the Commission consulted dozens of experts. In grappling with some of the more technical issues of particular interest to economists, it sponsored—jointly with the Brookings Institution—a two-day conference on July 31 and August 1, 1967, on budget concepts for economic analysis. The papers in the present volume were prepared for, or as a result of, that conference. Readers will note that this volume is reprinted from a larger Government publication, *Staff Papers and Other Materials Reviewed by the President's Commission on Budget Concepts* (1968), which contains most of the materials prepared in the course of the Commission's studies. Wilfred Lewis, Jr., who prepared the Introduction and acted as editor of this book, is a Senior Fellow of the Economic Studies Program at the Brookings Institution. He was on leave from Brookings from March to October 1967 as Research Director for the Commission.

The success of the conference was due in considerable measure to the organizing activities of Joseph A. Pechman and Samuel B. Chase, Jr., of the Brookings Institution, and Robert P. Mayo, who served as staff director of the Commission while on leave from the Continental Illinois National Bank and Trust Company of Chicago.

The conference was part of a special program of research and education on taxation and public expenditures, supervised by the National Committee on Government Finance and financed by a special grant from the Ford Foundation.

The various opinions are those of the authors and should not be attributed to the staff members, officers, or trustees of the Brookings Institution or the Ford Foundation or the institutions with which the authors are affiliated.

KERMIT GORDON
February 1968   *President*

THE BROOKINGS INSTITUTION is an independent organization devoted to nonpartisan research, education, and publication in economics, government, foreign policy, and the social sciences generally. Its principal purposes are to aid in the development of sound public policies and to promote public understanding of issues of national importance.

The Institution was founded December 8, 1927, to merge the activities of the Institute for Government Research, founded in 1916, the Institute of Economics, founded in 1922, and the Robert Brookings Graduate School of Economics and Government, founded in 1924.

The general administration of the Institution is the responsibility of a self-perpetuating Board of Trustees. The trustees are likewise charged with maintaining the independence of the staff and fostering the most favorable conditions for creative research and education. The immediate direction of the policies, program, and staff of the Institution is vested in the President, assisted by an advisory council chosen from the staff of the Institution.

In publishing a study, the Institution presents it as a competent treatment of a subject worthy of public consideration. The interpretations and conclusions in such publications are those of the author or authors and do not purport to represent the views of the other staff members, officers, or trustees of the Brookings Institution.

Studies of Government Finance

Studies of Government Finance is a special program of research and education in taxation and government expenditures at the federal, state, and local levels. This program, which is supported by a special grant from the Ford Foundation, was undertaken and supervised by the National Committee on Government Finance appointed by the trustees of the Brookings Institution.

MEMBERS OF THE ADVISORY COMMITTEE

Contents

WILFRED LEWIS, JR.
The Brookings Institution

Introduction

The papers in this volume fall into two major areas that were the subjects of a two-day conference of experts sponsored by the President's Commission on Budget Concepts and the Brookings Institution on July 31 and August 1, 1967. The first day dealt with the treatment of loans and financial transactions for which George F. Break of the University of California (Berkeley) prepared a background paper. The Break paper and two earlier papers that had been prepared by the Commission staff, reviewed earlier by the Commission itself, and subsequently furnished to the conference participants as well, appear in Part I of this volume along with invited comments by Richard Goode, Arthur M. Okun, and Herbert Stein. Part II includes papers dealing with fiscal impact discussed on the second day of the conference. These include Edward M. Gramlich's, "Measures of the Aggregate Demand Impact of the Federal Budget," and Harvey Galper's, "The Timing of Federal Expenditure Impacts," as well as the invited comments on these two papers prepared by E. Cary Brown, Warren L. Smith, and Paul J. Taubman. Later comments by conference participants Glenn Burress and Charls Walker, Samuel B. Chase, Jr., Gary Fromm, Michael E. Levy, Carl H. Madden, and Murray L. Weidenbaum, prepared within a few days following the conference, did not confine themselves entirely to one or the other of these topics but touched on both of them. These are reproduced in Part III.

The conference proceedings were summarized by David J. Ott whose report, reprinted in Part IV, was prepared for the benefit of Commission members unable to attend the conference or not represented by their own observers. The present introduction, therefore, is not another summary of the conference itself, but rather a series of further observations that are possible now that the Commission has made its decisions, filed its report, and received an indication of substantial acceptance of its recommendations by the Executive Branch of the Government. It also includes some comments and observations arising from the author's close association with the Commission during its short life.

LOANS: IN OR OUT?

One of the most difficult and time-consuming issues with which the Commission dealt, as well as a major topic of the conference with which the present volume is concerned, is how to treat Federal lending, borrowing, and similar financial transactions in the Federal budget. The question, stated in its most elementary terms, is whether Federal loan outlays should be treated like other Federal expenditures in calculating the overall budget surplus or deficit (as in the former administrative and consolidated cash budgets), or whether these should be excluded from the expenditure total, thus becoming offsets to Federal borrowing and other means of "financing" the budget deficit (as is implicitly the case in the Federal sector of the national income accounts [NIA]).

The major arguments on both sides of this question are well set forth in Parts I and IV. Goode and Stein prefer to include loans, while Okun strongly advocates their exclusion. Break's preference is to leave the loans in, but he would also put Federal borrowing "above the line," and he wants a clear segregation of the lending and financial categories. Break's approach would eliminate any simple overall surplus or deficit measure, substituting instead a full array of all income and outgo items including the financial ones.

A majority of the conference participants sided with Okun, a substantial minority with Goode and Stein, and very few with Break. I think it is not unfair to impute a certain amount of gamesmanship to this outcome, in the sense that several participants assigned high marks to Break's approach as perhaps the most "accurate," and even expressed a personal preference for it, but then recommended one of the more conventional approaches, even though second best, on the grounds that "the public" would not accept a budget statement that did not provide a simple clear surplus or deficit.

For those preferring the "loans out" (NIA) treatment, the compelling point—returned to again and again—is the need to analyze and explain the fiscal impact (that is, aggregate demand impact) of the budget in terms of direct income transactions. This need was not argued in terms of loans being less important than other expenditures, only sufficiently different in character as to require separate analysis. In this view, Federal loans admittedly have aggregate demand impacts, but so do other nonbudgetary transactions to which they are comparable, such as debt management and monetary policies, and should be analyzed in that context rather than as part of the budget.

The "loans in" advocates stressed that (1) the economic impacts of loans and other expenditures differ more in degree than in kind, and for "soft" loans there is hardly any difference at all; and (2) for managing the public finances, loans are as important as other expenditures in determining the gross needs for Treasury financing through taxes or borrowing. Perhaps not as much was made of another argument for "loans in" as could have been; namely, that (net) loans no less than transfer payments reflect use of resources under the direction of public policy, and ought therefore to be counted in describing the size of government and changes therein. This point is of no great analytical importance, perhaps, but undoubtedly relevant to congressional and public attitudes towards trends in public expenditures, a vital aspect of the President's budget in our peculiar system.

Stein argued that definitions of budget totals should be selected with at least some conscious attention to the effects of public and congressional attitudes on desirable levels and trends of Federal spending. In spite of the disclaimer by the "loans out" advocates that they do not mean to attribute any lesser importance to loan transactions, it is obvious that a fully below-the-line treatment of loans in the President's budget would not only produce lower totals but invite a distinct deemphasis of loans in public and congressional attention. Most participants, as well as the Commission members whom I observed, did not make any prejudices they may have held on this point very explicit. But casual observation suggests that those who think that government spending needs to be kept in as tight a check as possible were more likely to prefer a comprehensive budget including loans, while the "loans out" advocates were likely to have a more relaxed attitude towards government spending in general and loan outlays in particular. This is not to suggest any insincerity in the arguments put forward; only some predisposition, probably unintentional, in the importance attached to the different arguments.

All things considered, it is not surprising that in its report the Commission finally came down on both sides of the lending question, and proposed a budget format that presents the surplus or deficit both including loans and excluding them (see Table 1). It may be, then, that what now appears to be a consensus supporting the Commission's compromise may dissolve once again in controversy when the Government has had some experience with the new budget in actual use. However, while the Commission's approach is somewhat ambivalent, it does have one distinct advantage. It permits the two main purposes of a presidential budget—to explain the President's fiscal policy recommendations, and to present the array of his recommendations for appropriations for individual programs—to be pursued in a framework in which the relation between the two is clearer and more direct than now. This, in turn, may encourage some wholesome developments—a closer scrutiny by economists and the general public (as distinct from private interest groups) of the vital but mysterious appropriations process, and a closer attention by the Appropriations Committees of the Congress to the expenditure consequences and fiscal impact of their actions—matters historically of little apparent interest to them.

But this result will not come about unless the expenditure subbudget (the "receipt-expenditure account" in the Commission's jargon, more likely the "spending budget" or some such after once in use) is fully as useful for fiscal analysis as the NIA budget now is. This requires early attention to the important but unglamorous issue of seasonal adjustment that the Commission (justifiably, considering the time constraints under which it worked) ignored. Most users of the NIA Federal sector are really interested much more in the seasonally adjusted quarterly rates than in fiscal year totals. It is not easy to develop good seasonal adjustment methods for any official budget. Seasonal adjustment factors that lead to good results from an analytical standpoint

TABLE 1.—*Comparison of four types of budget*

[Fiscal years. In billions of dollars]

Type of Budget	1966 actual	1967 estimate[1]	1968 estimate[1]
Administrative budget:			
Receipts	104.7	117.0	126.9
Expenditures	107.0	126.7	135.0
Surplus (+) or deficit (−)	−2.3	−9.7	−8.1
Receipts from and payments to the public (consolidated cash budget):			
Receipts	134.5	154.7	168.1
Expenditures	137.8	160.9	172.4
Surplus (+) or deficit (−)	−3.3	−6.2	−4.3
Federal sector of national income accounts (NIA budget):			
Receipts	132.6	149.8	167.1
Expenditures	132.3	153.6	169.2
Surplus (+) or deficit (−)	+0.3	−3.8	−2.1
Commission's Recommended Budget:			
Receipts, expenditures, and lending:			
Receipt-expenditure account:			
Receipts	131.1	147.7	165.2
Expenditures (excl. net lending)..	135.7	155.5	171.1
Expenditure account surplus (+) or deficit (−)	−4.6	−7.8	−5.9
Plus: Loan account:			
Loan disbursements	14.6	18.3	19.0
Loan repayments	10.8	13.1	14.6
Net lending	3.8	5.2	4.4
Equals: Total budget:			
Receipts	131.1	147.7	165.2
Expenditures and net lending	139.5	160.6	175.5
Surplus (+) or deficit (−)	−8.4	−12.9	−10.3

[1] Figures consistent with January 1967 estimates.

not only often contain a number of subjective elements, but are subject to frequent—indeed annual—revision. These are tolerated and even appreciated when the motives of the statisticians making the adjustments are above suspicion. It is a somewhat different situation in the politically charged atmosphere surrounding official budgets. A possible solution would be for the Treasury and the Bureau of the Budget to issue only unadjusted monthly and quarterly data, and have a relatively apolitical agency such as the Office of

Business Economics in the Department of Commerce take responsibility for the seasonal adjustments.

The separate identification of loan subsidy amounts, discussed in one of the Commission staff papers in the present volume, was subsequently recommended by the Commission and accepted in principle by the Government, although not feasible for immediate implementation. This recommendation calls for splitting the principal amounts of new Federal loans into a "pure loan" element and a "subsidy" element by capitalizing the difference between the interest rate charged by the Federal Government and the Treasury borrowing rates on loans of comparable maturity prevailing at the time the loan is made.

If successfully implemented, this innovation might open a whole new approach to the tabulation and presentation of budget magnitudes. One can think of a number of other subsidy or subsidy-like elements on both the receipt and expenditure side of the Federal budget—and indeed, some now ignored in budget accounting altogether—which might lend themselves to a comparable treatment. For example, tax credits to achieve public policy objectives, of which there are several at the moment and more proposed all the time, might be treated as budget expenditures classified appropriately by program and function so that their competition with other uses of public funds would be made more explicit, rather than as negative taxes as they are at present—a treatment that draws little public attention to them and under which they receive no consideration as part of the Federal budget process.[1] The guarantee by the Federal Government of private loans is another candidate for somewhat comparable treatment. Guarantees are now excluded both from receipts and expenditures, since no cash changes hands between the Federal Government and the private economy (except in the event of default); but it would be possible to capitalize the amount of subsidy implicit in the more favorable borrowing rates made possible by the Federal guarantee, and to include this amount in a budget statement both as an imputed receipt and as an imputed expenditure.

Of course, a number of subsidies that might be more explicitly identified involve subjective and no doubt controversial estimating procedures and some of them, like loan guarantees, require imputations—a principle familiar to national income accountants, but one which would be distinctly revolutionary for the official budget. Therefore, the direct loan program is probably a good place to start; in this case the estimating procedures do not change the overall budget totals, but merely reapportion budget expenditure amounts from one category to another. Incidentally, the identification of loan subsidy

---

[1] For an interesting exploratory example, see "The United States Income Tax System—the Need for a Full Accounting," Remarks by Hon. Stanley S. Surrey, Assistant Secretary of the Treasury, before the Money Marketeers at New York, N.Y., November 15, 1967 (U.S. Treasury Department, November 16, 1967; processed).

amounts will not affect fiscal impact measures of the budget significantly since year-to-year changes are not large. But the recommended treatment is elegant conceptually, meets some of the arguments of the "loans in" advocates, and creates some disincentives for removing programs from the "spending" budget by redesigning them in the form of loans.

FULL EMPLOYMENT SURPLUS

Gramlich's paper addresses the question whether figures on budget results can be adjusted, arranged, and consolidated to yield a simple shorthand index of the impact of fiscal policy on the economy. Clearly, changes in the actual budget surplus or deficit won't do for this purpose for the now rather generally understood and accepted reason that actual budget results reflect not only what fiscal policy is doing to the economy, but also what the economy is doing to the budget through its effects on tax revenues and unemployment benefit payments.

It was to meet this difficulty that the full employment surplus (FES) concept was developed. Gramlich is critical of the FES calculation as usually presented (for example, in the annual issues of the *Economic Report of the President* from 1962 to 1965, in various monthly issues of the *Federal Reserve Bank of St. Louis Review,* and in a number of historical studies of fiscal policy). Although the presentations referred to do make the required distinction between movement along a schedule and shifts in the schedule, they do not weight different components of the budget by their respective demand impacts. Thus most of the usual presentations implicitly assume, for example, that a dollar's worth of corporate tax receipts reduces aggregate demand as much as a dollar's worth of defense purchases increases it.

Gramlich's recommendation is to calculate a weighted high employment surplus, for which he presents some alternative weighting systems constructed with the use of multipliers extracted from various well-known econometric models of the United States economy. Gramlich's paper, the formal and informal discussions following it, and Gramlich's further reply all deal with various aspects of the weighting question—whether or not to weight and, if so, what weights to use.

Without rehashing all this paper and the ensuing discussions, I will follow Warren Smith's advice and consider the weighting question in the context of the uses to which the FES measure could be put after it has been computed. Smith distinguished three possible uses of the FES: (1) to aid public understanding of fiscal policy; (2) to evaluate past fiscal policy; and (3) to support current analysis and policy prescription. For the last-mentioned purpose, I agree with Smith that, even if we were satisfied that the FES accurately measures fiscal impact, the use of procedures involving the FES would be an indirect and somewhat clumsy way to arrive at an estimate of the right fiscal policy. Selecting the right fiscal policy requires estimating the whole economy and choosing an appropriate monetary policy at the same time, and the selection would not be significantly advanced by calculating what the budget, *considered separately,* is contributing. Smith's first-mentioned use of FES—to aid public understanding of fiscal policy—is in my view by far the most important, and for this purpose a weighted measure seems clearly undesirable.

Weighting is undesirable not because of the complexity it introduces. Gramlich is right, I think, in pointing out that a weighted FES is not intrinsically any more difficult to comprehend than many other widely used concepts, such as the balanced budget multiplier. Moreover, if there were a "scientific" basis for weighting which was generally accepted by all or most technicians, there would be no more necessity for full public and congressional "understanding" of the weights themselves than there is for all present users of the Consumer Price Index to "understand" the weights that go into its calculation. The problem is rather that there is not yet, nor is there likely to be any time soon, a weighting scheme that would not be hotly disputed by other experts. This fact would expose the FES calculation, if not to manipulation for public relations purposes, at least to charges of manipulation, and this would unquestionably impair its usefulness for communicating executive branch fiscal policy recommendations to the Congress and the public.

If it turns out, therefore, that an unweighted FES calculation is so grossly inaccurate as to be misleading, we might well have to abandon the attempt to construct meaningful one-dimensional measures of fiscal impact altogether. In fact, many participants expressed the view that, at best, fiscal impact was so complicated a question that any attempt to describe it in a simple index would be more misleading than helpful. Alternatively, short of overwhelming agreement as to *best* weights, there might still be substantial agreement on *some* weights being better than none at all. The question would then be whether this set is enough better than not weighting as to justify the probable confusion and exposure to "finagling" charges.

However, gross inaccuracy of the unweighted FES was not demonstrated to the satisfaction of a majority of the conference participants. In fact, if changes in the FES from one period to the next rather than its absolute level at any one time are considered, weighting by various reasonable alternatives does not appear to make all that much difference most of the time, and the FES does not appear to be substantially less accurate than many other widely used aggregate economic measures. Aside from periods during which large changes in tax rates are legislated, the composition of the budget has rarely changed drastically enough to lead to large discrepancies on this account.

If, as I have argued, the unweighted FES is a reasonably good way to describe fiscal impact most of the time for public and congressional understanding, then it is *pari passu* reasonably good for the second purpose mentioned above, that of evaluating past fiscal policy. As Taubman points out, policy for past periods could be given a good or bad score simply by looking

at the supposed end products of fiscal and monetary stabilization actions—
that is, at the employment and price levels actually attained. This would
serve as a simultaneous test of the forecasting abilities of the policymakers as
well as their policy responsiveness, and an audience of professional economists
might well prefer this fuller test. On the other hand, this procedure would
not provide a means of saying anything about fiscal policy *per se*—as opposed,
say, to monetary policy and other measures. Moreover, there are good reasons
for wanting to know the extent to which the Federal Government is itself
a source of instability, as distinct from an imperfect compensator for private
instability. For example, the fiscal authorities, even if they deny omnipotence
to fiscal policy and eschew "fine tuning," can reasonably be expected in this
day and age to bear in mind as they make a budget that budget revenues grow
in a growing economy without any change in tax rates, and also to be aware
of induced effects on budget revenues of changes in the level of employment.
The unweighted FES provides a relatively simple and straightforward way of
allowing for both these things. It is less reasonable to criticize the authorities
for a failure to apply the proper multipliers to each component of the budget,
which is what would be implied if a weighted FES were used for this test,
especially considering that the proper weights to use are still controversial
and considering further that this is probably not the most efficient way to
make policy in the first place. Again, of course, there will be times when a
sharp change in tax rates or other major change in the composition of the
budget will make the unweighted FES less than completely reliable as an
indicator. However, these cases are probably better handled by verbal qualification of the results than by resort to refined numerical weighting.

Calculation of the FES—the main feature of which is to distinguish between active and passive budget changes—seems to imply that the Federal
Government has more responsibility to avoid being a destabilizing influence
itself than it has to compensate for private fluctuations. This distinction may
be in part for public relations purposes—that is, to make appropriate fiscal
policies more palatable in the face of real or imagined balanced-budget
dogma. There may be times, for example, when it is useful to show the
Congress and the public that a particular budget deficit has come about not
because of "fiscal irresponsibility" but rather for quite the opposite reason
of striving so hard for a surplus that the relation of tax rates to expenditure
levels is holding down the economy, with a perverse effect on budget revenues.

There could be another good reason for trying to distinguish between
active and passive budget results. It is possible to construct models of the
economy that behave as follows: once set on a stable growth path, and given
a stable growth of money supply and a constant approximately neutral fiscal
policy (that is, unchanged FES), the system responds to shocks with relatively
minor and quickly damped oscillations. It may be that the economy itself
would behave that way; the possibility has never really been tested. In short,
for those who prefer "rules" to "authority" in stabilization policy, one pos-

sible rule can be expressed in terms of a constant FES. Milton Friedman, better known for his monetary rules, suggested just such a rule for fiscal policy twenty years ago,[2] as did the Committee for Economic Development in its well known "stabilizing budget policy" (although the CED would apparently not have agreed with Friedman about abandoning discretionary use of monetary as well as fiscal policy).

Gramlich's other suggested change in the way the FES is usually calculated is to remove the induced effects of inflation on the budget. As he points out, a failure to remove the effects of inflation on budget revenues (and expenditures) could, in some periods, make the budget look restraining *ex post,* whereas an expansionary fiscal policy *ex ante* could be one of the underlying causes of inflation.

Of course, it is not all price effects that should be removed from the FES calculation, but only "excess" price effects. Prices rise somewhat in the United States even when unemployment is very high. The trend growth of revenues in the FES calculation should include the effects of such a price rise, since a failure of expenditures to rise by the full amount of potential revenue growth, including the part attributable to price rise, will, *ceteris paribus,* exert a restraining influence on the unemployment rate.

As Smith points out, it is not whether or not a price rise was *anticipated* that tells us how much of it should be incorporated in the FES calculation, but whether or not it was *acceptable.* Whether anticipated or not, an observed rate of price rise less than or equal to that rate of rise that would have caused a higher unemployment rate to be "acceptable" must *pari passu* also be considered "acceptable."

This argument implicitly assumes that "low unemployment" and "reasonable price stability" are compatible policy goals. They may not be, and indeed policymakers sometimes speak as though they didn't think they were. Recently, for example, some people seemed to hold that while an unemployment rate a fraction under 4 percent is not excessively low, the inflation that goes with it is "unacceptable." Fiscal policy or any other one policy is inadequate if there is more than one independent target—we need at least as many tools as targets—and under these circumstances the FES is also ambiguous. But if the acceptable pairs of price-change and unemployment rate include one pair that is also attainable, then the correct price adjustment for deriving an FES that approximately measures the extent to which active fiscal policy *per se* is pushing the economy toward or away from the target pair is one that includes the lesser of actual or acceptable inflation in the calculation of FES receipts and expenditures.

---

[2] "A Monetary and Fiscal Framework for Economic Stability," *American Economic Review,* Vol. 38 (June 1948), pp. 245–64. Reprinted in *Readings in Monetary Theory,* selected by a Committee of the American Economic Association (Blakiston, 1951), pp. 369–93.

It may be difficult to reach complete agreement on a precise definition of acceptable inflation. However, there are two reasons for thinking that this difficulty may not be too important in most actual applications. First, since 1948, we have seldom had any price inflation so severe that any large number of policymakers appeared willing to seek deliberately a higher unemployment rate in order to reduce inflationary pressures. Second, inflation affects expenditures as well as receipts: witness references to the behavior of the Consumer Price Index when legislative changes in social security benefits, veterans pensions, and military and civilian employee pay raises are under debate, to say nothing of induced changes on procurement prices. Hence, a failure to deflate may not lead to much inaccuracy in measuring the net differences between revenue and expenditure increases, even when an excess of actual over acceptable inflation has been observed.

Taubman, Gramlich, and others have made another criticism of FES that may be quantitatively minor most of the time, but which I believe to be conceptually valid. It could occasionally be significant, and it can be accommodated with a rather simple change in the usual methods of calculation. They point out that, when the economy is *in fact* some distance away from the full employment target growth path, trend revenue growth calculated at hypothetical high employment may emit misleading signals. For example, starting from a less-than-full employment position, a budget expenditure increase may be enough to provide a small net stimulus to the economy even though it falls short of revenue growth calculated at full employment—an entirely possible discrepancy considering that the marginal rate of taxation against national income under most tax structures tends to vary with the starting levels of income and revenue. This incongruity can be readily repaired by abstracting from *levels* of FES altogether, dealing directly with first differences, and calculating trend revenues at actual rather than hypothetical high employment income levels. If this is done, both "full employment" and "surplus" should be dropped from the name of the result and some term such as the budget's "net fiscal stimulus" should be substituted.

All things considered, there seems to be no good reason why public-private dialogue about budget policy should not be conducted in terms of a relatively simple measure of fiscal impact, as was the case during the period when the FES was routinely published in the *Economic Report of the President* from 1962 to 1965. Two improvements over the earlier measure seem to be appropriate: (1) elimination of "excess" inflation effects on revenues and expenditures (but only if, when, and to the extent that a retreat from employment targets is agreed on as an appropriate price for restraining unacceptable inflation); and (2) calculation of trend revenues at actual employment levels, without any reference to the hypothetical high employment levels. The resulting measure permits distinguishing, as unambiguously as it is reasonable to expect, observed changes in unemployment due to fiscal policy from those due to all other factors. Neither of the proposed changes is so cumbersome as to risk public and congressional understanding and acceptance by comparison with the earlier FES measure. Another possible change that could run such a risk—weighting the budget components by their respective demand coefficients—does not seem essential, although aberrations arising from changes in budget composition will once in a while be great enough to prevent a simple unweighted fiscal impact index from being interpreted too literally. But then the sound interpretation of any macro-economic measures requires modification on a judgmental basis from time to time.

EXPENDITURE TIMING

Another question discussed at the conference, for which the Galper paper served as point of departure, concerned ways to measure fiscal impact with the best possible regard to the timing of that impact. For many years, there has been criticism—usually associated with Murray Weidenbaum, but from others also—that the time of delivery of goods produced to government order, which is what tends to be reflected in the NIA budget, is a laggard and therefore misleading indicator of budget impact. The question especially concerns defense procurement, since defense accounts for the bulk of Federal goods procurement and is also, on occasion, among the more volatile of budget components.

Galper shows here that, given a fairly good equation linking contract awards with deliveries, the volume of defense production that enters the gross national product statistics in the guise of inventory investment rather than Federal purchases can be deduced. Moreover, for a few years for which overlapping data are available, Galper's defense inventory investment estimates are similar in magnitude to the change over the year in accounts payble by the Department of Defense. The fact that either of these measures shows a radically different picture of budget trends in a period of rapid change in defense expenditures, as during the Vietnam buildup and presumably again after the war in Vietnam is over, lends considerable support to the accrual basis for measuring expenditures that was eventually recommended by the Commission. Pending the full implementation of the Commission's accrual recommendations, which will undoubtedly take some time, Galper's procedure will produce some reasonably good "do-it-yourself" estimates for economic forecasters struggling with budget impact.

FINAL REMARKS

Throughout the proceedings, I was struck by a seeming paradox. Some of the strongest advocates of the need either to include or exclude Federal loans from the budget, as the case may be, were among those who felt that trying to refine the full employment surplus measure to provide a shorthand index of fiscal impact was doomed to failure because the minimum amount of information required to analyze the impact of the budget was far too large to be summarized in a simple one-dimensional measure. This paradox suggests the possibility of other motives for advocating "loans in" or "loans out" so strenuously. In this connection, possible views about the proper size of the Government, and the impact of budget totals and budget deficit figures on public reactions to Federal spending, have already been mentioned. Another motive that might lead someone to advocate "loans out" may be his confidence in national income theory compared to his confidence about monetary theory. There does seem to be more agreement on how income transactions of the Federal Government affect the economy than on how changes in credit flows and stocks of financial assets do. What this possibility seems to suggest is that a simple impact index of the FES type is badly needed to describe monetary and credit policy variables as well as direct income flows.

While I share the rather general view that the Commission's recommendations, when implemented, will represent a number of improvements, there remain some important items of unfinished business. The need for seasonal adjustment, and also the desirability of extending subsidy identification practices beyond the direct loan programs have been mentioned. Another has to do with the appropriate budget treatment of changes in commitments associated with Federal pay, pension, and transfer payment programs, in which changes in law bestow tangible wealth effects not adequately represented by current income transactions. Another, touched on briefly in the Commission's report, but not adequately in my opinion, is the need for at least slightly longer-run horizons in the budget presented by the President to the Congress. It seems quite possible, for example, that last year's violent budget controversy between the executive and the legislative branches was to some considerable extent beside the point, stemming from a lack of access by the Congress and the public to reasonable guesses about expenditure trends, and the relation between prospective revenues and expenditures, in years beyond the budget year. Our political system is such that it is not realistic to expect any great improvement in this area to come about through executive branch initiative. The initiative must come from the Congress, and might well take the form of requiring the addition of a few more columns, representing a few additional years into the future, in the President's annual budget. At least the future costs of program commitments already made, or proposed in the budget, should become part of the regular annual information on the budget.

PART I

Budget Treatment of Federal Lending and Borrowing

STAFF PAPER
President's Commission on Budget Concepts, May 21, 1967

Loans, Participation Certificates, and the Financing of Budget Deficits

INTRODUCTION

Probably no problem the President's Commission on Budget Concepts faces is more important or difficult than the need to reach sound conclusions and recommendations about the treatment of loans and financial transactions in the President's budget statement. In his initial letter to the members of the Commission, the President said:

> There has been particular question raised about the budgetary treatment of Federal lending programs, relating both to loan disbursements and to receipts from the sale or other disposition of loans. I hope the Commission will carefully review present budgetary practices with respect to these lending programs and recommend how loan disbursements and receipts should be treated in arriving at overall budget totals.[1]

This paper discusses the major issues in the treatment of loans and financial transactions in the budget totals and the pros and cons of the major alternatives.

LOANS AND LENDING

Present treatment of loans in consolidated cash budget

At present, loan outlays are treated the same as other expenditures in both the administrative and consolidated cash budgets. There are literally dozens of different loan programs included in the budgets for different agencies and functions. While a fair amount of detail on various aspects of Federal loan programs is presented in a separate special analysis made available with the budget, "Special Analysis E: Federal Credit Programs,"[2] the summary tables in the budget document itself, showing expenditures by agency or by major function, make no distinction between loans and other expenditures.

With few exceptions, Federal loan programs are funded and accounted for on a revolving fund or public enterprise basis, in which interest receipts, loan repayments, and other offsets are credited against outlays for new loans

---

[1] Letter of appointment to members of the President's Commission on Budget Concepts, The White House, March 17, 1967.

[2] *Special Analyses, Budget of the United States, Fiscal Year 1968* (1967), pp. 57–70.

and only net loan expenditures included in budget totals. (The Rural Electrification Administration, for which Congress has repeatedly rejected revolving fund legislation, is the one major example of a continuing loan program that is included gross, rather than net, in the budget totals.)

In addition to interest receipts and loan repayments, net expenditures for lending programs funded as public enterprises are also offset by the direct sale of loans and—increasingly in recent years—by the sale of participation certificates (PC's), which are shares in a "pool" of outstanding loans made by Government lending agencies.

Some lending agencies have authority to borrow to finance their activities by selling their own obligations. While agency debt obligations resemble participation certificates in many characteristics, they differ from participation certificates in that the proceeds from sales do not count as a revolving fund receipt (or negative expenditure) but as a means of financing an agency deficit.

Loans in the consolidated cash budget

Table 1 is a schematic presentation of the amounts included in consolidated cash budget totals for fiscal 1966–68 for loans, loan repayments, and other financial and financing items. The format of Table 1 does not resemble any of the summary tables actually provided in the budget documents (although the figures for total receipts, total expenditures, and surplus or deficit are the same as in the President's January budget). The information in the budget and in various supporting documents made available with the budget have been rearranged in the table to bring out explicitly the lending and financial components. It may be noted in passing that some of the information shown there is not easy to assemble for a general reader who may be interested in the relation of loans to budget totals.

Loans in the national income accounts budget

Loans and financial transactions generally are excluded altogether from receipts and expenditures in the national income accounts (NIA) budget because they do not directly enter anyone's income. Such transactions are viewed as a mere swap of assets. For example, in the case of a Government loan, the private borrower gets an asset (cash) but at the same time an offsetting liability. Similarly, if the Federal Government had a balance sheet comparable to that of most private businesses, the extension of a loan would be represented as the acquisition of one asset (loans receivable) in exchange for another (cash). In private accounting practice, proceeds of a loan—however advantageous to the borrower—are not "income" to him, nor are loan repayments "expenditures." Similarly, when the Federal Government itself borrows, the proceeds of its loans are not revenues (except in the special case of borrowing by the issuance of participation certificates), nor is the retirement of public debt an expenditure.

TABLE 1.—*Treatment of loans and financial items in consolidated cash budget, fiscal 1966, 1967, and 1968*

[In billions of dollars]

Item	1966 actual	1967 estimate	1968 estimate
Receipts from the public:			
Taxes, social insurance premiums, and miscellaneous receipts of administrative budget and trust funds [1]	134. 0	154. 0	167. 6
Interest receipts	. 2	. 3	. 3
Loan repayments [2]	. 3	. 4	. 2
Total receipts	134. 5	154. 7	168. 1
Payments to the public:			
Administrative and trust fund expenditures for purchases, grants, transfer payments, and subsidies, net of interest receipts treated as negative expenditures [3]	135. 3	157. 2	171. 4
Lending:			
Loan disbursements	17. 6	22. 2	21. 7
Deduct:			
Loan repayments and direct sale of loans	−12. 9	−16. 0	−16. 5
Sale of participation certificates (net of retirements) [4]	−2. 2	−2. 5	−4. 2
Equals: Net lending	2. 5	3. 7	1. 0
Total expenditures and loans	137. 8	160. 9	172. 4
Cash surplus (+) or deficit (−)	−3. 3	−6. 2	−4. 3
Financing of budget deficit:			
Decrease in cash balances	. 1	3. 4	. . . . . .
Exercise of monetary authority (seigniorage)	. 6	1. 1	. 5
Net cash borrowing by Treasury and other Federal agencies from the public and the central bank	2. 6	1. 7	3. 8
Total financing	3. 3	6. 2	4. 3

[1] Excludes seigniorage and intragovernmental transactions.

[2] Consists only of those loan repayments coming into budget receipts (most loan repayments are deducted from loan expenditures).

[3] Excludes intragovernmental transactions, debt issuance in lieu of checks, revolving fund receipts from exercise of monetary authority, and increase or decrease in outstanding checks.

[4] Excludes Commodity Credit Corporation certificates of interest and trust fund purchases of participation certificates.

Source: *The Budget of the United States Government for the Fiscal Year Ending June 30, 1968* (1967), and supporting documents and unpublished data provided by the Bureau of the Budget.

As a matter of fact, the difference between the surplus or deficit in the consolidated cash budget and the NIA budget in most years is traceable in large part to the inclusion of loans, loan repayments, and PC sales in the cash budget and their total exclusion from the NIA budget. The exclusion of loans and financial transactions from the NIA budget is perhaps the most frequently cited "advantage" by those who prefer that measure for analyzing the overall economic impact of Federal activity. At the same time, however, the exclusion of loans is cited as a disadvantage of the NIA budget by other economists who prefer to analyze the impact of Federal activity by using the more comprehensive cash budget.

The case for excluding loans from the budget

Several reasons have been given at one time or another for treating loans at the very least as something other than ordinary budget expenditures or for excluding them altogether from the calculation of budget surplus or deficit. The reason for excluding loans in the NIA budget—that these are not income items in ordinary accounting practice—has already been stated.

The same conclusion seems to be suggested if we consider the net economic effect if the Federal Government simultaneously makes a loan and finances the loan by borrowing. We will set aside for the moment the case where bonds are sold to the central bank, which is the financial equivalent of printing new money. If the Government borrows by selling bonds, its lending and borrowing of equal amounts very largely wash out in net economic effect, depending somewhat of course on the type of security sold and the type of loan made.

Much of the Federal Government's borrowing and relending is a form of activity quite different in economic character from the levying of taxes and the purchase of goods and services for public programs. In many cases, the Government is simply acting as a conduit for funds borrowed from areas or capital markets with loanable funds to spare, passing them on to private, State and local government, or foreign parties who are not able to borrow directly themselves. In this sense, the Government is engaging in financial intermediation, like a bank, a savings and loan association, or other financial intermediary. By borrowing and relending, these institutions bring the interests of savers (lenders) and borrowers into balance. When Government lending activity is viewed this way, then it seems logical to treat loans differently from ordinary taxes and expenditures—indeed even exclude them completely—in calculating the budget surplus or deficit.

Other arguments for excluding loans from the budget totals have been put forward by Commission member Robert Turner, Arthur M. Okun of the President's Council of Economic Advisers, and others who point out that Federal credit activity is not restricted to direct lending but encompasses a large volume of Federal guarantee and insurance of private loans as well. At the end of fiscal year 1966, for example, there were outstanding $99 billion of federally guaranteed or insured private loans, three times the $33 billion of direct Federal loans outstanding at that time. The budget totals reflect only a token of Federal guarantee or insurance activity, that associated with the costs of administering the program and picking up defaults.

There is no easy way to reflect loan guarantees and insurance in the budget totals in a manner which does justice to their full significance. Including direct loans in budget totals, however, while loan guarantees and insurance are excluded, gives a misleading impression of the over-all volume of Federal credit activity. Moreover, continuing pressures on both Congress and the Executive to hold down the level of apparent Federal spending and the budget deficit establish artificial incentives to shift from direct loans to indirect lending whether or not the guarantee or insurance of private loans represents a fully satisfactory substitute. This tends to distort program choices between direct and indirect lending in a way that could be avoided, some argue, if direct loans were also excluded from the budget totals.

The case for including loans in the budget

Advocates of including loans in the calculation of budget surplus or deficit point out that when the Government makes loans, it is not just acting as a bank or financial intermediary. If financial intermediation were all that were required, the private sector could well take care of balancing the interests of borrowers and lenders in a country with such highly developed capital markets as ours. Clearly something else is involved, specifically a recognition that without Federal intervention, important public objectives would not be accomplished through the ordinary working of the capital markets.

From this point of view, Federal loan programs represent a redirection of national resources to comply with social priorities. They establish claims on resources and demands for current output of the economy that are very hard to distinguish from the demands and claims that arise from Federal expenditures for grants, transfer payments, or subsidies—transactions which are clearly included in anyone's measure of Government "expenditures." "Soft" loans by the Agency for International Development to developing countries repayable in local currency, and nonrecourse loans to farmers made by the Commodity Credit Corporation (CCC) for which there is no legal obligation to repay if the farmer prefers to forfeit his collateral, are only extreme examples of so-called "loans" which are particularly hard to distinguish from ordinary Government expenditures. In any event, the burden on the Treasury to finance loans through taxes or borrowing is not less than—or different from—the burden associated with financing any other Government expenditure.

Some may be tempted to try to distinguish between true loans and "loans" that are really only disguised grants, subsidies, or transfer payments, and to recommend different budget scorekeeping rules in the two cases. It is perhaps not too difficult to make such a distinction in theory: a loan is expected to be repaid, while an outlay for which there is no reasonable expectation of repayment is not really a loan. In practice, however, it would be impossible to try to apply any such distinction. There are many cases in which a "loan" which cannot reasonably be expected to be repaid must nevertheless be carried on the Government's books as an asset. No formal admission can be made that the loan is not recoverable. For diplomatic and other reasons, for example, the United States Government is still carrying on its books some World War I loans to its military allies that everyone knows are uncollectible.

To some, the pressures to minimize budget expenditures and the budget deficit provide an argument for excluding loans so that the choice between direct and indirect loans can be made solely on their respective merits. But if loans were excluded from the budget, these same pressures might well lead to an even worse distortion of program choices. The misnaming of grants, transfer payments, and subsidies—to get them out of the budget totals—might be greatly stepped up. Moreover, some would argue that, wherever feasible, it is desirable to have incentives that encourage the guarantee or insurance of private loans rather than direct Federal loans. In this connection, it may be noted that there have been several suggestions for centralizing the borrowing and lending activities of the various Government agencies now engaged in loan activities in a central credit agency, under Treasury supervision, both as a means for improving the coordination of the Federal Government's activities in capital markets and as a device for making more explicit the extent of Federal subsidy in various loan programs. Both these objectives are also served whenever there is a shift from direct loans to Federal guarantee or insurance of private loans, which is more apt to happen if loans are counted as ordinary budget expenditures.

Participation Certificates in the Federal Budget Picture

As the Federal Government's loan programs grow in importance, so does the significance of the way they are handled—and the way loan financing is handled—in the Federal budget. Until very recent years the financing of net Federal loan expenditures has been accomplished for the most part either by the sale of regular direct public debt obligations of the United States Government, or by the sale of obligations of the lending agency itself, such as the Federal National Mortgage Association (FNMA) and the various farm credit agencies. In recent years, however, the sale of participation certificates has been an increasingly important means of financing Federal credit programs.

For many years, the Commodity Credit Corporation has financed certain of its commodity loans, primarily loans on cotton, by pooling them and issuing participation certificates to commercial banks, thus permitting the banks to continue fulfilling their longstanding practice of financing the domestic cotton crop. Similarly, when the Reconstruction Finance Corporation went into liquidation, most of the many thousands of outstanding loans in 1954 were pooled and certificates of participation sold to the banks. The Export-Import Bank, beginning in 1962, sold PC's in a pool of outstanding loans. Typically, the agency issuing the participation certificates fully guaranteed their payment by substituting new loans should one in the pool go into default. Since the agencies were wholly owned by the United States Government, there was at least as much implied backing by the Treasury as in the case of the direct obligations of Government agencies.

By the end of fiscal 1964, PC's outstanding totalled $1.2 billion. These have been recorded in the Federal budget in exactly the same way as if the loans were physically sold—that is, as a negative expenditure which in turn reduced the stated Federal deficit.

In recent years, however, the use of participation certificates has been considerably broadened in scope and size. The Housing Acts of 1964 and 1965 provided for the FNMA to sell participation certificates not only in its own mortgage holdings but also in those of the Veterans' Administration—all of them Government-insured or guaranteed mortgages.

In his January 1966 budget, President Johnson took a further step by proposing that the use of the pooling technique be extended to a number of other Federal agencies which hold financial assets. This proposal subsequently became the Participation Sales Act of 1966. This Act capitalized on the experience of the FNMA by giving that agency responsibility for managing and coordinating the pooling and sale of assets in the capacity of trustee for the other agencies. The Act did provide for congressional review of the pooling of assets, thus enabling Congress to retain its traditional influence and control, through the regular budget process, over the scope and administration of the lending programs. The Act extended the use of the participation sales technique to include assets of the Farmers Home Administration, the Office of Education's academic facilities loan program, the college housing program, the public facilities loan program of the Department of Housing and Urban Development, and the Small Business Administration.

Under these enlarged programs, the volume of PC's outstanding rose from $1.2 billion in June 1964 to $4.4 billion in June 1966 and, if present budget estimates are realized, to $11.5 billion by June 1968—or just short of ten times the volume of four years ago. As a result, the net expenditures of Federal loan programs have been correspondingly reduced in the way they are currently reported, and the Treasury has been able to claim that the upward course of Federal direct lending programs has been arrested. Table 2 indicates how the apparent trend of Federal lending is affected by whether or not PC sales are counted as negative loan expenditures. In the three years from 1966 to 1968, between $9 and $10 billion have been deducted from budget expenditures due to PC sales, thus reducing the actual and proposed budget deficits—either on an administrative budget or on a cash budget basis—by an equivalent amount. Table 3 shows the administrative budget deficit as estimated in January would be 50 percent higher if the sale of PC's were excluded and the consolidated cash deficit for next year would be double its budgeted level.

TABLE 2.—*Net expenditures of Federal lending programs, fiscal 1962-68*

[In billions of dollars]

Fiscal year	Expenditures reported [1]	Net sales of participation certificates	Expenditures adjusted
1962......................	2.6	0.3	2.9
1963......................	1.7	.2	1.9
1964......................	2.1	.3	2.4
1965......................	1.6	.5	2.1
1966......................	.3	2.2	2.5
1967 (estimated).............	.9	2.5	3.4
1968 (estimated).............	− .5	4.2	3.7

[1] Administrative budget expenditures. This amount does not reflect loan repayments reported as receipts.

Source: Bureau of the Budget, and *The Budget of the United States Government for the Fiscal Year Ending June 30, 1968* (1967).

TABLE 3.—*Effect of exclusion of net participation certificate sales on the budget deficit, according to three different budget concepts, fiscal 1962–68*

[In billions of dollars]

Fiscal year	Administrative budget		Consolidated cash budget		National income accounts [1] budget
	Reported	Excluding participation certificates	Reported	Excluding participation certificates	
1962..............	−6.4	−6.7	−5.8	−6.0	−2.1
1963..............	−6.3	−6.5	−4.0	−4.2	−1.2
1964..............	−8.2	−8.5	−4.8	−5.1	−1.4
1965..............	−3.4	−3.9	−2.7	−3.2	+2.3
1966..............	−2.3	−4.4	−3.3	−5.4	+.3
1967 (estimated)....	−9.7	−12.2	−6.2	−8.7	−3.8
1968 (estimated)....	−8.1	−12.3	−4.3	−8.5	−2.1

[1] Unaffected by PC accounting.

Source: Table 2 and *The Budget of the United States Government for the Fiscal Year Ending June 30, 1968* (1967).

Participation certificate sales and Federal credit programs

It is clear that the executive branch of the Government considers the Participation Sales Act as a tremendous breakthrough in financial management of Federal lending programs. It is also clear to many that Federal lending will be an increasingly important vehicle for the expression of public priorities in coming years. As Joseph W. Barr, Under Secretary of the Treasury, stated in an address last October:

> The pooling of loans and the sale of participations, when these techniques are in full use after the current inflationary threat passes, cannot fail to underscore the differences among Federal funds spent, say, for an Army rifle, which is expendable and has a strong tendency toward obsolescence; funds spent for a national park, which will be an asset to be enjoyed by our grandchildren; and funds lent to credit-worthy borrowers who will pay back every cent, with interest. This will have an important effect on the budgeting process.

> Competition for the available Federal budget dollar is keen—particularly when the whole range of great unsatisfied needs of our society is considered. The Great Society means, in part, meeting the greatest of those needs.

> It is only necessary to name a few areas—health and education, poverty, the rebuilding of blighted urban areas, water pollution, air pollution, transportation—to see that future national needs will create great future demands for capital.

> We gain some perspective in the area of future capital needs from the recent National Planning Association study, *Goals, Priorities and Dollars,* a study of the cost of achieving our national goals for 1975. The study estimates that, by 1975, our annual expenditure level for urban development should reach nearly $130 billion, in 1962 prices.

> In transportation, the study concludes our 1975 expenditure level should be almost $75 billion, and in housing, $62 billion. All these are double the actual 1962 expenditures.

> The study further estimates that, in 1975, annual investment in private plant and equipment should reach almost $152 billion—triple the actual 1962 level. Gross private domestic investment as a sector of hypothetical Gross National Product in 1975 is projected at $205 billion, more than two and one-half times the actual 1962 level.

> Another National Planning Association study estimated the cost of transforming the Nation's metropolitan centers into what the study considered to be "viable" communities over a period of 20 years. Their estimate was $2.1 trillion, in both public and private expenditures. These figures give us some idea of the order of magnitude of the need for capital which we will face in less than a decade.

> The Participation Sales Act did not authorize any new programs or any additional loan funds for existing programs. But its passage was of vital importance in assuring local communities, educational institutions, and individuals that loan programs authorized by the Congress would be adequately funded. Further, it provides assurance to many others—individuals, communities, and institutions—that future programs to alleviate their most severe problems will be financially feasible.

> Things in government seldom remain fixed and static for long. We took a long step forward with the Participation Sales Act. But I would not be surprised if, in a matter

of a few years, that step led to still more comprehensive progress in the future financing of Federal lending programs.[3]

In a memorandum prepared by Budget Director Charles L. Schultze and Secretary Henry T. Fowler supporting the 1966 Participation Sales Act, they put forward an additional rationale for treating the sale of PC's as sale of assets even though title to the asset and all servicing arrangements on the loans remain with the original lender, or with the FNMA as trustee. They indicated that the basic purpose of issuing participation certificates was to "encourage the substitution of private for public credit in various major Federal credit programs. Given the desirability of drawing in greater private participation in the Federal credit programs, the sale of interests in pools of assets is the most satisfactory and economical means that has been devised to meet this end." [4]

The memorandum went on to say:

A guiding principle of these programs is that Federal credit should supplement or stimulate private lending rather than substitute for it. This is a matter of basic economic philosophy, as well as a recognition of the fact that the private market should, and will, continue to account for the bulk of all credit extensions.

Federal credit programs, working through the private market, help to make the market stronger, more competitive, and better able to serve the economy's needs over the long-term, than if the Federal credit programs unnecessarily preempted functions that private lenders could perform effectively. In addition, use of private market facilities frequently can ease the problem of administering Government programs and make Government aid, where appropriate, more available to potential borrowers.

Carrying through these principles and recommendations, increased emphasis has been placed in recent years on greater use of Government guarantees of private credit and on direct sales of individual Government loans to private lenders. More recently, sales of individual loans have been supplemented by pooling large numbers of loans and selling certificates of participation in such pools.[5]

The memorandum also cited the advantages to the Government of a unified financing approach, particularly for loans with submarket interest rates, and in addition, observed that:

A further advantage of the pool arrangements is in their ability to draw into the financing of public credit programs practically all sectors of the capital markets. Many segments of the market cannot deal in individual mortgages. Other sectors are not able to purchase individual business or college housing loans. But almost all segments of the market are potential investors in pool certificates. Two consequences flow from this: *first,* the market for a number of particular types of credit instruments is substantially

---

[3] *Financial Management of Federal Credit Programs in the Great Society,* Remarks of the Hon. Joseph W. Barr, Under Secretary of the Treasury, before the Third Annual Corporate Pension Conference, The University Club (New York City, October 6, 1966).

[4] Memorandum for the President prepared by the Secretary of the Treasury and the Director of the Bureau of the Budget in support of the President's transmission of the Participation Sales Act of 1966, attached to White House Press Release dated April 20, 1966.

[5] *Ibid.*

broadened; and *second,* sales of participations do not disrupt particular segments of the capital markets, as might be the case if the mortgages or loans were sold individually.[6]

In support of the use of the PC device, the Administration also cites the 1961 Report of the Commission on Money and Credit, and the report of President Kennedy's Committee on Federal Credit Programs, chaired by Secretary Douglas Dillon.[7]

Participation certificate sales and Treasury financing problems

Financing of Federal lending programs by direct Treasury debt issuance, of course, means financing under the public debt limit. Financing by agency issues is outside of the debt limit. Therefore, in addition to the obvious desirability of having a business-type enterprise stand on its own feet, a further incentive for agency borrowing is that it gets around a debt limit that often pinches the Treasury rather badly.

There is a practical limit, however, to how far individual agencies can go in borrowing directly from the public. A proliferation of agencies borrowing in relatively small amounts would merely add to the overall interest cost of Government because of the confusion it would cause among investors and the large number of small issues. In addition, the administrative cost to the Government of setting up individual marketing arrangements for smaller agency borrowing operations would obviously be wasteful.

There is also a practical limitation to the extent to which the Treasury can encourage the Federal agencies to sell loans out of their own portfolios to private investors. Many of these loans carry submarginal rates of interest (such as the Rural Electrification Administration, the college housing program, and many Agency for International Development loans). These could be sold to investors only at a deep discount. Although this would have the advantage of calling attention rather dramatically to the degree of subsidy involved, it would likely give rise to a tremendous outcry that the Federal Government was "giving its assets away" to bankers, other financial institutions, and affluent investors. The discount on such sales below the share value of the loan would be accentuated by the odd terms and amounts, and different maturity dates of many of the issues involved. The unfavorable results of an attempt by the Small Business Administration to sell specific loans a year ago is a good example of what can happen. The sale of certificates of participation in pools of agency assets neatly meets many of these problems.

Perhaps understandably, in view of its relative inability to control Federal spending directly once appropriations have been made, Congress insists on a restrictive public debt limit as a device to convey an image of congressional control and as a means of forcing review of overall spending by the

---

[6] *Ibid.*

[7] Commission on Money and Credit, *Money and Credit* (Prentice-Hall, 1961).

executive branch of the Government. At the same time, it is understandable why the Treasury in particular may be attracted to devices which assist in ferreting out sources of funds that permit it, as the ultimate issuer of checks, to pay the Government's bills and to make sure that the Government's obligations are met. The Treasury could find itself in a position where it was forced to delay bill payment if it were squeezed too hard.

In addition to giving the Treasury flexibility to engage in financing operations outside of the public debt limit, the PC provides borrowing flexibility of another sort as well. Agency borrowing is not subject to the legal prohibition against selling Treasury bonds of more than five years' maturity at interest rates in excess of $4\frac{1}{4}$ percent. This interest rate ceiling was enacted fifty years ago under World War I conditions. The Congress has, however, consistently refused to remove it despite the fact that during much of the time during the past eight years the Treasury has been prevented from selling securities beyond five years' maturity. As a result, there has been a substantial shortening of the average length of the public debt and a warping of what might be considered a logical maturity structure of the public debt. Borrowing by Federal agencies directly in the market, however, can be at any interest rate or maturity required for the successful marketing of the new issues. This is also true of participation certificates, so the emergence of the PC as a full-blown method of financing permits the Treasury an additional way of getting around the $4\frac{1}{4}$ percent ceiling and financing through the agencies beyond the five-year area. Thus it does indirectly what the Congress will not permit directly. Both the Administration and the Congress are concerned about this problem, and the Ways and Means Committee in June 1967 proposed that the $4\frac{1}{4}$ percent ceiling apply only to securities issued with more than a seven-year, rather than five-year, maturity.[8]

Some of the criticism of PC's has been directed at this evasion of both the public debt and Treasury interest rate ceilings. The Commission may not wish to make recommendations about the propriety of legal ceilings on the public debt and interest rates which Treasury bonds may carry. These are both areas of longstanding controversy. However, the Commission will probably wish to recognize, internally, during its deliberations of other aspects of budget scorekeeping, that these ceilings are inefficient if not harmful, and it will undoubtedly regard as natural and understandable the attractiveness of devices—such as PC sales—which avoid both ceilings.

Criticism of the use of participation certificates

The Commission's primary responsibility lies in the area of recommending how various transactions should be treated in budget scorekeeping, and not to review the merits of the transactions themselves. On the other hand, there is no doubt that present budget scorekeeping rules have played some role

---

[8] *Report to Accompany H.R.* 10328, 90 Cong. 1 sess. (June 2, 1967), p. 2.

in bringing these instruments into existence, although as seen above, there are other factors working in the same direction. It is therefore appropriate to review, at least briefly, some of the criticism of the PC instruments themselves. It should be quickly pointed out that, just as the use of PC's has been bipartisan, so the criticism is not particularly partisan.

Criticism of PC sales as an evasion of the public debt and interest rate ceilings has already been mentioned. Much additional criticism of the use (as distinct from the treatment) of participation certificates has been directed at the Treasury's ill-fated timing last year when the first big issue growing out of the Participation Sales Act ran squarely into one of the tightest money market periods in our history. This, together with the market's anticipation of large future issues, contributed substantially to the near-crisis conditions in the money markets in late summer. Interest rates rose to the highest levels in more than a generation. The Treasury was also criticized for failing to make the bonds attractive to investors. They were not available in coupon form and were ineligible for Federal Reserve wire transfers. They represented too many maturities and carried other less than attractive features, many of which were later corrected. Although such financing details are beyond the scope of inquiry by the President's Commission on Budget Concepts, in all fairness they should be mentioned here because they account for a significant part of the criticism of the PC device.

Participation certificates have also been criticized because they carry higher interest rates than Treasury bonds of comparable maturity and, therefore, increase Treasury borrowing costs. This point has been answered as follows in the previously mentioned Treasury Budget memorandum:

It has been pointed out on some occasions that the sale of Federal credit program financial assets, whether through participation certificates or other means, is more expensive than financing through the direct issue of Treasury obligations. This is true, although the cost difference has proved to be relatively minor. For example, FNMA participation certificates have been sold at rates roughly ¼ of 1 percent above Treasury issues of comparable maturity; and it is entirely possible that the margin may diminish as the market gains experience with these high-quality credits.

Moreover, carried to its logical conclusion, this argument would have the Treasury financing directly all of the Federal insurance and guarantee programs, since it can obviously do this more cheaply than the private market. Other types of credit, now handled entirely in the private market, could also be financed more "cheaply" by the U.S. Treasury. We certainly wish to retain, however, the principle that the allocation of credit for essentially private purposes should be a function of the private market. That was the philosophy of the Commission on Money and Credit and of the President's Committee on Federal Credit Programs. It is a sound philosophy, and I believe we should continue our efforts to strengthen the private market as a means for achieving program objectives with a minimum of Government interference.[9]

---

[9] Memorandum for the President prepared by the Secretary of the Treasury and the Director of the Bureau of the Budget, *op. cit.*

Criticism of the budget treatment of participation certificates

The strongest criticism has been directed, however, not at the use of PC's but at the way they are reflected in budget totals. There was substantial criticism of the Eisenhower Administration in its use of the CCC certificates of interest some years back. This criticism took the form of congressional complaint that it was a deliberate evasion of the public debt limit, and there were widespread complaints by the academic community and the general public, as well as by Congress, that the PC's resulted in a deliberate understatement of the true level of expenditures and the deficit of the Federal Government.

Those criticisms seem mild, however, compared to those which have arisen as a result of the expansion of PC's under the Participation Sales Act of 1966. Valid or not, treatment of the now sizable PC sales as a reduction in budget expenditures and budget deficit has perhaps done more to undermine public and congressional confidence in the integrity of budget totals than any other single issue.

The following statement from a 1966 *Survey* by the Morgan Guaranty Trust Company of New York is not unrepresentative:

> The opportunity which Federal credit agencies have to finance some portion of their activities from non-Treasury sources complicates evaluation of overall budget trends. This can be so even if the volume of new lending activity remains relatively stable from year to year. Confusion can be introduced simply if Federal agencies collectively vary their financing mix as between Treasury and non-Treasury sources. If, for example, after several years of substantial reliance on self-financing by means of the sale of assets and the use of loan repayments, Federal credit agencies suddenly shift to major reliance on the Treasury as a source of funds, the effect will be to push up the budget's expenditure total. Conversely, a sudden increase in the proportion of loans which are self-financed will result in a downward push on budget expenditures. Neither of these occurrences will necessarily be of much significance in terms of government's overall spending and lending impact on the economy. But that fact is not generally appreciated. It is quite likely that the average citizen, whose knowledge of budgetary trends comes chiefly from general news coverage of simple budget totals, will often gain an erroneous impression as to the economic impact of the government's financial operations.[10]

It is probably fair to deduce that concern over the budget treatment of PC's is in turn due to concern over the level and trend of Federal lending activity. If the net cost of new loans can be offset by selling PC's, there is likely to be less pressure to hold down this form of Federal activity than under a different budget treatment. This, of course, gets to the very root of why anyone should worry about budget scorekeeping in the first place, and about congressional and public understanding of the score. The Morgan Guaranty *Survey* article cited previously is again indicative of this viewpoint:

> It is obvious that the PC technique has added significantly to the possibility of confusion—and on a major scale, since of the $33-billion total of direct loans that were

---

[10] *Monthly Survey*, Morgan Guaranty Trust Company, October 1966.

outstanding on June 30, 1965, approximately one-third were in the portfolios of agencies presently eligible to participate in the PC program. The PC technique represents a further means by which agencies can acquire funds without going to the Treasury, one which is free of some of the important limitations that attach to present methods of self finance.[11]

What is Government borrowing?

A longstanding principle of budget scorekeeping for the Federal budget is that proceeds from the sale of debt instruments are not receipts, and debt retirement not expenditures. Participation certificates escape from this rule on the justification that they represent the sale of assets, comparable to the direct sale of loans, rather than the sale of Treasury'debt instruments. The sale of assets (such as surplus commodities, or the sale of loans from agency portfolios) have always been regarded as receipts (or negative expenditures) rather than as financing items.

Again, quoting from the Morgan Guaranty *Survey* article:

> Whereas the Eisenhower Administration placed emphasis primarily on the sale of financial assets themselves—something that where successful involved an actual transfer of assets to a private buyer—the sale of PC's gives a buyer only a beneficial interest in a grouping of assets. And this distinction is crucial. Legal title to the items in a PC pool remains with the government—specifically with Fanny Mae as trustee—and the originating agency meanwhile retains custody of the loans and continues to serve them. The total of loans outstanding on the books of Federal credit agencies is precisely the same before and after a sale of PC's. The "banking" role of the government in extending and holding loans is in no meaningful way changed. Instead of being sold to private parties, the assets themselves serve essentially as collateral for the PC's. And the importance of even this function can be questioned, since in practical terms the safety of the PC's from the standpoint of the person buying them depends principally on Fanny Mae's guarantee as to the timely payment of principal and interest and on their ultimate backing by the Treasury. What is being sold, therefore, is in reality the credit of the United States.
>
> Presumably no one would seriously contend that a loan extended by a Federal credit agency to, say, a small business involved private credit if the funds used had originated with the sale of a Treasury bond to a private investor. Instead, agreement would be general that the lending activity was being carried on with public funds. And precisely the same thing is true if, alternatively, the funds employed originate with the sale of PC's. All the money used by government and its agencies, whether it is tax money or borrowed money, has to originate privately, but that in itself provides no basis for alleging that governmental activities are in any significant sense private activities.[12]

Congress has also been quick to point out that since the Attorney General has ruled that "FNMA's guaranty of a participation certificate brings into being a general obligation of the United States backed by its full faith and credit," the executive branch has in effect erased the last vestige of distinction between a participation certificate, on the one hand, and a direct public

---

[11] *Ibid.*
[12] *Ibid.*

debt obligation, on the other.[13] It is obvious that the Ways and Means Committee was thinking of this when it sent the new debt limit bill to the floor of the House in June with the provision that the $365 billion limit requested by the Secretary of the Treasury should specifically include those participation certificates issued during the fiscal year 1968. Interestingly enough, the Committee warned that this action was purely a temporary expedient and that, in accordance with the request of the Secretary of the Treasury and the Budget Director, a full-dress consideration of the participation certificate issue was being held off until the final report of the President's Commission on Budget Concepts.[14]

While it is hard to differentiate participation certificate sales from the sale of Treasury bonds in terms of economic character, it is also very hard to differentiate them from the direct sale of loans, the proceeds of which have always been treated as budget receipts or, more frequently, negative expenditures. The transition from the direct sale of loans to the sales of PC's in a pool of loans has been gradual and not altogether without logic. The difference between selling loans and selling PC's arises not from the economic character of the transaction but from the fact that, in a legal or accounting sense, the Federal Government retains the title to the loans in the case of participation certificate sales; when it sells loans from its portfolios, it actually relinquishes the asset. It may also be argued that not treating proceeds from the sale of Treasury debt as "receipts" is a matter of convention rather than irrefutable logic. The sale of long-term bonds to private nonbank purchasers may have very nearly as much restraining impact on the private economy as the collection of taxes, and some countries do in fact treat borrowing (other than borrowing from the central bank) as budget revenues.

If the criterion for distinguishing between revenues and borrowing were to be the economic impact of the transaction, then there is considerably more logic in treating borrowing outside the banking system (particularly long-term borrowing) as a revenue than not. Of course, borrowing from the banks, particularly the central bank, resembles nothing so much as the printing of new money—a sovereign right of central governments, to be sure, but one which few would wish to count as a budget revenue.

Major Alternative Treatments

Clearly, the issue of how to treat loans and PC sales takes on much of its controversial character because of the effect on the budget surplus or deficit. Before examining major alternatives, it is perhaps well to recognize that the labeling of some income as "receipts" and some outgo as "expenditures" (and the difference between the two as the budget surplus or deficit) has

---

[13] Letter from Attorney General to the Secretary of the Treasury, September 30, 1965.

[14] *Report to Accompany H.R.* 10328, *op. cit.*, p. 10.

historically been more a matter of convention than of logic. The elements of cash income and outgo, from among which alternative combinations of "receipts" and "expenditures" can be selected, can be listed in a comprehensive array in which total income and outgo are equal, with no surplus or deficit. Table 4 does just this, by a slight rearrangement of the elements of the consolidated cash budget figures for fiscal 1967 shown in Table 1. To simplify the presentation, all loan repayments, whether counted as receipts or as negative expenditures in the cash budget, are here treated as negative expenditures; PC sales are treated as income items rather than negative expenditures.

TABLE 4.—*Comprehensive income and outgo presentation of consolidated cash budget totals, fiscal 1967*

[In billions of dollars]

Income	Amount	Outgo	Amount
Taxes, social insurance premiums, and miscellaneous receipts.........	154.3	Purchases, grants, transfers, and subsidies.......	157.2
Sales of participation certificates..............	2.5	Loans:	
Treasury and agency borrowing..............	1.7	Disbursements...22.2	
Decrease in cash balances..	3.4	Repayments.. −16.1	
Exercise of monetary authority..............	1.1	Direct sales.... −.3	
		Net lending........	5.7
Total............	163.0	Total............	163.0

Source: Same as Table 1.

Alternative I: Treating loans as expenditures, and PC sales as borrowing

This alternative would be preferred by many who find no particular difference between PC sales and regular Treasury borrowing, and who also find loans more like other expenditures than not. Comparing this with the present cash budget, the principal change is the elimination of PC sales as negative expenditures, which would increase the level of expenditures and budget deficit. A schematic presentation of the results for fiscal years 1966–68 appears in Table 5.

Alternative II: Keeping both loans and PC sales in budget totals, as at present

This alternative is presented schematically in Table 6. The budget deficit remains the same as that in the cash budget (although PC sales are treated here as receipts rather than negative expenditures).

TABLE 5.—*Alternative I presentation of consolidated cash budget totals*

[Fiscal years. In billions of dollars]

Transaction	1966 actual	1967 estimate	1968 estimate
Receipts:			
Taxes, social insurance premiums, and miscellaneous receipts............	134. 2	154. 3	167. 9
Expenditures:			
Purchases, grants, transfers, and subsidies.........................	135. 3	157. 2	171. 4
Net lending......................	4. 4	5. 7	5. 0
Total expenditures and loans........	139. 7	163. 0	176. 4
Surplus or deficit......................	−5. 4	−8. 7	−8. 5
Financing of deficit:			
Sales of participation certificates.......	2. 2	2. 5	4. 2
Treasury and agency borrowing.......	2. 6	1. 7	3. 8
Decrease in cash balances...........	. 1	3. 4	....
Exercise of monetary authority........	. 6	1. 1	. 5
Total financing..................	5. 4	8. 7	8. 5
Addendum: Surplus or deficit in present consolidated cash budget..............	−3. 3	−6. 2	−4. 3

Source: Same as Table 1.

Alternative III: A "capital budget" for loans

This alternative excludes both loans and participation certificate sales from the calculation of surplus or deficit in the basic budget. These items appear "below the line" in a separate "lending" budget. If loans are excluded from the budget, then at least the losses on loans (or a suitable allowance for losses if an accrued treatment is preferred) would enter as an expenditure in the basic budget and as a credit in the lending budget. The deficit in the "basic" budget would be smaller than that in the present consolidated cash budget, at least for the three years shown here, but the overall financing requirements (and sources of financing) would be equal in magnitude to the deficit in the present cash budget, although it would presumably be called "financing requirements" rather than "deficit." The format for this alternative is presented as Table 7. Conceptually, this budget resembles the present NIA budget in definition of receipts and expenditures (although by spelling out the lending and financing aspects of the budget "below the line," this alternative presents more information than the present NIA budget).

TABLE 6.—*Alternative II presentation of consolidated cash budget totals*

[Fiscal years. In billions of dollars]

Transaction	1966 actual	1967 estimate	1968 estimate
Receipts:			
Taxes, social insurance premiums, and miscellaneous receipts.............	134. 2	154. 3	167. 9
Sales of participation certificates.......	2. 2	2. 5	4. 2
Total.........................	136. 3 ·	156. 8	172. 1
Expenditures:			
Purchases, grants, transfers, and sub- sidies..........................	135. 3	157. 2	171. 4
Net lending......................	4. 4	5. 7	5. 0
Total expenditures and loans.......	139. 7	163. 0	176. 4
Surplus or deficit......................	−3. 3	−6. 2	−4. 3
Financing of deficit:			
Treasury and agency borrowing.......	2. 6	1. 7	3. 8
Decrease in cash balances............	. 1	3. 4	......
Exercise of monetary authority........	· 6	1. 1	. 5
Total financing..................	3. 3	6. 2	4. 3.
Addendum: Surplus or deficit in present consolidated cash budget..............	−3. 3	−6. 2	−4. 3

Source: Same as Table 1.

Other alternatives

It should be pointed out that all the discussion in this paper and the three major alternatives presented above treat the coverage of the Federal budget pretty much along present lines. There is no attempt to include the income and outgo of the Federal Reserve System such as a budget statement for the whole Federal sector of the economy might do. As in present Treasury and United States budget statements, Treasury borrowing from the Federal Reserve has been treated implicitly as not different from other forms of borrowing from the public.

It should be borne in mind, however, that the Federal Reserve System, broadly viewed, is part of the Federal Government, and that most of the income and outgo of the Federal Reserve System arises from its sales and purchases of Treasury securities—transactions which closely parallel the lending and borrowing of Federal credit agencies discussed in this paper. In

TABLE 7.—*Alternative III presentation of a "capital budget" for loans*

[Fiscal years. In billions of dollars]

Transaction	1966 actual	1967 estimate	1968 estimate
Regular budget:			
Receipts:			
Taxes, social insurance premiums, and miscellaneous receipts.......	134.2	154.3	167.9
Expenditures:			
Purchases, grants, transfers, and subsidies....................	135.3	157.2	171.4
Allowance for losses on loans [1].....	.4	.4	.4
Total expenditures..............	135.7	157.6	171.7
Budget surplus or deficit.................	−1.4	−3.3	−3.8
Lending budget:			
Loan disbursements.................	17.6	22.2	21.7
Credits against loan programs:			
Loan repayments...............	12.8	16.1	16.4
Direct sale of loans...............	.4	.3	.3
Sales of participation certificates...	2.2	2.5	4.2
General fund contribution to cost of loan programs (allowance for losses) [1]....................	.4	.4	.4
Total credits...................	15.8.	19.3	21.3
Net cost of loan programs.........	1.9	2.9	.4
Financing:			
Requirements:			
Budget deficit...................	1.4	3.3	3.8
Net cost of loan programs.........	1.9	2.9	.4
	3.3	6.2	4.3
Sources:			
Decrease in cash balances.........	.1	3.4	....
Exercise of monetary authority.....	.6	1.1	.5
Cash borrowing from the public...	2.6	1.7	3.8
	3.3	6.2	4.3

[1] Amounts assumed for illustrative purposes.

Source: Same as Table 1.

a budget in which both Treasury and Federal Reserve "borrowing" and "lending" were consolidated, sale of Treasury securities to the Federal Reserve (principally through the vehicle of Federal Reserve acquisition of Treasury debt instruments in the open market) would be netted out; "borrowing" by the consolidated Federal sector would represent net changes in public debt held outside both the Treasury and the Federal Reserve System.

For the purpose of analyzing the economic impact of Treasury borrowing operations, a consolidated Treasury-Federal Reserve budget statement of this kind may have some merits. It would focus attention on the undisputed fact that Treasury borrowing from the central bank is substantially different in economic character from other forms of Treasury borrowing. Some countries, in fact, explicitly distinguish between Treasury borrowing from the central bank and other borrowing, and count the latter as budget revenues. Treasury borrowing from the central bank, on the other hand, is a form of exercise of the monetary powers of central governments, equivalent to seigniorage or the printing of new banknotes, and would be a means of financing the budget deficit even if other borrowing were treated as revenue.

This last combination is not presented here as a practical alternative comparable to the three major alternatives mentioned above, since there are a number of related technical questions that go beyond the scope of this paper which should be considered at the same time. However, exploration of these technical questions may be desirable in preparation for a future meeting of the Commission.

CONCLUDING REMARKS

Financial intermediation—borrowing and relending—by the Federal Government will almost certainly grow at a brisk pace in coming years. There are many reasons for thinking that an increasing share of Federal activity in pursuit of national goals and priorities may take the form of loans or loan guarantees or other intervention in the capital markets rather than that of tax-supported and direct Federal administration of new programs. This not only explains the very deep concern in many quarters for proper budget "scorekeeping" rules for loans and loan financing, but lends urgency to the Commission's findings and recommendations in this area.

It is also clear that the problem of how to treat loans and participation certificates takes on added interest from the high degree of concern in Congress, the press, and elsewhere, with the level of budget surplus or deficit as a shorthand index for success or failure in Government budgeting and stewardship of public funds. This implies that the Commission probably has a responsibility to make recommendations in its final report on what meaning and significance—if any—should be attached to the surplus or deficit resulting from the application of the rules it recommends for the calculation of budget receipts and expenditures.

The implication of rules for the treatment of loans and participation certificates for the definition and measurement of the public debt should also be kept in mind by the Commission. The Commission may or may not wish to recommend changes in the public debt ceiling. But it should have in mind that whatever rules it recommends for budget treatment of loans and participation certificates will carry implications for the logical definition of the public debt as well. For example, if participation certificates are to be treated as borrowing but loans as expenditures, the present public debt definition should be modified to include participation certificates. If both loans and participation certificates are excluded from budget totals, then loans held by the Federal Government should logically be counted as offsets to Treasury borrowing in the calculation of net public debt.

STAFF PAPER
President's Commission on Budget Concepts, June 23, 1967

Problems in Implementing a Capital Budget for Loans

At its last meeting, the President's Commission on Budget Concepts showed considerable interest in exploring the feasibility of a divided budget system that would recognize the difference in character between loans and other Federal expenditures by treating loans in a separate budget. The Commission, however, seemed to prefer this approach only if the regular budget would still include a relatively full measure of subsidies and other costs of loan programs, including subsidies involved in lending at low rates of interest, subsidies involved in making "soft" (high-risk) loans that cannot really be expected to be recovered fully, and the costs of administering the loan programs.

PREVIOUS RECOMMENDATIONS ON SUBSIDIES

In advocating fuller disclosures of subsidies on loan programs, the Commission has many precedents. The second Hoover Commission in 1955 recommended that the Treasury charge interest on advances or contributions to Federal lending agencies equal to the going rate of interest paid by the Treasury on its own obligations of comparable maturity.[1] The Commission on Money and Credit recommended that loan programs be self-supporting unless a deliberate subsidy was intended.[2] And more recently, the Committee on Federal Credit Programs recommended:

(a) All proposals to create new credit programs or to broaden existing credit programs should be accompanied by an appraisal of the relationship between the interest rate charged in the program, the rate which would be charged by competitive and efficient private lenders and the rate necessary to cover the Government's costs.

(b) The normal reviews of all existing Federal credit programs should include discussion of these relationships.[3]

---

[1] *Lending Agencies*, Report of Commission on Organization of the Executive Branch of the Government, H. Doc. 107, 84 Cong. 1 sess. (1955), Recommendation No. 43.

[2] Commission on Money and Credit, *Money and Credit* (Prentice-Hall, 1961), Chap. 7.

[3] *Report of the Committee on Federal Credit Programs to the President of the United States, February 11, 1963* (U.S. Govt. Printing Office, 1963), pp. 27 and 28.

Subsidies and a Divided Budget

A capital budget for loans is not a necessary prerequisite for the disclosure of subsidies. The present participation certificate (PC) device, whatever its other merits or demerits, certainly marks a step forward in disclosure by requiring annual appropriations for the difference between interest earned on pooled assets and interest paid on participation certificates. Moreover, if the agency concerned, the President, and the Congress are all willing, there is no reason why losses and risk of losses could not be recognized under the existing budget arrangements and adequate loss reserves established. Admittedly, however, present arrangements are not overly conducive to such recognition and disclosure.

Similarly, taking loans out of the budget does not automatically guarantee greater disclosure. The questions which the Commission should consider are (1) whether separate budgeting for loans makes the disclosure of subsidies more or less likely than present arrangements, and (2) how good the chances are of relatively full disclosure.

As the Commission is aware, significant failure to disclose present and probable future losses greatly reduces the appeal of the capital budget format. This could open the door to the juggling of budget totals by the renaming or redesignation of expenditure programs in the form of "loan" programs in order to reduce apparent expenditures and the deficit in the regular budget. On the other hand, since charging the regular budget in full for subsidies and losses would not have a favorable effect on budget totals, there would be no incentive to redesign programs in the form of loans.

Different Types of "Subsidy"

First and most obviously, the practice of charging an interest rate below the rate which the Treasury pays when it borrows can be a very substantial subsidy to the borrower. For example, the present value of a 35-year 2 percent loan (typical Rural Electrification Administration terms) discounted at $4\frac{1}{2}$ percent is approximately 70 percent of face value. In this case, the borrower is in effect receiving an asset worth, say, 100, and at the same time a liability worth only 70. The difference of 30 is every bit as much an expenditure as any ordinary grant, subsidy, or transfer payment and should be recognized as such in the regular budget.

Lending at interest rates below Treasury borrowing costs, however, is not a full measure of the benefits of many programs, since it does not take into account the very large difference in risks between a Treasury security and the loans extended by the Government. This additional benefit could theoretically be measured approximately if it were known at what interest rate private credit institutions would be willing to make the same loan. Often, of course, this can only be conjectural, since usury laws—if not tradition—would deny these borrowers access to the capital markets were it not for Government intermediation.

A final cost element in direct Federal loans concerns the agency costs of administering the loan programs. These can sometimes be quite substantial, depending on the type of loan and the type of borrower. The interest rate charged by the Government often covers only part, if any, of such costs, and it is frequently difficult to discover just what the true administrative costs are. In a few cases, loan programs are administered along with other nonlending programs of the same agency, and there is no full cost accounting of the associated salaries, space, and so on.

It is not clear how much of the total benefits to Government borrowers can properly be taken into the budget as costs, since they probably should not all be viewed as costs to taxpayers. While they are not unanimous on this point, most economists seem to recommend the use of Treasury borrowing costs on loans of comparable maturity as the appropriate measure of the budget costs. In this view, the additional costs measured by the rate of interest that would be demanded by private lending institutions for the same loans represents costs to the general public in their capacity as competitive users of capital rather than as taxpayers. While all costs should be considered in weighing the benefits of a proposed new program or the continuation or expansion of an existing program, these should be part of the Planning-Programming-Budgeting system calculus rather than budget expenditures per se. On the other hand, a failure to count probable losses as ordinary budget expenditures would no doubt lead to some juggling of budget totals by substituting risky loans for outright grants or transfer payments.

It should also be borne in mind that not all the difference between lending rate and the alternative rate at which private loans would be available can properly be considered as undesirable. Part of this difference is the price knowingly and explicitly approved by the Congress for social objectives such as the preservation of family-sized farm units, the promotion of home ownership, the beneficial side effects of urban renewal, public housing, and so on. It is true that these costs should be counted as budget expenditures rather than as loans. It is important, however, to avoid giving the impression that the main purpose of making "subsidy" elements explicit in the budget is to charge borrowers the full costs. Clearly that cannot be the intent, or there would be few Government loan programs in the first place. Rather the purpose is to improve the flow of information to decisionmakers and, for this purpose, the amount charged against the ordinary budget should perhaps be given a more neutral expression, such as "general fund contributions to the costs of loan programs."

RECOGNITION OF SUBSIDIES AND OTHER COSTS

The outlook for formal recognition of all subsidies in Government lending programs is not good. In fact, there is considerable evidence that this is unlikely. For example, administrations for the last decade have requested authority to fund the Rural Electrification Administration on a revolving fund basis. But the Congress has been adamant in its opposition to this change, partly because it did not want the subsidies made explicit.

The history of interest rates used in calculating benefit-cost ratios on water resource projects is also discouraging. From the beginning (dating from the issuance of Bureau of the Budget Circular A–47 in 1952) the water resource agencies have been constrained to discount future benefits on prospective projects by a formula which results in artificially low interest rates and a corresponding overstatement of the present value of future benefits. The formula used takes the average coupon rates on outstanding Treasury bonds which were originally long-term issues. Numerous recommendations by both the Treasury and the Bureau of the Budget to switch over to formulas using actual yields and actual maturities on outstanding Treasury bonds have not proven saleable, even within the executive branch. And these benefit-cost ratios are not even part of budget expenditures, but are rather only part of the analytical background in determining project priorities. It would presumably be even more difficult to win acceptance of a formula that increased budget costs of these projects.

Aside from the problem of recognizing possible future losses, it has often not been possible under present practices even to recognize actual past losses. For example, Congress has refused to allow the General Services Administration to cancel its obligations to the Treasury for funds loaned to the Nicaro Nickel Plant in Cuba. Although the plant was nationalized some years ago, the Congress did not wish to "endorse" the nationalization. Similarly, for diplomatic and political reasons, the United States continues to carry its loans to First World War allies on the Treasury books and in official statements of its foreign exchange assets—although no one else recognizes them.

Some loans probably should not be written down even when it is obvious that collection risks are high. For example, it is highly questionable whether the Government can actually recover the full amount of capital to be advanced to private industry for the development of the supersonic transport aircraft. However, it would not be appropriate for the Government to admit to the industry that it does not expect to be repaid.

A similar situation exists with respect to many foreign aid loans to developing countries. Everyone knows there will be large attrition on these loans. As a matter of policy, however, it is good to have the borrowing country take the loan seriously, and to strive for the economic development that would permit it to service the loans at some future time. In many such cases, a policy of establishing reserves for losses, and making regular payments to the reserves, appears feasible and desirable on a broad formula basis, particularly if loans are to be taken out of the budget.

With many new loan programs, there is not sufficient comparable experience from which to calculate probable future losses with any precision.

Almost each new program involves a new class of borrowers in new situations. Under these circumstances, both the Congress and the executive branch are likely to underestimate probable losses on new loan programs if doing so will reduce the apparent budget costs of programs they prefer. For programs it likes, the Congress may be expected not only to resist having subsidies made explicit, but is quite likely to pass laws prohibiting any budgetary treatment which would make it appear as though the borrowers were being "subsidized."

The actual loss experience on past Government loan programs can be very misleading. Some of the best repayment records are apparently maintained by agencies with extremely soft programs which manage to prevent actual defaults by refunding or further liberalizing the terms whenever a default threatens. Some of the Farmers Home Administration loans are of this character—that is, there is a good loss experience because potential defaulters are carefully aided by the lending agency. The Export-Import Bank never has had a default, in part because it negotiates a refunding when faced with threatened default. Of course, refunding does hold down losses, and is not to be eschewed. But a loan which is *never* repaid is an expenditure, not a loan.

For all of these reasons, it does not appear likely that "subsidies" will be fully recognized at the time of initial loan extension when there is some incentive not to do so. A reduction in apparent budget expenditures is certainly such an incentive.

FOREIGN LOANS AND COMMODITY CREDIT CORPORATION NONRECOURSE LOANS

Some of the worst abuses can be avoided by keeping foreign loans and nonrecourse loans, such as Commodity Credit Corporation (CCC) advances to farmers, in the regular budget, from the outset, rather than in the lending budget. Loans abroad differ in character from domestic loans, quite apart from the fact that they include many "soft loans." Since they give foreigners an immediate claim against U.S. resources, and for this reason enter the balance of payments deficit, foreign loans can logically be treated as expenditures rather than investment. Similar arguments can be made regarding subscriptions to international lending institutions and these, too, should be kept as expenditures in the regular budget.

It is interesting to note that CCC nonrecourse loans are not regarded as loans in the national income accounts budget but, in fact, are treated there as Federal purchases of goods and services. Essentially, these are advances on eventual purchases.

ALTERNATIVE APPROACHES

Several choices are available for handling a recognized difference between Treasury borrowing rates and agency lending rates. The amount might be charged annually over the life of the loan, or it could be given recognition all at once, to the extent of the discounted present value of the difference, at the time the loan is first made. Within each of these possibilities, it is further possible (1) to appropriate on a program-by-program basis; (2) to seek blanket congressional authorization (that is, a permanent indefinite appropriation for all present and future loan programs as a group, such as is now done for interest on the public debt, an expenditure category that is similar in several respects) ; or, finally (3) to include accounting adjustments in the budget totals without any congressional authorization.

Before comparing available alternatives, it is first necessary to recognize that the regular budget already includes—and would continue to include even in a divided budget—the current costs of subsidies arising from past lending at below Treasury borrowing rates. Interest on the public debt is higher than it would be if the Government's interest income equaled the cost of Treasury capital tied up in outstanding loans. To this extent, then, the identification of interest subsidies is not a matter affecting budget totals, even in the context of a divided budget—but only a question of how budget expenditures are classified. (The same is true of administrative expenses. These are already in the regular budget, and would remain there. Identification would involve only a reclassification of expenditures, not a change in budget totals.)

Capitalizing interest subsidies in advance, however, at the time the loans are extended, involves changing budget totals. This allowance would presumably take the form of a regular budget payment to the loan budget, which would have the effect of reducing net lending and increasing ordinary budget expenditures.

Several arguments have been advanced for pay-as-you-go, rather than capitalized-present-value, treatment of interest subsidies. One argument is that the present unified budget approach discriminates against loan programs vis-à-vis, say, grants that might accomplish the same program goals. Since loans now enter budget expenditures to the full extent of their face value, pressures to hold down budget totals tip the scales in favor of outright grants for one year's costs of a multi-year program, and against a loan for the full cost of the program. This argument seems to overlook the point that if the beneficiary needs the funds only a year at a time, the annual installments could take the form of loans rather than grants—and probably would if grants were in the budget and loans were not.

Another argument is that capitalizing interest subsidies in advance would seem to require, for consistency, capitalizing other streams of future Government expenditures, such as a change in a pension or grant or benefit formula which promises future as well as current expenditure increases. Against this argument, it can be pointed out that, at most, the identification of some portion of "loans" as current rather than capital outlay will result in regular budget expenditures of less than the cash amount actually being paid out this year. This is not comparable to a promise to pay cash in future years.

Finally, it is argued that some loans have lasting benefits for society, and to capitalize the interest subsidy would overstate the current cost. However, this is an argument for removing from the budget not merely loans but investments in physical assets and, indeed, health, education, and manpower expenditures which increase the supply of "human capital" as well.

All in all, recognition of the full discounted present value at the outset seems distinctly preferable, logically, to annual payments. If the Government makes a loan of 100, at an interest rate which is so low that the present value of interest and amortization charges is worth only, say, 70, the other 30 is clearly a Government expenditure indistinguishable in substance from a grant or a transfer payment. This should be recognized in the budget totals.

If the device of a regular budget payment to the loan budget, equal to the present value of interest subsidy on new loans, is used, then implicitly "loans outstanding" would be written down proportionately, the balance having been treated as a current expenditure rather than a loan. In such a case, part of the "repayments" that come in subsequently would actually represent interest, and this portion of repayments would become a receipt (or negative expenditure) in the regular budget rather than the loan budget. If loan programs were not expanding, and if interest rates remained constant over a long period, there would be no significant difference in the budget totals between capitalizing the subsidy on new loans, or taking the subsidy on a current basis on the entire portfolio of loans outstanding. Even if loans outstanding were increasing, the difference would apparently not be significant (rough quantitative estimates are given in a later section of this paper). This appears to argue for the pay-as-you-go approach, since it is somewhat easier to explain and present. On the other hand, the capitalized-present-value approach would provide much stronger disincentives for re-designing ordinary expenditures in the form of, say, 50-year interest-free loans in order to reduce budget totals.

With a divided budget approach, defaults—which do not now affect the budget totals (other than to reduce receipts below expectations)—would become charges to the regular budget and credits to the loan budget. Here, too, the preferable approach would be to establish reserves for losses at the outset. Various experts familiar with Government loan programs believe this is quite feasible on a reasonably realistic basis for most existing Federal credit programs, and that this would provide a means of circumventing the reluctance to recognize actual losses. Again, however, the character of present loan programs might not be a fully adequate guide to the feasibility of making accurate risk assessments on new loan programs of an unfamiliar character.

On the issue of what form of authorization to seek, it seems unlikely, indeed impossible, to expect Congress to appropriate program-by-program according to any consistent formula over time. On the other hand, if the Congress understood that only a bookkeeping payment from the regular budget to the lending budget was involved, and not a real exchange of money, it might be willing to recognize once and for all the abstract principle of "equal treatment" for all loan programs, and provide permanent indefinite authorization for the appropriate adjustments to budget totals. It is not inconceivable that the executive branch could make a statistical adjustment to budget totals without congressional authorization, but it seems clearly preferable for Congress to accept this in principle before it is attempted.

If defaults occurred in excess of amounts set aside as reserves for losses, and if such defaults were recognized, the regular budget would be charged with an additional "contribution to the cost of loan programs" which—like interest subsidies and contributions to reserves for losses—would be a lending budget receipt. If the default were not formally recognized, the capitalized formula approach recommended here would still automatically capture part of the effect of the default as a regular budget expenditure. As a result of the default, interest receipts would cease and the difference between the Treasury borrowing rate and interest received would increase. Moreover, strict adherence to the formula might capture a relatively large portion of the effect of the default since it is the whole present value of the future interest rate differential which is being charged. If the new expected repayment date were in the indefinite future, the amount which became payable from the regular budget to the loan budget would equal the entire amount of the unpaid principal.

One of the advantages of the funding arrangements described here is that the budget totals both in the regular budget and in the lending budget would take on an analytical significance which is not now readily available from any present tabulations of the budget. A ready Government-wide comparison could be made between interest received on Government loans and the imputed cost of capital tied up in these loans. Likewise, the "cost" of new loans would be split between the amount which can really be considered as the acquisition of a Federal asset and the amount which is written off currently as an ordinary budget expenditure.

FINANCING OF THE LOAN BUDGET

Even with a divided budget, a decision must be made about which of the various gadgets that have been invented to finance loan programs, such as sales of participation certificates, should be counted as "receipts" in the loan budget and which as "financing items" below the line. It seems appropriate to count PC sales as a financing item rather than as a receipt so that a better measure of net new lending activity will come out of the totals of the loan budget. It must be recognized, however, that there are several borderline transactions which are very difficult to classify. For example, CCC sales of certificates of interest are a form of PC sales and presumably a financing term. On the other hand, if the CCC guarantees private (commercial bank) nonrecourse loans to farmers, it is very hard to distinguish the net effect of this transaction from the sale of a certificate of interest to the bank, or the reissuance of a nonrecourse loan to the farmer directly by CCC. The national income accounts budget, in fact, recognizes no difference in these two transactions and treats both as Federal purchases of goods and services.

Another borderline transaction occurs when the Farmers Home Administration packages outstanding loans and "sells" them in large blocks to private financial institutions, backed by a 100 percent guarantee. The new owners of the loans do not, however, deal directly with the borrowers, and the FHA continues to service the loans. It is hard to see a difference in economic effect between this transaction and the sale of a participation certificate, although an accounting distinction can be made between the sale of individual loans, in the one case, and sale of rights in a pool of loans in the other.

The Budget Deficit Under a Divided Budget

The more imputations loaded into the regular budget on a statistical basis in the form of general fund contributions to the cost of loan programs, the more difficult it is to interpret the significance of the level of budget surplus or deficit so far as economic impact of the budget is concerned. On the other hand, most would argue that changes in the budget surplus or deficit are more significant than the absolute level anyway. And since year-to-year changes in the imputed items may not be all that large (unless a big loan loss, for example, is suddenly given recognition in one year's budget totals), the interpretation of the significance of *changes* in the budget surplus or deficit as an index of the stimulative or restraining impact of the budget on the economy may not be seriously impeded by the inclusion of imputed items.

It should also be noted that in a consolidation of the regular budget and the lending budget, in so far as the over-all level of receipts from and payments to the public, and the over-all surplus or deficit, are concerned, the imputed items would all cancel out as intragovernmental transactions.

Calculation of "Subsidies" and Effect on Budget Totals

Table 1 shows, for various assumed interest rates and maturity schedules, the degree of subsidy involved in lending at below Treasury borrowing rates. The figures in this table have all been calculated around an assumed Treasury borrowing rate of 4½ percent. Thus, for example, if Treasury capital costs 4½ percent, the table indicates that a 3 percent fifty-year loan should really be considered 23.2 percent subsidy and only 76.8 percent pure loan. On the other hand, a five-year loan at 4 percent, using the same assumed Treasury borrowing rate, involves a subsidy equal to only 1.4 percent of the face value of the loan.

These factors have been used to calculate for fiscal 1966 the subsidies implicit in major Federal credit programs. Although most programs include a variety of loans at different terms, it was necessary to select a single interest rate and maturity as "representative" for each major credit program. The results shown in Table 2 are therefore only very rough estimates. Nevertheless, we believe that these calculations represent a rough order of magnitude of Federal interest rate subsidies.

TABLE 1.—*Present value, discounted at 4½ percent, of $100 repayable in equal annual installments over selected periods at selected interest rates*

Maturity in years	Percent												
	0	½	1	1½	2	2½	3	3½	4	4½	5	5½	6
1......	$95.69	$96.17	$96.65	$97.13	$97.60	$98.08	$98.56	$99.04	$99.52	$100.00	$100.47	$100.95	$101.43
5......	87.80	89.12	90.45	91.79	93.14	94.49	95.86	97.23	98.61	100.00	101.40	102.80	104.22
10......	79.13	81.32	83.54	85.80	88.09	90.41	92.76	95.14	97.56	100.00	102.47	104.98	107.51
15......	71.60	74.49	77.46	80.49	83.58	86.74	89.96	93.25	96.59	100.00	103.47	106.99	110.58
20......	65.04	68.51	72.08	75.77	79.55	83.44	87.43	91.52	95.71	100.00	104.38	108.85	113.41
25......	59.31	63.25	67.33	71.57	75.95	80.48	85.16	89.97	94.92	100.00	105.21	110.54	116.00
30......	54.29	58.61	63.12	67.83	72.73	77.83	83.10	88.56	94.20	100.00	105.96	112.08	118.34
35......	49.89	54.50	59.37	64.49	69.85	75.44	81.26	87.30	93.55	100.00	106.64	113.45	120.44
40......	46.00	50.87	56.04	61.51	67.27	73.30	79.61	86.17	92.97	100.00	107.24	114.68	122.30
50......	39.52	44.77	50.42	56.46	62.89	69.68	76.81	84.25	91.99	100.00	108.25	116.72	125.38
60......	34.40	39.90	45.91	52.41	59.37	66.77	74.57	82.74	91.22	100.00	109.03	118.27	127.70
100......	21.95	27.95	34.83	42.52	50.93	59.95	69.46	79.37	89.56	100.00	110.59	121.30	132.09

Source: Office of Debt Analysis, U.S. Treasury Department.

TABLE 2.—*Gross loan disbursements and estimated interest subsidies for major Federal credit programs, fiscal 1966*

[Dollar amounts in millions]

Agency or program	Gross loan disburse- ments	Assumed representative loan terms		Percentage of loan representing interest subsidy [1]	Allocation of gross loan disbursements	
		Interest rate (percent)	Maturity (years)		Interest subsidy	Pure loan
Commodity Credit Corporation	$1,537	3½	1	(2)	(2)	(2)
Foreign loans:						
Military assistance credit sales	81	4½	5	0	$0	$81
Agency for International Development	1,406	2½	30	22.17	312	1,094
Export-Import Bank	685	4⅞	15	0	0	685
Total foreign loans	2,172				312	1,860
Domestic recoverable loans:						
Office of Economic Opportunity	32	4	20	4.29	1	31
Rural Electrification Administration	361	2	35	30.15	109	252
Farmers Home Administration	1,068	4	15	3.41	36	1,032
Economic Development Administration	45	4	25	5.08	2	43
Maritime Administration	8	4	20	4.29	0	8
Office of Education	233	3	8	5.38	13	220
Public Health Service	22	3½	10	4.86	1	21
Federal National Mortgage Association (administrative budget)	327	varies	varies	0	0	327
Federal National Mortgage Association (trust fund)	1,804	varies	varies	0	0	1,804

Federal Housing Administration	365	4½	25	0	0	365
Public housing program	199	4⅝	1	0	0	199
College housing program	344	3	40	20. 39	70	274
Urban renewal program	285	4⅞	varies	0	0	285
Other housing and urban development programs	103	3½	30	11. 44	12	91
Reclamation and irrigation loans	18	2	50	37. 11	7	11
Loans to District of Columbia	71	4	35	6. 45	5	66
Veterans Administration:						
Administrative budget	461	4	30	5. 80	27	434
Trust funds	114	4	25	5. 08	6	108
Small Business Administration	510	4	10	2. 44	12	498
Banks for cooperatives	1, 585	4	20	4. 29	68	1, 517
Federal intermediate credit banks	6, 140	5	7	0	0	6, 140
Other agencies or programs and adjustments	−167			0	0	−167
Total domestic recoverable loans	13, 928				369	13, 559
Total all programs	17, 637				[3] 681	[3] 15, 419

[1] See Table 1.

[2] Not available.

[3] Excludes $1,537 of CCC loan disbursements.

Sources: "Special Analysis E," *Special Analyses, Budget of the United States, Fiscal Year 1968* (1967), and *Federal Credit Programs,* Report by the Secretary of the Treasury to the Congress as required by the Participation Sales Act of 1966, Committee Print, Committee on Banking and Currency, 90 Cong. 1 sess. (1967), pp. 42–49.

Certain points stand out from these calculations. For domestic recoverable loans, the total subsidies implicit in new credit extensions for fiscal 1966 are surprisingly small—approximately $350 million on gross loan disbursements of $13 billion, an average of only about 3 percent of face value. With this type of measure, many large loan programs would not show up as involving a "subsidy," since agency lending rates are often higher than Treasury borrowing rates. The Federal Housing Administration, public housing, urban renewal, and Federal intermediate credit banks are in this category. For some programs, of course, the percentage subsidy is relatively small. The Rural Electrification Administration, the college housing program, and the banks for cooperatives involve the largest subsidies. These three programs account for about two-thirds of the total interest rate subsidy on domestic recoverable loan programs, at least according to the methods used here.

The remaining tables—Tables 3 to 5—are designed to show the effect on fiscal 1966 budget totals of alternative ways of estimating and budgeting for subsidies and other costs of loan programs. These are meant to be analytical tables rather than suggestions about how the loan programs would actually be labeled and presented in a summary tabulation of receipts and expenditures. As a start, Table 3 shows the way in which loan program transactions now affect the consolidated cash budget totals. In Table 4, the present amounts have been rearranged as a "benchmark" against which the subsequent alternatives can be compared. Table 4 differs from Table 3 in only two respects:

> a. For uniformity, loan repayments and interest receipts are treated as negative expenditures rather than miscellaneous receipts, as some of them now are;
> b. To emphasize the major issues, sales of participation certificates (other than CCC certificates of interest) are treated as financing items rather than as receipts or negative expenditures.

In Tables 3 and 4, loan amounts are taken at full face value as shown in "Special Analysis E" in the budget documents, and there is no explicit identification of subsidies.

Table 5 presents budget totals for three alternative treatments of loan cost amounts in comparison with the benchmark figures from Table 4. Alternative 1 is a unified budget presentation in which CCC loans are taken as expenditures rather than loans; no distinction is made between foreign and domestic recoverable loans; and administrative expense, interest rate subsidies, and defaults are shown on a year-by-year basis as incurred, with no advance reserves for losses.

TABLE 3.—*Treatment of loans and financial items in present consolidated cash budget*

[In billions of dollars]

Transaction	1966 actual	1967 estimate	1968 estimate
Receipts from the public:			
Taxes, social insurance premiums, and miscellaneous receipts of administrative budget and trust funds [1]	134.0	154.0	167.6
Interest receipts	.2	.3	.3
Loan repayments [2]	.3	.4	.2
Total receipts	134.5	154.7	168.1
Payments to the public:			
Administrative and trust fund expenditures for purchases, grants, transfer payments, and subsidies, net of interest receipts treated as negative expenditures [3]	135.3	157.2	171.4
Lending:			
Loan disbursements	17.6	22.2	21.7
Deduct:			
Loan repayments and direct sale of loans	−12.9	−16.0	−16.5
Sale of participation certificates (net of retirements) [4]	−2.2	−2.5	−4.2
Net lending	2.5	3.7	1.0
Total expenditures and loans	137.8	160.9	172.4
Cash surplus (+) or deficit (−)	−3.3	−6.2	−4.3
Financing of budget deficit:			
Decrease in cash balances	.1	3.4	
Exercise of monetary authority (seignorage)	.6	1.1	.5
Net cash borrowing by Treasury and other Federal agencies from the public and the central bank	2.6	1.7	3.8
Total financing	3.3	6.2	4.3

[1] Excludes seigniorage and intragovernmental transactions.

[2] Consists only of those loan repayments coming into budget receipts (most loan repayments are deducted from loan expenditures).

[3] Excludes intragovernmental transactions, debt issuance in lieu of checks, revolving fund receipts from exercise of monetary authority, and increase or decrease in outstanding checks.

[4] Excludes CCC certificates of interest.

Sources: Derived from *The Budget of the United States Government for the Fiscal Year Ending June 30, 1968* (1967); Bureau of the Budget, "Statement of Miscellaneous Receipts in the 1968 Budget," January 1967 (offset); and "Special Analysis E," *Special Analyses, Budget of the United States, Fiscal Year 1968* (1967).

TABLE 4.—*Benchmark treatment of lending programs, comparable to present situation*

[In billions of dollars]

Transaction	1966 actual	1967 estimate	1968 estimate
Receipts:			
Taxes, social insurance premiums, and miscellaneous receipts other than loan repayments and interest............	134. 0	154. 0	167. 6
Expenditures and loans:			
Purchases, grants, transfer payments, and subsidies (net of interest received).	135. 0	156. 9	171. 1
Lending:			
Loan disbursements..............	17. 6	22. 2	21. 7
Deduct loan repayments..........	−13. 1	−16. 4	−16. 7
Net increase in loans outstanding.	4. 5	5. 8	5. 0
Total expenditures and loans...	139. 5	162. 7	176. 1
Budget surplus (+) or deficit (−)..........	−5. 5	−8. 7	−8. 5
Financing of budget deficit:			
Decrease in cash balances............	. 1	3. 4	......
Exercise of monetary authority........	. 6	1. 1	. 5
Sales of participation certificates.......	2. 2	2. 5	4. 2
Sale of Treasury and agency securities to the public and the central bank....	2. 6	1. 7	3. 8
Total financing.................	5. 5	8. 7	8. 5

Source: Derived from Table 3.

In Alternative 2, loan principal amounts for domestic recoverable loans are shown in a separate "lending" budget, with foreign loans remaining, however, in the regular budget; and a reserve for losses is charged to the extent of 1 percent of new loan disbursements on all loan programs. Interest subsidies and administrative expense, however, are shown only on a year-by-year basis as incurred.

In Alternative 3, loan principal amounts for domestic recoverable loans are again shown in a separate lending budget while foreign loans remain in the regular budget; a reserve for losses is charged to the extent of 1 percent of new loan disbursements; and administrative expenses are earmarked within the regular budget as in the previous alternatives. Interest rate subsidies, however, are treated by making a payment from the regular budget to the loan budget equal to the capitalized present value of interest rate subsidies on new loans. This last item has the effect of transferring from loan budget expenditures to regular budget expenditures that portion of new loan principal amounts which represents a current expenditure rather than a loan due to a difference between borrowing and lending rates. In this alternative, "repayments" on old loans must be apportioned accordingly between "interest" and pure "repayments," since part of nominal repayments actually represent interest rather than return of capital.

In all the alternatives, certain common assumptions and treatments have been made. Participation certificate sales are treated as borrowing rather than negative lending, while loan repayments, sales of loans, and interest receipts are all treated as negative expenditures rather than revenues. Direct sales of loans have been lumped with loan repayments and the two together are included under the term "repayments." To make the calculations, interest rates on both Treasury borrowing and agency lending are assumed to be approximately constant over a long period with the result that the percentage subsidy is the same for new disbursements as for outstanding loans of the same program. Arbitrarily, administrative expense has been taken at one-fourth of 1 percent of loans outstanding, and payments to the reserve for losses at 1 percent of new loan disbursements. Actual defaults have rather arbitrarily been taken at $0.2 billion for 1966 on domestic recoverable loans, and $0.3 billion on foreign loans. These defaults in turn have been assumed, arbitrarily, to exceed by $0.1 billion each reserves that might have been established previously if the divided budget had been in effect earlier. One final arbitrary adjustment has been made in taking total CCC loans as non-recoverable, although part of CCC lending is not nonrecourse in character. This was done because figures were available for CCC nonrecourse loans only on a net basis, which was not adequate for preparing the other estimates in the table.

TABLE 5.—*Fiscal 1966 budget totals under alternative treatments of loan programs*

[In billions of dollars]

Transaction	Present	Alternative 1	Alternative 2	Alternative 3
REGULAR BUDGET				
Revenues..........................	134.0	134.0	134.0	134.0
Expenditures and loans............	139.5	139.5	136.3	136.5
Expenditures......................	135.0	134.8	134.7	135.1
Credit programs...................	.....	.3	.2	.6
Portion of "loans" taken as current outlay:				
CCC (net).......................		−.7	−.7	−.7
Capitalized interest subsidy on new loans....	.....	.....	.1	.7
Administrative expenses..........		.1	.1	.1
Additions to reserves for losses on new loans..		.	.2	.2
Defaults in excess of past reserves..		.5	.2	.2
Interest on capital invested in outstanding loans..		1.8	1.8	1.5
Deduct:				
Actual interest receipts.........		−1.4	−1.4	−1.4
Portion of loan "repayments" which is actually interest..		.....	.....	−.3
All other expenditure programs..........	135.0	134.5	134.5	134.8
Loans (increase in net loans outstanding)......	4.5	4.7	1.6	1.4
Gross loan disbursements.................	17.6	16.1	2.2	2.2

Deduct:				
Portion of face value "expensed"				
Loan repayments (excl. "repayments" which represent interest)	−13.1	−10.9	−.4	−.3
Contributions to reserves for losses			(1)	(1)
Defaults in excess of past reserves		−.5	−.1	−.1
Budget surplus or deficit	−5.5	−5.5	−2.3	−2.5
LENDING BUDGET				
Gross disbursements (domestic recoverable loans only)			13.9	13.9
Deduct:				
Portion of face value "expensed"				−0.4
Loan repayments (excl. "repayments" which represent interest)			−10.5	−10.3
Contributions to reserves for losses			−.1	−.1
Defaults in excess of past reserves			−.1	−.1
Net increase in domestic recoverable loans outstanding			3.2	3.0
CONSOLIDATED BUDGET				
Revenues	134.0	134.0	134.0	134.0
Expenditures and loans	139.5	139.5	139.5	139.5
Surplus or deficit	−5.5	−5.5	−5.5	−5.5

[1] Less than $50 million.

Source: Derived from Table 4 (see text).

Conclusions

1. In setting up a divided budget in which loan programs are funded separately from other expenditures, some of the worst distortions can be avoided if it is agreed from the start that nonrecourse loans (such as CCC advances to farmers) and loans abroad, whether repayable in local currency or in dollars, continue to be counted as ordinary budget expenditures and not relegated to the lending budget. There are practical reasons for doing this in both cases. The national income accounts budget counts CCC nonrecourse loans as Federal purchases, and loans abroad as different in character from domestic loans, since (a) they depend on more than solvency of the borrower for repayment in dollars, and (b) the Federal Government as lender does not have the same legal remedies in the event of default.

2. For domestic loans, it is most unlikely—one is tempted to say, impossible—to expect the budget and appropriations processes to provide objective or reasonably full measures of total expected future losses over the life of the program at the time the loan commitments are made, if the cost of doing so is an increase in budget expenditures. At present, many of the Government's bad debts are not written off even after it is obvious that the loans have gone sour, even though budget costs are not involved. A policy of establishing reserves for losses would make it possible to give considerably greater recognition to default losses than now. These would not likely be commensurate with probable losses, however, in particularly "soft" programs. Failure to recognize probable losses in advance would create distinctly greater distortions in a divided budget than it does in the present unified budget.

3. It also appears feasible for some portion of interest rate subsidies and for administrative costs to be recognized explicitly. In fact, it would probably be easier to do this in a divided budget context than in the present unified budget context. The recognition of interest rate subsidy is more logically entered on a once-for-all basis when the loan is initially made, although quantitatively the difference between recognizing interest subsidies on a capitalized once-for-all basis, compared to a pay-as-you-go basis, is not large for the present mix of programs. While this is a more complicated approach, the capitalized present-value approach would create larger disincentives to renaming programs in order to get them out of the budget.

4. A significant part of the interest rate subsidy can be derived statistically on a formula basis. The formula would calculate the differences between interest rates to be received and the Treasury's borrowing costs on securities of comparable maturity. Of course, there is an additional element of subsidy because the Treasury borrowing rate does not take full account of the risks of the particular loan and is, therefore, below the rates that would be charged on comparable loans by private lenders. However, at least some part of this additional subsidy element is properly regarded as a social cost rather than

a budget cost, and the remainder could be recognized when and as defaults actually occurred or by charging the budget for reserves for losses, or both.

5. It is well to recognize that loans below the hypothetical "market" rate (or even below the Treasury's borrowing rate) are usually made deliberately for what are more properly regarded as social objectives than "subsidies," such as the promotion of home ownership, the preservation of family-sized farming units, spillover benefits from urban renewal and public housing, and so on. Making this contribution explicit will presumably help hold benefits in line with what is intended, but should not appear to be aimed at eliminating these benefits.

6. Program-by-program legislation or appropriations to pay for subsidy elements seems most infeasible. A uniform formula approach—consisting simply of the difference between the actual lending rate and the Treasury borrowing rate—might, however, win legislative approval.

7. The administrative costs associated with loan programs might also be handled on a flat formula basis, even though there would often be many difficulties in trying to measure and appropriate for these on a program-by-program basis.

8. A formula payment consisting of the difference between the Treasury borrowing rate and the interest rate actually received would partially make up for any failure to recognize losses or risk of losses. For example, if a loan soured and interest receipts ceased altogether, the formula approach would automatically require an additional general fund contribution to the lending budget.

9. If the budget is to be divided, budget expenditures to cover interest subsidy would presumably require appropriations. The most attractive approach would be to seek a permanent indefinite appropriation to cover existing and possible future loan programs before adopting the divided budget approach.

10. With a divided budget, it appears feasible to give recognition at least to the measurable part of interest rate subsidies. In fact, the divided budget approach would seem to provide both the incentives and the opportunity to be much more explicit about interest rate subsidies than the present unified budget. It is also possible, through reserves for losses, to give greater recognition to default risks than is now the case. Given the probable inability to recognize potential future losses fully in a divided budget approach, there is some danger, however, that programs would be renamed or redesigned in order to reduce budget expenditures and the budget deficit.

GEORGE F. BREAK

Department of Economics, University of California, Berkeley

The Treatment of Lending and Borrowing in the Federal Budget

Considerable dissatisfaction has been expressed in recent years with Federal budget accounting, much of it centering around the Federal loan programs. Since these programs have important economic effects, their omission from the national income accounts (NIA) budget seriously lessens this budget's usefulness to policy makers. On the other hand, the full inclusion of these loan programs in the consolidated cash budget apparently distorts the economic picture presented in that document. The effect of new loans on aggregate private spending is more indirect, and possibly less vigorous, than that of other kinds of Federal expenditures.

Within the past five years, increasing use of existing Federal financial assets as a source of budget receipts, both by the outright sale of loan paper and by the use of participation certificates in Federal loan pools, has also raised numerous pointed questions whether these transactions, which reduce the size of the reported cash budget deficit, are really very different from new Treasury borrowing, which does not.

The expert who wishes to evaluate Federal stabilization policies may be able to circumvent these deficiencies by making his own adjustments in reported budget figures, but the general public has neither the ability nor the desire to do so. As a result, people may be led to believe that the Federal government is exerting an inflationary impact on the economy when in fact it is doing the reverse, or they may naively greet with approval a surplus budget that in fact will, when enacted, push prices sharply upward. Perhaps even worse, having learned that there are three different budget surpluses and deficits, and having observed that now one is stressed and now another, they may come to believe that Washington is simply not to be trusted.

The central questions posed in this paper are whether it is possible to define a single budget surplus or deficit figure that can provide a basis for intelligent public discussion of Federal stabilization policies, and if so, what kind of budget statement would produce that figure. It would be foolish to assume that one ideally simple, precise formula is about to be revealed. Nevertheless, in the discussion that follows, a number of improvements in budgetary organization and presentation are identified. Their adoption, it is

58

argued, would help both to clarify public understanding of Federal governmental activities and to provide a sounder base for the analysis and integration of fiscal and monetary policies designed to maintain high employment and stable price levels. The focus throughout this paper is on the usefulness of the official budget for macroeconomic discussions and analyses—that is, for problems of stabilization policy. Other purposes which the budget must also serve, such as the facilitation of cost-effectiveness analysis and growth policy formation, are separable problems beyond the scope of this paper.

The first section describes briefly the analytical macroeconomic budget statements that economists use to determine the need for, and the effects of, alternative stabilization policies. These statements are, of course, much too complex to be usable in the official budget document. Moreover, there is considerable disagreement among the experts over the appropriate quantities to be entered in them. A "good" official budget statement, however, should be related to these analyses because it must provide surplus and deficit figures that do not seriously mislead the public about the effects the Federal government is having on total spending. On the theoretical basis provided in the first section, therefore, rests the subsequent discussion of alternative budget arrangements.

The second section considers the case for a unified budget statement, such as the NIA and cash budgets, and argues that a multipart budget would be preferable. The third section deals at length with the application of this concept to Federal transactions in direct loans, loan guarantees and loan insurance, and Treasury securities. The section closes with a discussion of the use, and possible abuse, of a multipart summary budget statement in the event that one is ultimately adopted. Finally, the fourth section summarizes the conclusions about the best treatment of Federal lending and borrowing in the official budget.

Analytical Macroeconomic Budget Statements

In order to predict the impact on aggregate demand of any set of fiscal or monetary operations, economists must first estimate the separate impact of each component of the policy set and then combine these into a positive or negative net total. In effect, all of the relevant financial transactions are classified into subsets, each containing like elements whose impact on aggregate demand differs from that of the members of any other subset; estimates are made of the net impact of each subset during the time period under consideration; and these estimates are then combined into one final figure or, if the estimates are uncertain, into a range of most probable total effects.

In Table 1, a highly simplified illustration emphasizing Federal lending and borrowing, it is supposed that four subsets have been agreed upon and arranged in descending order of importance as far as their effects on aggregate demand are concerned. To each category is attached a set of economic impact coefficients, k_{it}, which, when multiplied by the amounts of any financial transactions falling in that category, yields estimates of the impact of those transactions on aggregate demand in all future time periods, t. If, for example, a new tax-financed program of direct loans is under consideration and interest centers on the effects on private spending two years later, the desired estimate is $k_{22}LP-k_{12}T$. If the two coefficients are 1.8 and 2.5, respectively, and if the amount of the transaction is 100, the prediction is that two years later aggregate demand will be reduced by 70.

Table 1.—*Illustrative classification of Federal transactions*

Group	Economic impact coefficient [1]	Expenditures (+)		Receipts (−)	
		Item	Amount	Item	Amount
1	k_{1t}	Purchases of goods and services and transfers.	GT	Taxes.	T
2	k_{2t}	Purchases of risky, illiquid securities (direct lending).	LP	Sales of risky, illiquid securities (loan sales; principal repayments).	LS
3	k_{3t}	Purchases of safe, liquid assets (retirement of Treasury debt).	DP	Sales of safe, liquid securities (Treasury debt issue).	DS
4	k_{4t}	Reduction of risk and illiquidity of private securities (issue of new loan guaranties).	IG	Increase of risk and illiquidity of private securities (retirement of guaranteed loans).	RG

[1] $k_1 > k_2 > k_3$ and $k_4 = a(k_2 - k_3)$, $0 < a \leqq 1$, for all t.

It is easy to see from this the nature of the problems that budget makers face. If the economic impact coefficients (EIC's) differ materially among themselves, and there is every reason to believe that they do, conventional budget statements are unlikely to reveal the true macroeconomic effects involved. Balanced budgets may be either expansionary or contractionary; a surplus budget may be strongly inflationary; and a deficit budget may be sharply deflationary. Clearly, one must try to find some way out of such an Alice-in-Wonderland world, where things are seldom what they seem. The route, unfortunately, is a tortuous one.

UNITARY BUDGET STATEMENTS

In terms of the concepts of the preceding section, a conventional unitary budget statement, such as the current NIA and cash budgets, results from dividing a comprehensive listing of all sources and uses of Federal funds into two parts. Above the line are placed those transactions that have important, and approximately similar, impacts on aggregate demand; and below the line go all remaining transactions, the presumption being that they have relatively unimportant, and also approximately similar, macroeconomic impacts. The emphasis here should be on the word "approximate." No one pretends that a simple two-way classification of this sort can give a very precise picture of the complex economic world. The important question is whether it is good enough for the purposes for which the general public typically wants to use it. Does it, in the first place, always and only show a deficit when the Federal Government is exerting an expansionary impact on aggregate demand? And conversely, does it always and only show a surplus when the Government's aggregate impact is negative? These answers will be affirmative if the economic impact coefficients (EIC's) of *all* of the above-the-line transactions are significantly greater than the EIC's of any of the below-the-line transactions. If k_{it} is defined as the set of EIC's for above-the-line items and k_{jt} as the set of EIC's for below-the-line items, the requirement is that:

$$k_{it} > k_{jt}, \text{ for all } i, j, \text{ and } t.$$

A second requirement for general usefulness is that the budget include all governmental transactions that have an important impact on the economy. Placement below the line, then, means exile to the limbo of economic factors that can for the most part be disregarded, and we shall need to consider at a later point whether Treasury borrowing operations should continue to be relegated to that undistinguished position.

The question to be asked about Federal lending programs, therefore, is whether or not they fit nicely into the one category or the other. In terms of Table 2, for example, should item 2 be placed above the line, as it is in the consolidated cash budget, or should it be placed below the line, as it is in the NIA budget? It would be easy to answer this question if the econometricians could only provide reliable estimates of the EIC's for Federal lending and borrowing programs. Unfortunately, they apparently have not yet done so, though there is considerable hope for the future.[1] Lacking these estimates, one must attempt to derive their equivalent indirectly, by studying the economic characteristics of Federal loan programs and relating these to the behavior of private borrowers and lenders.

---

[1] For an interesting recent report on such research see Carl F. Christ, "A Short-Run Aggregate-Demand Model of the Interdependence and Effects of Monetary and Fiscal Policies with Keynesian and Classical Interest Elasticities," *American Economic Review,* Vol. 57 (May 1967), pp. 434–43.

TABLE 2.—*Federal sources and uses of funds statement, consolidated cash basis, fiscal 1966*

[In billions of dollars]

	Uses		Sources	
1	Purchases of goods and services; transfer expenditures; subsidies..	135.5	Taxes and other receipts.....	134.5
2	Loan disbursements.....	17.6	Loan repayments...........	12.3
			Loan sales................	.4
			Sale of participation certificates...................	2.6
3			Decrease in cash balances....	.1
			Seignorage................	.6
			Net cash borrowing by Treasury from public and Federal Reserve System...........	2.6
	Total............	153.1	Total...............	153.1

Sources: *The Budget of the United States Government for the Fiscal Year Ending June 30, 1968* (1967), Table 2, p. 42, and Table 11, p. 52; *Special Analyses, Budget of the United States, Fiscal Year 1968* (1967), Table E–3, p. 63, and Table E–4, p. 65.

There can be no doubt that loans are different. Two basic features that distinguish them from Government purchases and transfers are commonly cited by those who favor exclusion of loans from the regular budget. The first is that Government purchases and transfers are income-expenditure, or flow, transactions, whereas loans are asset-liability, or stock, transactions. While this is a perfectly logical reason to exclude loans from the NIA budget, which deals only with income-expenditure transactions, it is not a sufficient reason for excluding loans from the official budget, which must include all Federal activities that have an important impact on private spending.

Asset-liability transactions may well qualify under the "importance" test, though the contrary view is implied by the following statement made by George Jaszi in a defense of the NIA exclusion of Federal loans: "In the analysis of economic behavior, we must make a distinction between forces that influence economic units by changing their income, and forces that influence them by *merely* changing the composition of their assets and liabilities" (my italics).[2] Use of the word "merely" seems to prejudge the issue before the evidence is in.

The second distinguishing feature concerns the mechanism by which the macroeconomic effects of Government operations are transmitted. Federal

[2] George Jaszi, "The Federal Budget on National Income and Product Account," *Review of Economics and Statistics,* Vol. 44 (August 1962), p. 336.

purchases and transfers affect the private parties to the transactions directly by changing their incomes; Federal loans, it is argued, exert their effects indirectly by altering the terms and availability of credit to private borrowers. The distinction, in other words, is between fiscal programs which concentrate their first-stage effects on the immediate transactors and monetary programs which disseminate their first-stage effects broadly over private credit markets. Since fiscal transactions also have their indirect monetary effects, the presumption is created that the macroeconomic effects occur more quickly and in greater magnitude. If this were uniformly the case, loan programs should be placed in a separate category in the budget, and if their effects were also judged to be minor, they should be excluded entirely. In the latter case a unitary budget statement, with direct loan programs placed below the line, would be appropriate.

Consider, first, the problems involved in separating direct loan programs from Federal purchase and transfer operations. The main difficulties arise for so-called "soft" loans and for loans designed for borrowers who lack access to private credit markets. Examples of the former are loans to foreign borrowers with very long maturities, low interest rates, and permission to make principal repayments in local currencies. To distinguish these from straight gifts, which everyone agrees are above-the-line fiscal transfers, is a difficult task indeed. Similar transfer qualities, in the form of partial forgiveness features, have characterized National Defense Education Act (NDEA) student loans from the beginning and have recently been authorized for Federal borrowers who become the victims of major disasters.[3] Placement of direct loans below the line in a unitary budget would create strong incentives for the conversion of above-the-line grant programs into loans with lenient repayment terms, thereby circumventing some of the constraints that Congress or the Bureau of the Budget might like to see applied to those programs. Similar, though presumably weaker, incentives would exist in a multipart budget that placed loans in a separate category. Ways of minimizing this effect are discussed in the next section.

Whenever a Federal loan is extended to a borrower who lacks access to private credit markets, the full amount of that loan constitutes a net addition to his disposable funds. To this extent it resembles a straight Federal

---

[3] NDEA student loans are forgiven (up to a maximum cancellation of 50 percent) at the rate of 10 percent of the loan principal plus accrued interest for each year that the recipient teaches full time. In 1965 the Southeast Hurricane Disaster Relief Act (PL 89–339) authorized partial cancellations of certain Small Business and Farmers Home Administration loans made to victims of Hurricane Betsy, and in 1966 the Disaster Relief Act (PL 89–769) authorized interest payment waivers on Small Business Administration disaster loans to private institutions of higher education, as well as loan payment suspensions of up to five years on refinancings of Veterans' Administration and Housing and Urban Development loans made previously to victims of major disasters.

grant. The repayment feature of the loan, it is true, may lead the borrower to behave differently from the grantee, but this difference need not detract from the relative income-generating powers of the loan. Indeed, whereas the grantee may take his time about spending his gift, the borrower is likely to feel some pressure to invest his loan proceeds quickly so as to increase his prospective income stream and hence his ability to meet the periodic loan payments. In principle, then, one might well decide that loans granted to submarginal borrowers are primarily fiscal transactions and should be placed above the unitary budget line, while loans granted to nonmarginal borrowers are primarily monetary transactions and should be placed below the line.[4] The problem, of course, is to identify the Federal loans that do in fact go to submarginal borrowers. Both variety and ambiguity characterize the statutory and administrative regulations that govern the relation between Federal lending agencies and private lenders. This is evident from the following summary, prepared by the House Committee on Banking and Currency in 1963, of the determinations that Federal lenders must make before extending their own credit to an applicant:

> For two programs . . . the determination requires a finding that private financing is not available. For 20 programs . . . the determination requires a finding that private financing is not otherwise available on reasonable terms. For another five programs . . . the determination is on a basis that private financing is not available on terms equally favorable to those available under the Federal credit program. For five programs the determination is on a basis of terms and conditions which the borrower "could reasonably be expected to fulfill." Under the remaining 42 credit programs . . . the Federal credit agency is not required to make any determination as to the availability of private financing.[5]

Needless to say, opinions differ about what constitutes "reasonable terms of private credit." As long as Federal lending agencies operate under such vague constraints it will be impossible to make a sharp distinction between loans to submarginal and loans to nonmarginal borrowers. This strengthens the case for treating all direct loans in the same way for budgetary purposes and also provides one argument for not excluding them entirely.

Another, more important, argument is provided by recent experience in

---

[4] Nonmarginal loans may well affect other borrowers more than they affect the persons who actually receive the Federal funds. Consider, for example, a Federal loan of $100 extended to a borrower who otherwise could have obtained $80, on more stringent terms, from private lenders. The Federal borrower, therefore, experiences a net increase in his disposable funds of only $20, but private lenders have $80 more to lend than they otherwise would have had. Federal loans of this sort clearly resemble closely the monetary policy tools used by the Federal Reserve to ease private credit markets.

[5] *A Study of Federal Credit Programs,* House Subcommittee on Domestic Finance of the Committee on Banking and Currency, 88 Cong. 2 sess. (1964), Vol. 1, p. 77.

this country with countercyclical monetary policy. The postwar record indicates rather clearly that monetary ease has helped significantly during recessions and that monetary restraint, notably in 1966, is capable of restraining aggregate demand. If this is so, it is hard to believe that Federal loan programs have such insignificant economic effects that they should be placed below the line in a unitary Federal budget. It may be objected that there is likely to be very little net impact once the stimulating effects of direct Federal loans are offset by the opposite effects of the Treasury debt sales that finance them. In rebuttal one may argue that the lending operation will cause a shift of funds from the buyers of the new Treasury bonds to the recipients of the Federal loans, leading to a net increase in private spending for new output. In other words, the EIC for Federal loans (k_2) is taken to be significantly greater than the EIC for Treasury debt operations (k_3), though the empirical evidence on this score is far from unequivocal.

More fundamentally, however, one may object that it is a gross oversimplification to assume that Federal loans are always, and more or less automatically, financed by Treasury borrowing. For this to be true there would have to be no interaction between loans and other types of Federal spending, or between loans and the revenue side of the budget. Though these fiscal offsets, as I have called them,[6] are impossible to quantify, they do exist and they are too important to be ignored. The Vietnam war provides an especially dramatic illustration both of the downward pressures that one expanding Federal spending program can place on others, such as the poverty program, and of the impact of higher Federal spending on tax policy. *Ex ante,* then, we cannot tell to what extent new loan programs will be financed by higher taxes, by lower nonloan expenditures, or by increased Treasury borrowing; and *ex post,* though we can say that a deficit is financed by borrowing, we cannot say which particular expenditure programs gave rise to that deficit and hence were in fact debt-financed. Clarity about fiscal affairs can best be achieved by keeping expenditure operations separate and distinct from financing operations, as was done in the discussion of economic impact coefficients in the first section.

A final reason for excluding loans from the Federal budget has to do with the scope of that document. (This applies equally well to Treasury debt operations.) Since the Federal Reserve System is not included in the budget, a complete picture of Government monetary operations cannot be given. It may be argued that no picture at all is better than a partial one. A partial picture is likely to be misleading, however, only if the monetary offsets are so fully operative that Federal lending and borrowing exert no net impact on the economy. This would happen in either of two ways. Disliking the mone-

---

[6] George F. Break, *Federal Lending and Economic Stability* (Brookings Institution, 1965), pp. 19–27.

tary effects of Federal loan and debt operations, the Federal Reserve might completely offset them; or approving of the effects, it might simply refrain from producing them itself.

This view of the policy world, however, exaggerates the powers of the central bank. It will not always be able, or willing, to offset fully the effects of Federal lending and borrowing. When it does not, those operations qualify for inclusion in the budget. Programs that sometimes have important net effects and sometimes do not, however, are not very satisfactory members of the budget family. It seems preferable to expand the Federal budget to include Federal Reserve open market operations. This should help to clarify the true monetary picture—namely, that Federal lending does have important effects but that these, on occasion, may be partially or fully offset by Treasury or Federal Reserve transactions of an opposing nature. This is discussed more fully in the next section.

All factors considered, then, direct Federal loans are too different from Federal purchases and transfers to be placed above the line in a unitary budget, but are too important economically to be placed below the line. The only solution appears to be the adoption of a multipart budget statement.

MULTIPART BUDGET STATEMENTS

The conversion of existing unitary Federal budgets—either the NIA or cash versions—into a single, comprehensive, multipart budget statement raises several important questions:

   1. Should direct loan repayments, loan sales, and participation certificate sales all appear in the lending budget or should one or more of these transactions be placed elsewhere?
   2. Should guaranteed and insured loans be placed in the multibudget, and if so, how?
   3. Should Treasury borrowing and Federal Reserve open market operations be shown in the budget?
   4. Should all direct loan disbursements be placed in the lending budget, or should some of them appear elsewhere?

These problems are discussed below.

Participation certificates and other loan program receipts

With the Federal Government's direct loan portfolio close to or above $30 billion in recent years there have been numerous questions in Congress and elsewhere concerning the desirability of selling off some of these assets. Such a policy has the attraction of substituting private for public credit. Whenever Federal expenditures exceed Federal receipts, this policy offers the enticing prospect of reducing the size of the reported deficit, hopefully without incurring some of the undesirable effects of expenditure cuts or tax increases.

The chief difficulty has arisen over the terms on which the loans may be sold. Since the great majority were initially extended on more lenient terms than private lenders would have been willing to give the same borrowers, subsequent sales are possible only at a discount below par unless, in the meantime, interest rate levels have fallen sufficiently. A Budget Bureau memorandum of early 1963, for example, estimated that as of the middle of that year, when the Government's holdings of direct loans were expected to reach $30.0 billion, some $22.7 billion of them would generally not have been suitable for sale at all; among the remaining $7.3 billion were many loans that could be sold only at large discounts.[7] A systematic program of loan sales was in fact under way, but the expected volume was only $0.9 billion for fiscal 1963 and $1.8 billion for fiscal 1964 (see Table 3).

TABLE 3.—*Direct and participation sales of Federal loans, fiscal 1963–68*

[In millions of dollars]

Fiscal year	First budget estimate [1]		Second budget estimate [1]		Actual	
	Total sales	Participa- tion sales	Total sales	Participa- tion sales	Total sales	Participa- tion sales
1963.........	......	....	926	....	1, 142	....
1964.........	1, 846	....	1, 593	....	1, 077	....
1965.........	2, 274	....	2, 227	....	1, 564	750
1966.........	3, 108	....	3, 307	2, 635	2, 961	2, 601
1967.........	4, 739	4, 205	3, 922	3, 580	......	....
1968.........	5, 275	5, 000	......	....	......	....

Source: *The Budget of the United States Government*, "Special Analysis E, Federal Credit Programs," various issues.

[1] The first budget estimate for 1964, for example, is the one given in the official budget for that year; the second estimate appeared a year later in the budget for fiscal 1965; the actual figure was reported 2 years later in the budget for fiscal 1966.

The prospects for a successful, large-scale loan sales program, consequently, were not encouraging, as long as it was based on the separate disposition of individual loans. Previous experience had been gained, however, by both the Reconstruction Finance Corporation and Export-Import Bank with the use of participation certificates by means of which beneficial interests in pools of Federal loans could be sold to private investors even though few of the loans in the pool were saleable individually. It was a flexible device both for spreading risks and for sharing them between the Government and the private lender, and it reached its ultimate refinement,

---

[7] *Continuation of Present Debt Ceiling*, Hearing before the House Committee on Ways and Means, 88 Cong. 1 sess. (1963), pp. 66–71.

amid considerable controversy, in the Participation Sales Act of 1966 (PL 89–429).[8] As Table 3 indicates, participation certificates are now being used to an important extent. Their treatment in the Federal budget is therefore a matter of considerable consequence.

The 1966 Act authorized six Federal lending agencies[9] to place part or all of their outstanding loan portfolios in pools to be administered by the Federal National Mortgage Association (FNMA). It authorized FNMA to sell participation certificates, subject to an annual ceiling amount to be set by Congress in an appropriation act, even if the interest payments on these certificates exceeded the interest payments due on the pooled loans. Any deficiencies that FNMA might experience on this account were to be made up by "timely payments" on the part of the lending agencies concerned; and the Act authorized the appropriation, without fiscal year limitation, of the funds required for such payments.

The effect of this ingenious arrangement was to make participation certificates virtually indistinguishable from ordinary Treasury securities. As the Banking and Currency Committee stated in their report on the Act: "Purchasers of participations would be assured of timely payments of principal and interest without further action by the Congress."[10] The minority report of that committee described the arrangement more vividly:

> The purchaser of the participation does *not* acquire title to the pooled asset. He does *not* even acquire a pro rata interest in the assets pooled. All he acquires is the right to have his investment repaid with interest at the rate stated in the participation certificate. The agency pooling the loans retains the right to any excess payments that may be received in the trust on account of principal or interest from the loans pooled. . . . The agency pooling the loans continues to bear the responsibility and burden of servicing the loans. The agency pooling the loans remains exposed to the risks of default.
> . . . The investment quality of the participations is established by the FNMA guarantee of the participations, in turn backed by an *unlimited draw on the U.S. Treasury,* rather than by whatever the quality of the assets pooled.[11]

Finally, even the most conservative investor who is more suspicious of an FNMA guarantee than he is of a standard Treasury security should be reassured by the following statement in the recent Fowler report on Federal credit programs:

> The Attorney General has ruled in several instances that in the absence of statutory provisions to the contrary, a guarantee by a Federal agency contracted pursuant to a

---

[8] For further discussion of this Act and its implications for the budget, see "Loans, Participation Certificates, and the Financing of Budget Deficits," this volume, pp. 15–36.

[9] The Farmers Home Administration, the Office of Education, the Department of Housing and Urban Development, the Veterans' Administration, the Export-Import Bank, and the Small Business Administration.

[10] *Sale of Participations in Government Agency Loan Pools,* H. Rept. 1448, 89 Cong. 2 sess. (April 25, 1966), p. 5.

[11] *Ibid.,* pp. 18 and 22.

congressional grant of authority is an obligation fully binding on the United States, whether or not a source of funds for fulfillment of the guarantee obligation has been specified.[12]

Participation certificates issued under the 1966 Act, we may conclude, should be treated in the budget in the same way that new issues of Treasury debt are treated. They should not, in other words, be entered on the receipts side of the lending sub-budget, along with principal repayments and ordinary loan sales.

The next question, then, is whether ordinary loan sales have a sufficiently greater (negative) impact on aggregate demand to justify their inclusion in the lending sub-budget. That there is a difference in the nature of the two sets of assets is clear. Outstanding Federal loans are risky, illiquid securities, whereas Treasury debt, guaranteed agency securities, and participation certificates are all riskless and frequently highly liquid. Whether these differences produce a significant divergence in the economic impact coefficients is debatable, but my own preference is to place loan sales in the lending budget until it can be demonstrated that they do not, in fact, contribute any more monetary restraint than an equal volume of participation sales or new Treasury debt issues. In any case, the budget should provide sufficient detail to permit the user to reclassify loan sales if he wishes to do so.

Guaranteed and insured loans

A strong case can be made for including federally-guaranteed or insured loans [13] in the budget in one or more separate categories. Many of these loans, though made with private funds, have economic effects that are very similar to those of direct Federal loans.[14] As the Secretary of the Treasury recently noted:

---

[12] *Federal Credit Programs,* A Report by the Secretary of the Treasury to the Congress as Required by the Participation Sales Act of 1966, Senate Committee on Banking and Currency, Committee Print, 90 Cong. 1 sess. (1967), p. 7.

[13] No sharp distinction is made officially between guaranteed and insured loan programs. Generally, however, an insurance operation is intended to be self-supporting while a guaranty program frequently is not. *Ibid.,* pp. 10–11.

[14] Gerhard Colm has been a longtime advocate of adding guaranteed and insured loans to the budget. According to Colm:

> The economic impact of Federal Loan Insurance and guaranty activities should be stated in a supplement to the modified [by the addition of direct loan programs] National Income Account. The economic impact of these programs may be of substantial importance even though they are reflected only with negligible amounts in budget expenditures. All these activities should be readily visible when reviewing the total impact of the government's activities in any one year. In general, it must be left to the user of the information to decide what part of the loans would be extended even if there were no Federal insurance or guarantee.

See Gerhard Colm and Peter Wagner, "Some Observations on the Budget Concept," *Review of Economics and Statistics,* Vol. 45 (May 1963), p. 124.

The sharp distinction between the role of the Federal Government in direct loans and its role in guaranteed or insured loan programs has been disappearing over the past decade or so, as many new techniques have modified the types of participation by the Federal Government and by private lenders.[15]

In its direct lending programs the Federal Government normally originates the loan, services it during its lifetime, finances it, and bears the full risk. With insured loans it need not perform any of the first three functions, and it need assume only part, though usually a major one, of the total risk involved. In the event, however, it has chosen not to keep the two types of loans so neatly separated. Most of the insured loans of the Farmers Home Administration are originated and serviced by that agency, and the full risk is borne by the Federal Government, as it is also in the guaranty programs operated by the Commodity Credit Corporation, the Urban Renewal Administration, and the Public Housing Administration.

The economic effects of Federal loan insurance and guarantees are similar to those of direct Federal loans in two ways:

1. When granted to submarginal borrowers, both types increase the disposable funds of the recipients by the full amount of the loans.

2. When directed to nonmarginal borrowers, both types exert their impacts mainly by liberalizing lending terms and increasing the availability of credit for a broad group of potential borrowers. Their effects, in short, are primarily monetary rather than fiscal.

The two types do, however, differ in their sources of financing. Direct loans, as we have seen, may be financed in a variety of ways—by Federal taxpayers; by beneficiaries of competing Federal spending programs; by private borrowers who, because of the credit stringency created by new issues of Treasury debt, are rationed out of the credit market; by money creation by the Federal Reserve; or by the activation of idle money balances. Insured and guaranteed loans, on the other hand, must for the most part be financed either by monetary expansion or by other borrowers. Expanding insurance and guaranty programs *might,* it is true, exercise some restraint on Federal expenditures or induce some tightening of tax policy, but since the budgetary reviews and restraints that apply to fund-using programs are absent, it seems unlikely that these fiscal offsets would be important. If this is so, it adds another reason for assigning insured and guaranteed loans their own special budgetary niche.

Adding the loan insurance and guaranty programs to the regular budget would increase the availability of comprehensive information about important governmental economic activities. This benefit would not be without its cost, mainly in the form of rather high uncertainty about the significance of

---

[15] See the Secretary's Report on *Federal Credit Programs, op. cit.,* p. 5.

the new figures.[16] How many lenders, it may be wondered, use the insurance and guaranty programs simply because they are there, making loans that they would have made in any case, though on somewhat more stringent terms. Some of the uncertainty, to be sure, is no greater than that which characterizes the direct loan programs. Guaranteed loans to submarginal borrowers, for example, are in principle at least as income-generating as Government transfer payments, but in practice, as noted earlier, it is difficult to identify them unequivocally. Perhaps the most intractable programs, at least for the present, are those of the Federal Housing and Veterans' Administrations. To measure their effects on the level of residential construction requires both an estimate of their impact on mortgage credit terms and then an estimate of the effect of that credit-term change on the demand for new housing. My own exploratory studies in this area, made in 1957–59, yielded a set of estimates with an uncomfortably wide variance, though the smallest did indicate an expansionary force of $1.4 billion a year, about 40 percent of the average annual change in FHA and VA loans outstanding in 1957–59.[17] A more recent study, covering the 1946–63 period, places the current impact of the programs at the considerably lower level of about $1.0 billion a year, or only about 25 percent of the average annual increase in FHA and VA loans outstanding during 1963–66.[18] Since the FHA and VA programs dominate Federal loan insurance and guaranty operations, uncertainty in that area is particularly bothersome.

There are, however, four guaranty programs about which there should be little doubt. These are the agricultural price-support loans of the Commodity Credit Corporation, the local authority notes and bonds guaranteed by the Public Housing and Urban Renewal Administrations, and guaranteed defense production loans. Each is subsidiary to a much more important Federal spending program. Their effect is mainly to postpone Federal expenditures that would have been made in any case.[19]

In a Federal budget that is measured on a cash basis, these guaranteed loans should simply be omitted since their purchase or retirement will show up automatically in cash expenditures. If the budget is placed on an accrual basis, however, these four programs should be placed in the fiscal sub-budget, and the net change in the amount of their guaranteed loans outstanding added to, or subtracted from, other Federal expenditures for goods and

---

[16] In addition, there might be some mistaken inferences about the amount of Federal money involved in the programs. These could presumably be minimized by a carefully designed tabular presentation of the insurance and guaranty programs.

[17] George F. Break, *The Economic Impact of Federal Loan Insurance* (Washington: National Planning Association, 1961), pp. 25–26, 58–65, and 225–54.

[18] A. H. Schaaf, "Effect of Federal Mortgage Underwriting on Residential Construction," *The Appraisal Journal*, Vol. 35 (January 1967), pp. 54–69.

[19] For a detailed analysis of the four programs see *The Economic Impact of Federal Loan Insurance, op. cit.*, pp. 18–20, 80–113, 132–38, and 211–15.

services or transfers.[20] The economic impacts in question occur when the loans are guaranteed rather than later when the Federal expenditures are made.

Treasury security transactions

In the modern multibudget there appears to be ample room for both Treasury borrowing and Federal Reserve open market operations. Economists have long argued that borrowing from the central bank and borrowing from the general public have different economic effects. It is time for this important distinction to be clarified, rather than obscured, by the Federal budget. Suppose, for example, that in a given year Federal expenditures exceed revenues by $5 billion and that the Treasury issues new debt of an equal amount. The economic effects of these Government operations will be one thing if the Federal Reserve is also selling Treasury securities on the open market and quite another if it is a substantial buyer of those securities. Such differences cannot be found in any of the existing Federal budgets, but they would be revealed if a separate sub-budget were created for all transactions in Treasury securities between the Government and the private sector of the economy. Table 4 illustrates how the examples given here would appear in such a sub-budget.

This proposal does not mean that the Federal budget should, or indeed could, show all of the effects of national monetary policy. The Federal Reserve does not live by open market operations alone, and the use of its other instruments cannot readily be shown in the budget accounts. What is recommended, however, is that the Federal budget be made into a comprehensive financial document which nets out all intragovernmental debt transactions, such as those between the Treasury and the trust funds and between the Treasury and the Federal Reserve, but which shows fully all debt transactions with non-Federal investors. Only thus can a complete and realistic picture be given of the economic effects of Federal financial transactions.

There is, however, one major obstacle that appears to preclude a full implementation of the proposal. It seems clear that the Federal Reserve will not wish to provide projections for its open market operations comparable to those now given in each budget for the remainder of the current, and the whole of the following, fiscal year. These entries in the Federal debt sub-budget (or supplementary statement if that form seems more desirable) could simply be left blank, or if there is a stable trend to Federal

---

[20] Whether the budget should be placed on a cash or accrual basis is not at issue here, but it may be noted that in the 1963 Symposium on Budget Concepts the experts qualified their answer to this question, preferring an accrual budget for some purposes and a cash budget for others. See "Budgetary Concepts: a Symposium," *Review of Economics and Statistics,* Vol. 45 (May 1963), especially the comments by Colm and Wagner (pp. 123–24), Otto Eckstein (p. 127), Richard Goode (pp. 131–32), and Carl S. Shoup (p. 139).

TABLE 4.—*Illustrative budget treatment of Federal Reserve transactions*

[In billions of dollars]

Transaction	Deficit financed by debt		Deficit financed by new money	
	Expendi-tures (−)	Receipts (+)	Expendi-tures (−)	Receipts (+)
Net Treasury debt issue (+) or retirement (−)............	......	5.0	......	5.0
Net Federal Reserve open market sales (+) or purchases (−)...............	......	1.0	6.0	......
Total net change in Federal debt held by the "public" [1].....	......	+6.0	−1.0	......

[1] The "public" here includes private investors, both domestic and foreign, as well as State, local and foreign governments. It covers, in other words, everyone other than the Federal Government itself.

Reserve net purchases or sales at full employment levels of GNP, these "normal" figures could be used instead of actual forecasts.[21] If to this were added information about the maturity dates of outstanding Treasury securities, the budget user would be able to estimate the impact of projected Federal Government operations on private credit markets.

It appears that the present budget would be more useful if a summary budget account were added that consolidated all Federal debt transactions, and separated those that involve the trust funds and the Federal Reserve from those involving other investors. If this change is made, the definition of "public debt held by the public" should be altered to include only Treasury securities held by non-Federal investors (shifting the Federal Reserve from the public to the Federal sector of the economy) and, further, the summary budget table dealing with the public debt should be redesigned to reflect this altered definition.[22]

---

[21] In a recent discussion of the 1968 budget, for example, Michael E. Levy specified a "normal" absorption of Treasury securities by the U.S. trust funds and the Federal Reserve together of $3.5 billion between July 1 and December 31, 1967. See his "Fiscal 1968 Deficit—a Policy Dilemma," in the National Industrial Conference Board's *Business Trends*, July 10, 1967, p. 110.

[22] *The Budget of the United States Government for the Fiscal Year Ending June 30, 1968* (1967), Table 11, p. 52.

Special types of direct loans

We have already noted the ambiguous budgetary nature of loans made to submarginal borrowers and loans extended on especially lenient terms. Though a good case can be made for placing loans to submarginal borrowers in the fiscal, rather than in the lending, sub-budget, it seems impossible, at least for the present, to identify clearly the loans that should be so treated. It is recommended, therefore, that no such distinction be attempted, but rather that those programs that are intended primarily for marginal borrowers be identified as a separate category in the lending sub-budget. This procedure may also avoid some difficult arguments over what is, and what is not, a submarginal borrower program, since placement in the fiscal, rather than the lending, sub-budget might subject a program to more stringent budgetary controls. How great that risk is likely to be is difficult to judge. Clearly the risk should be less with the kind of multipart budget being recommended here than it would be for a unitary budget with loan programs placed below the line. In the multibudget the deficit or surplus shown in the lending segment would inevitably receive considerable official and public attention, but less significance would presumably be attached to it than to the deficit or surplus shown in the fiscal sub-budget. Downward pressures, consequently, might well turn out to be somewhat less for lending, than for fiscal, programs.

One of the potential drawbacks of a separate budget for Federal loan programs, then, is the incentive it might provide for the conversion of grants and subsidies into lenient-term loans that would accomplish approximately the same purpose. This could be done by setting a very long period until maturity, by charging low interest rates, by allowing the suspension of loan payments under certain contingencies, or by providing for the outright waiver of loan principal and interest payments if the borrower meets some predetermined conditions. All of these devices are currently employed, and their use might well expand if a multipart budget were adopted. There is, however, one relatively simple means of counteracting these tendencies. Since it is discussed in some detail in another chapter in this book, it need only be mentioned briefly here.[23] In essence, the proposal is to value Federal loans, for budgetary purposes, not at cost to the Government but at what they would sell for on a market that evaluated all future income streams at the Federal borrowing rate—that is, the interest rate that the Treasury would have to pay if it issued securities with maturities comparable to those of the direct Federal loans being valued. Though this procedure, if consistently applied to all direct loans, would produce both accrued capital gains and accrued capital losses, recognition in the budget is proposed only for the losses. This would be done by showing the market value of low interest rate loans in the lending

---

[23] See "Problems in Implementing a Capital Budget for Loans," a staff paper of the President's Commission on Budget Concepts, in this volume.

budget and entering the accrued capital loss in the fiscal budget as a subsidy. If a 40-year, 2 percent, $100 Federal loan were made to some fortunate borrower, for example, and if the Federal borrowing rate were 4½ percent, under the proposal the loan would be shown as worth only $67 in the lending budget, while a $33 subsidy expenditure would be charged to the fiscal budget. A 10-year, 4 percent loan, on the other hand, would have an imputed subsidy of only $5.

While questions can be raised concerning the use of the Federal borrowing rate to evaluate direct loan programs,[24] they are not germane to this discussion. The proposal described would shift a larger and larger portion of a direct loan to the fiscal budget as the terms of that loan were made more and more lenient. Its adoption, therefore, would help to counteract whatever incentives there might be with a separate lending budget to show a less conspicuous deficit by converting grants and subsidies into lenient-term loans.

A prototype multibudget statement

Table 5 shows the general form which a multipart summary budget statement might take. The rationale underlying most of its components has already been given, but a few additional comments may be helpful:

1. Items A1, A2, and A3 are not shown in greater detail because their budgetary treatment is not under discussion in this paper.

2. Item A4 would, of course, include the income-expense transactions of both the direct and the insured and guaranteed loan programs.

3. Item A5 would be shown, for reasons noted above (see section on guaranteed and insured loans), if the budget statement were given on an accrual basis.

4. The case for including estimates of the subsidies implicit in the direct loan programs was discussed in the immediately preceding section.[25] Similar computations could also be made for the loan insurance and guaranty programs, as well as for Government enterprises that sell their output to the public.

5. The direct lending account could show the capital transactions of its component programs in either or both of two ways: (1) recording the amounts of loans outstanding at the beginning and at the end of each fiscal year; or (2) showing for each year gross loan disbursements, principal repayments, and loan sales and writeoffs. As indicated earlier, participation certificate sales should be excluded from this account and shown in the Treasury and agency debt account.

[24] See, for example, my own discussion of this question in *Federal Lending and Economic Stability, op. cit.,* pp. 19–46.

[25] For a detailed discussion of the integration of item A6 with the direct lending account, see "Problems in Implementing a Capital Budget for Loans" in this volume.

6. In the loan insurance and guaranty account it probably would be sufficient to show the amounts of the major types of loans outstanding at the beginning and end of each fiscal year.

7. Federal receipts from the sale of securities are divided between the direct lending and the Treasury and agency debt accounts on the basis of the riskiness and liquidity of the assets involved. Since these qualities can vary more or less continuously from one end of the spectrum to the other, arbitrary distinctions are probably inevitable. Reclassifications may also be required from time to time. The unguaranteed securities of some Federal agency might become risky enough to warrant placing them in the lending account, or participation certificates might qualify for that account by requiring that their purchasers bear a portion of the risks attached to the pool of loans in which they buy an interest. One of the great virtues of the multibudget format, however, is that it tends to minimize the importance of arbitrary distinctions.

Finally, a few words should be said about the use and interpretation of the multibudget. Clearly this would be a more difficult task for the layman

TABLE 5.—*A prototype multipart summary budget statement of Federal financial operations*

Item	Receipts (+)	Expenditures (−)
A. Fiscal operations:		
A1. Cost of nonpriced Government output (Federal purchases of goods and services)...........		
A2. Priced output (expenditures and receipts of Government enterprises).................		
A3. Transfers (grants, income subsidies, interest payments, taxes, and so on)..............		
A4. Lending programs: Transactions on current account (administrative expenses; interest income; changes in loss reserves; writeoffs)...		
A5. Lending programs: Special capital transactions (Public Housing Administration, Urban Renewal Administration, Commodity Credit Corporation, and defense production direct and guaranteed loans)..................		
A6. Implicit subsidies:		
Government enterprise operations........		
Direct lending operations..............		
Loan insurance and guaranty operations..	———	———
Surplus (+) or deficit (−) on fiscal account......................	═══	═══

TABLE 5.—*A prototype multipart summary budget statement of Federal financial operations*—Con.

Item	Receipts (+)	Expenditures (−)
B. Monetary operations:		
B1. Direct lending account:		
B11. Foreign loans......................		
B12. Defense loans......................		
B13. Domestic, civil loans...............		
Marginal borrowers...........		
Unrestricted................		
Other......................		
Surplus (+) or deficit (−) on lending account.....		
B2. Loan insurance and guaranty account:		
B21. Foreign loans.....................		
B22. Defense loans.....................		
B23. Domestic, civil loans..............		
Marginal borrower programs...		
FHA and VA housing loans....		
Other......................		
Increase (−) or decrease (+) in the amount of insured and guaranteed loans outstanding.......		
B3. Treasury and agency debt account:		
Net Treasury and agency borrowing from:		
B31. U.S. trust funds..............		
B32. Federal Reserve System........		
B33. Non-Federal investors:		
Foreign................		
Domestic..............		
Increase (+) or decrease (−) in:		
Gross debt outstanding (B31+B32 +B33).......................		
Intragovernmental debt outstanding (B31+B32)....................		
Net debt outstanding (B33)........		

than if a single, unitary budget were used.[26] Several different accounts would
be shown, each with its own separate balance, and questions would undoubtedly arise about what each meant, and whether they could be added
together, and so on. Many people would need help in making up their minds,
and this might seem an unfortunate state of affairs. It is, however, the way
the world is. All of us need help, and the trouble with the unitary budget is
that it misleads some and makes it harder for others to find the information
they need in order to understand what the Federal Government is really
doing. The multibudget, on the other hand, is comprehensive enough to
include everything of importance in the Federal financial sector and flexible
enough to permit each expert to derive, with a few appropriate adjustments,
his own estimate of the net macroeconomic' impact of the Federal
Government.

CONCLUSIONS

It has long been recognized that no one budget arrangement will serve
all of the purposes for which Federal financial data are needed. This paper
has dealt with the design of a summary budget statement that would show,
with reasonable accuracy and without excessive complexity, the net impact
of the Federal Government—particularly of its lending and borrowing
activities—on the level of aggregate demand in the country. Since Federal
financial activities are far from homogeneous in this respect, a unitary
budget, such as the consolidated cash or NIA budget with its single surplus
or deficit, does not provide a satisfactory answer to the problem. Different
program groups need recognition of their distinctive macroeconomic impacts.
Each should be shown separately in the summary budget statement, with its
own surplus or deficit serving as an indicator of the group's net contractionary or expansionary impact. In principle, these group surpluses and
deficits could be converted into comparable units if they were multiplied by
a suitable set of economic impact coefficients and then combined into a single
consolidated surplus or deficit. Given the present degree of uncertainty about
the effects of various Federal programs, however, it seems best to leave the
consolidation for the budget user and simply to present a budget of many
parts. With these parts, the multibudget does not imply that all Federal
activities are equally important from the point of view of national stabilization policy. Though their arrangement would indicate the best official judgment about their relative income-generating powers, the user would be able
to make whatever rearrangements he thought desirable.

The general conclusion, then, is that each of the three existing Federal
budgets is incomplete and ill-organized. Their scope should be expanded to
include the open-market operations of the Federal Reserve System, the loan

---

[26] A single multibudget, however, might well be less confusing than the present set
of three, competing unitary budgets.

insurance and guaranty operations of the Federal Government, and the debt operations of the Treasury. A number of basic rearrangements, such as the establishment of a separate capital account for the direct loan programs and the shifting of participation certificate sales from that account to the borrowing account of the Treasury, are also recommended. With these changes, it is hoped, the budget document would facilitate public understanding both of the economic significance of different Federal financial transactions and of the complex inter-relationships between fiscal and monetary policy.

COMMENTS BY DISCUSSANTS

Richard Goode [27]

International Monetary Fund

George Break's paper impresses me as an illuminating treatment of the subject of Government lending and borrowing. It helps dispel the twilight surrounding these aspects of Government finance. I find Break's point of view congenial and his analysis good; nevertheless, I have some reservations about his recommendations on budget presentation.

Break's proposal of a multipart budget statement rests on several analytical propositions and generalizations about institutional arrangements. Some of these are explicit and others are implicit. Regarding direct lending by Government agencies, he holds that on the average these loans increase aggregate demand significantly but by less than equal amounts of expenditures for goods and services or transfer payments. Borrowing from the public is contractionary but generally affects spending less than equal amounts of negative lending (that is, loan sales or principal repayments). Borrowing from the Federal Reserve system, on the other hand, has no direct influence on demand. Break believes that sales of participation certificates should be classified as borrowing from the public rather than as negative lending.

All of these propositions are plausible as statements of central tendencies. Taken together, they support a classification of transactions along the lines suggested in Break's prototype multipart budget statement. I am sure, however, that Break would agree that there is a wide dispersion within categories and a considerable overlapping of categories. The effects of transactions, particularly of direct lending and borrowing, will depend, moreover, on economic conditions and especially on monetary conditions and policies.

No simple summary can take account of the full variety of transactions and conditions, and Break's multipart budget statement should not be faulted for its failure to do so. The question is whether a simple summary can be made informative and, if that is possible, how Break's multipart statement

---

[27] Opinions expressed are my own and do not purport to represent the views of the International Monetary Fund.

compares with other statements. My judgment is that a simple budget summary has value, though it will be incomplete and ambiguous in certain respects. Break's sectoring of the accounts is useful for experts, but I am uneasy about his departure from the unitary budget principle and his refusal to give guidance to laymen about what the parts of his statement mean and whether they can be added together.

The principle of budget unity and comprehensiveness, which has been firmly supported by specialists for a long time, is derived mainly from considerations of political accountability and allocative rationality rather than stabilization policy, but in my opinion there is no irreconcilable conflict between this principle and the requirements of informed public opinion on stabilization policy. The needs of specialists can be met, without departure from the unitary principle, by an elaboration and refinement of a balanced statement of sources and uses of funds, along the lines of Break's Table 2, with an annexed statement of the public debt and Government loan guarantees and insurance.

The general public will not be satisfied by a sources and uses statement. There is legitimate interest in the size of total Government expenditures and in the surplus or deficit. If the executive branch does not provide a suitable set of summary figures, others will produce figures which may or may not be sensible.

The practical question, as I see it, is whether the summary figures should take in only what Break calls "fiscal operations" or should be more comprehensive. My preference would be to go further and to combine "fiscal operations" with the direct lending account by adding together parts A and B1 of Break's prototype multipart budget statement (Table 5). The debt account (part B3 of Break's statement) would go below the line and the loan insurance and guaranty account would be relegated to an annex. The outcome would be approximately the present consolidated cash budget, but with the sale of participation certificates classified as Government borrowing rather than as negative lending or receipts. I leave to one side the question of the time of recording of transactions, that is, the relative merits of cash and accrual accounting.

My reasons for wishing to include direct lending in the basic budget summary are similar to Break's arguments about why it is economically too important to be placed below the line. While I agree with Break that direct Federal loans are in general different from Federal purchases and transfers, my adherence to the unitary principle leads me to combine the outlays in defining total expenditures and the deficit or surplus. Admittedly the distinction between direct lending and loan guarantees and insurance is arbitrary in some instances, but I do not consider this a decisive objection.

An important issue is whether there is in practice enough difference between direct lending and Government borrowing operations to justify placing the former above the line and the latter below the line. This is, of course, one of the main issues in choosing between the consolidated cash budget and the national income accounts budget. It could be argued, however, that the best course would be not to omit direct lending from expenditures but to move certain kinds of borrowing above the line, as is the practice in some countries.

A sharp distinction between direct lending and Government borrowing will be most appropriate when direct lending does most to stimulate investment and consumption and Government borrowing does least to retard spending. Direct lending is likely to add to aggregate demand when soft loans are extended or, generally, when borrowers would find it hard to obtain credit from nongovernmental sources. Alternative credit sources may be least accessible during a depression, because the borrowers are considered poor risks; in wartime, because of credit rationing; or during a boom accompanied by credit stringency. Government borrowing will have the least effect on spending when lenders are most liquid, as during a depression when banks have excess reserves; in wartime when consumption and investment are subject to direct controls; and whenever the central bank is willing to supply additional reserves to commercial banks on easy terms in order to maintain orderly conditions, to keep down interest rates, and to stimulate or protect private investment.

Under other conditions the case for a sharp distinction between direct lending and borrowing is weaker but not without merit. A cash deficit computed by placing direct lending above the line and borrowing below the line will indicate the Government's demand for credit and money creation. The experience of the United States and many other countries suggests that governments usually expect their credit needs to be given priority over other demands and frequently persuade the monetary authorities to accommodate governmental requirements without increases in interest rates that are considered unusual or excessive. Actions that increase the cash deficit of the Government, including additional direct lending by Government agencies, commonly augment liquidity and are expansionary in this way regardless of their immediate impact on income flows.

In connection with liquidity effects, I fully agree with Break that emphasis should be placed on the absorption of Government securities by the Federal Reserve System. However, I would not try to consolidate the open market operations of the system with the budget accounts. The most important part of the budget is the estimates for the year in progress and the coming year; and, as Break notes, realistic projections of future open-market operations could hardly be included. Furthermore, there is advantage, in my opinion, in maintaining the institutional distinction between monetary and fiscal policies and operations, though their coordination is highly desirable. It may be appropriate, of course, for the President's budget message to refer to open-market operations and other factors in discussing the previous year's budget results and the probable effects of the new budget.

In conclusion, I should like to say that Break's able paper seems to me to make a good case against excluding direct lending from Government expenditures. Since I believe a unitary budget summary is highly desirable, his paper strengthens my preference for a coverage similar to that of the cash budget as distinguished from the NIA budget. This preference is subject to the important qualification that participation certificates be treated as Federal debt instruments. I am speaking only of the items to be included in the summary and am leaving aside the question of the time at which transactions should be taken into account.

Even if the estimates are made with uniform assumptions about the level of activity, a simple unitary budget summary cannot meet the high standards set up in the first section of Break's paper—nor, may I add, does Break's own multipart statement. It is possible to imagine combinations of expenditures and receipts such that one budget, involving certain total expenditures and cash deficit, is less expansionary than another budget in which expenditures and the deficit are substantially smaller. Such differences in composition may greatly complicate comparisons extending over a long period of time, but the year-to-year or quarter-to-quarter comparisons required for the ordinary purposes of fiscal policy are less likely to be affected by changes in the composition of expenditures and revenues. On an incremental basis, changes in the high-employment cash surplus or deficit usually can be interpreted with a fair degree of confidence.

Arthur M. Okun

Council of Economic Advisers

The *Annual Report* of the Council of Economic Advisers has focused on the national income accounts (NIA) version of the Federal budget for many years. NIA is not a perfect tool for fiscal analysis in a number of ways. It needs to be supplemented by balance sheet (or flow-of-funds information) about Federal financial activities. It should be reformed so that it can emerge primarily as the product of an accounting system rather than of statistical estimation. The defining characteristics of an income-generating expenditure need to be carefully reviewed. Nevertheless, in its present form, NIA is a far more meaningful statement of Federal fiscal activities than any other budget concept. In particular, there are important reasons for preferring NIA over the consolidated cash budget.

Among the differences between the cash and NIA budgets, those involving the timing of receipts and expenditures deserve some discussion, but they are not of great importance. The matter of chief significance is the treatment of loans and other financial transactions.

Accrual of receipts. The logic of NIA is to treat the timing of Federal receipts so that they show up as the mirror image of the charges on the books of the corporations and persons who pay those receipts to the Federal

Government. The Government should be recorded as earning receipts when business firms or individuals regard themselves as incurring tax payments.

Corporations do, in fact, accrue their liabilities for taxes to the Federal Government, and that is the logic of accruing the receipts in the Federal accounts. To the extent that cash payments lag behind liability, there is implicitly a loan extended by the Federal Government to the business firm. In a sense, therefore, the choice of accrual versus cash in timing receipts should be dictated by the general treatment of loans, which is discussed in detail below.

In point of fact, however, given the essentially current basis on which tax receipts will be collected by the Federal Government once changes in the rules on timing collections are completely implemented, there will be little practical difference between the volume of accrual and cash receipts. The only significant difference arises when the rules for the timing of collections are changed, as they have been in recent years. Apart from adjustments to correct for any further changes in collection rules, NIA could live with a cash concept of all receipts by fiscal year 1970; this would have the practical advantage of avoiding a statistical estimate of accruals. But any such modification should be recognized as a compromise of the practical over principle, which still points to an accrual concept.

Accrual of expenditures. The only significant differences between Federal cash payments and accrued expenditures arise in the payment of interest and in purchases from business. Interest is recorded as an expenditure as it accrues rather than when paid. In the NIA, deliveries are the basic concept in timing purchases from business. Deliveries lag behind work done on Government account as business produces to fill defense orders. In fact, given the system of progress payments now in effect, the cash expenditures of the Federal Government for such items run ahead of deliveries during a defense buildup.

Recently some critics have argued that the cash payments are a better measure of Government defense impact because they show less of a lag behind private production. This is not a persuasive argument. Under the present system, production on defense contracts is recorded, prior to delivery, in private inventory investment. Then, upon delivery, the goods show up as a Government purchase, and as a reduction in private inventories. The same delivery concept is applied for private equipment, with full recognition that an inflow of new orders for machine tools adds to inventory accumulation in the machinery industry before it is recorded as an increase of fixed investment in new equipment.

There is nothing sacred about the delivery concept in NIA. It would be possible to modify NIA to allow for purchases to be recorded on a different basis, so long as there were corresponding modifications in the treatment of business inventories. But there is no particular and obvious merit in any alternative thus far suggested. The cash budget has the important disadvantage of creating variations in timing as a result of purely administrative changes in the way the Department of Defense pays its bills.

Loans and financial assets. The big issue between the two budgets is the handling of loans and financial assets. The cash budget shows as an increase 'in expenditures any direct lending and acquisition of financial assets by the general fund and trust funds, net of repayments and sales of such assets (but, of course, not netting out sales of direct Federal debt). The NIA budget excludes these because they are not income-generating expenditures.

The NIA treatment is not meant to deny that Federal credit programs have important effects on the economy. It is meant to signify that (a) these effects are not properly assessed by the entry in the cash budget, which amounts to the excess of direct lending and acquisition of financial assets over sales and repayments; and (b) however these effects are summed up, the total is not properly additive to income-generating expenditures.

The cash budget does not measure satisfactorily the impact of Federal credit programs. It omits the most important effects of the Federal Government on financial markets, namely those that work through insurance and guarantee programs. New commitments for guaranteed and insured loans of fiscal year 1968 are estimated at close to $30 billion, three times the magnitude of the nearly $10 billion of direct lending scheduled for the year. Similarly, the outstanding total of guaranteed and insured loans is expected to be $115 billion at the end of fiscal year 1968 compared with $43 billion of direct loans.

A private credit demand can be turned into a Government-backed demand on financial markets by either of two routes: (1) by guarantees and insurance, or (2) by direct Government loans covered by Federal borrowing. The cash budget draws a hard and arbitrary line between these two techniques. The fact that this is not a meaningful boundary line may be most evident in the case where the Federal Government makes direct loans and then sells off the assets with a Federal guarantee. The resale of the asset wipes the direct loan off the cash budget, and it then gets treated like a guarantee. Suggestions not to net out participation certificate sales (or other types of sales of Federal assets) miss the point: the fact is that the loans involved aren't very different from guarantees whether the Federal Government holds onto the assets or sells them off.

The inclusion of net loans as expenditures in the cash budget (especially if combined with provisions against netting out the resale of certain assets) would lead to a strong preference in the budgetary process for guarantees over direct loans. There are other convincing grounds for that preference, and it is reflected in our programs. Perhaps more should be done to limit direct lending. But overstating the meaningful total of expenditures in order to hold down the total of direct loans is a curious and inefficient form of discipline on the budgetary process. There must be a better way to arrive at the appropriate judgments between guarantees and insurance, on the one hand, and direct lending, on the other.

Direct loans are thus similar to guarantees and insurance. But they are generally very different from income-generating expenditures. To be sure, there are cases where loans could have effects similar to income-generating Federal expenditures (or tax reductions). If the Small Business Administration lends to a borrower with a demand for goods and services and with no available alternative means of financing, the direct Federal loan creates an opportunity to spend on output. To the small businessman in that position, the loan may not be very different from a tax cut or a windfall profit. But this model does not fit the bulk of direct Federal lending programs. And it does fit some part of the total of Federal guaranteed and insured loans— student loans may be a good example.

In short, the net figure on lending and financial assets that enters the cash budget is in no sense a meaningful summary of Federal financial impact or an equivalent of Federal income-creating expenditures. More analytical work should be done to evaluate Federal financial impact, covering direct lending, guaranteed and insured credit, debt management, repayments, and sales of Federal assets. The accounting framework which would focus attention on these issues is a balance sheet (or flow-of-funds table) for the Federal sector, including contingent liabilities and categorizing assets and liabilities by liquidity. Such a statement, in combination with an NIA budget, would give the economist the needed inputs for fiscal and financial analysis. The cash budget, however, in trying to tell the fiscal and financial story simultaneously, fails to communicate either in a comprehensible way.

Herbert Stein

Committee for Economic Development

We ask Professor Break whether loan transactions should be in or out of the Federal budget, and he says, in effect: "Both. I'll give you all the numbers and you can combine them or not, weight them or not, as you wish." This is a sensible answer, but I am not sure that it is the answer to the question we are called upon to consider.

As I see it, the problem is this: We are interested in certain fiscal policy decisions, particularly, I suppose, in general, over-all decisions. These decisions will be influenced by a great many factors, but for convenience I will group these influences into three:

1. Considerations applicable to particular expenditure programs or revenue sources. For these considerations—which may range from cost-benefit analysis to pure political pressure—the definition of the budget is unimportant. The desire of the people of Biloxi for a new bridge, or its benefit to them, does not depend on how the bridge is classified in the budgetary accounts.

2. Econometric analysis of policies needed to achieve certain general goals—stability, high employment, growth, and so on. For this purpose the best possible model of the whole economy is necessary. The number of variables in the model would presumably be large, limited only by their contribution to the reliability of the results. The number of separate variables drawn from or related to the budget would probably also be large. What these variables would be, I don't know. I gather that the econometricians are also uncertain. But probably one total for expenditures or for the deficit, or one for expenditures and one for loans, would be quite inadequate. In any case, the econometricians—in their own mysterious way—will decide what budgetary variables to use and I don't suppose the President set up a Commission of citizens to decide that for them.

3. The feeling or prejudice that people have about something they regard as "The Budget," about its total size, and especially about its deficit or surplus. This feeling seems to be shared to some degree by all Presidents, all or most congressmen, and a great many other people. The nature of this feeling is such that the larger the prospective deficit the less likely is any increase in those expenditures which count in the budget and the more likely is any increase of any revenues of the kinds included in the budget. These attitudes are not immutable, and in fact I think they have weakened substantially. At least, the threshold of alarm about deficits seems to have risen to the neighborhood of $25 to $30 billion. The preference still exists, however, and is recognized to be useful in some circumstances. For example, the current arguments for a tax increase are first, that it will prevent inflation, second, that it will prevent tight money, and third—and apparently separate and additional—that it will hold down the budget deficit.

While there is, I believe, a clear—although weakening—preference in the country for balanced budgets, there is no very clear preference for any particular definition of the budget. The attitude seems to be that we don't care what you include in it but we would like it to be balanced. Despite a number of changes in the definition of the budget in the past forty years and some grumbling from the financial press, by and large the changes have been accepted and have not changed public attitudes about the budget. I'm convinced that if public opinion polls were taken over the past generation they would reveal a clear and consistent public preference: seventy percent in favor of balancing the budget, and fifty percent who do not know what it means.

Thus, there is an opportunity to affect budget policy by changing the definition of the budget. The influence of the preference for budget-balancing can be made less harmful, or more beneficial—depending on one's point of view—according to how the budget is defined. That is what the Committee on Economic Development was trying to do twenty years ago when it proposed the high-employment budget. In my opinion this is the most fruitful redefinition of the budget that has yet been suggested. That, I think, is the kind of opportunity now before the President's Commission on Budget Concepts.

If this opportunity is to be realized, however, the Commission must leave the public preference for a balanced budget with something to focus on. That is, the Commission must arrive at a budget that can be called "balanced" or "not balanced." We could produce a statement of sources and uses of Federal funds which was balanced by definition. This would be saying to the public that we don't think the concept of deficit or surplus is meaningful and it shouldn't influence policy. If we don't believe that, or don't think the public will accept it, then I don't think we have any stopping-point short of defining *a* budget which reveals *a* deficit or surplus. If we present a budget with two parts, A and B, without saying that *the* budget is A or B or A plus B, then someone else will answer the question.

What I am saying is that a budget with two parts has too few parts for the purposes of the econometrician, and one too many for all other purposes. I may be wrong about this, and I will return to that possibility later. Now I would like to turn to the question whether, if there is to be only one budget, it should include or exclude loan transactions. I don't find this an easy question to answer, and I am quite willing to be persuaded. In fact, until I read Professor Break's paper, I was perfectly satisfied to look at the budget in terms of the national income accounts, which excludes the loan transactions. Now I am less satisfied.

We can start, as Professor Break does, with the economic stabilization consequences of budget policy. Given the public's preference for a balanced budget, will that preference be more constructive from the standpoint of economic stability if it is guided by a budget that excludes or includes loan transactions?

One crude way to look at that question is to consider the historical record. We can compare the series of national income accounts surpluses with the series of such surpluses minus Federal net lending. If the numbers had been interpreted so that a surplus induced relaxation and a deficit induced tightening, which of these series would have given clearer signals for a stabilizing fiscal policy? Refined analysis might squeeze something out of these data, but for the present I am unable to convince myself that it would have made much difference. In retrospect, the major fiscal policy error in the past twenty years was to allow the Federal budget to become rapidly more restrictive after the 1958 recession and to delay correction for so long. I think it is quite clear that the inclusion or exclusion of net lending would not have affected that decision. I think the same can be said about the decision not to have a general tax increase after the Vietnam step-up. The fact is that the amount of net lending—and particularly its annual change—has been too small to have had much influence on fiscal decisions. Besides, the variations are irregular.

Alternatively, we can approach the problem analytically, and ask—as Professor Break does—in order for the budget deficit to provide an adequate picture of the economic impact of the budget, under what conditions is it preferable to include or exclude lending transactions? Break describes the objective as a budget about which it can be said that a deficit always signifies an expansionary impact. I have been used to saying that we seek a budget in which equal deficits signify equal impacts and in which bigger deficits or smaller surpluses have more expansionary impacts. A more general statement might be that we seek a definition of the budget such that its deficit correlates as closely as possible with the economic impact of the budget. However, these different formulations are probably not important in the present context.

Professor Break emphasizes what he calls the economic impact coefficient as the main criterion for the safety or wisdom of putting a certain category of transactions below the line delimiting the budget. Presumably, if a certain category of transactions is to be put below the line and excluded from the budget, the economic impact coefficients of that category of transactions should be uniformly lower than for the transactions above the line.

Two other factors also seem of possible significance in deciding whether the value of the budget as a measure of economic impact is increased or reduced by the inclusion of a certain category of transactions. One is the likely size and range of variation of the deficit or surplus in that category of transactions as compared with the size and variability of the deficit or surplus in the total of other above-the-line transactions. Thus, if Federal net lending varied from $10 billion to minus $10 billion, and the surplus on all other Federal transactions ranged from plus $2 billion to minus $2 billion, we might conclude that Federal lending should be included in the budget even though its economic impact coefficient per dollar was relatively low. A second factor influencing the significance of including or excluding the category in question is the degree of correlation of its deficit with the deficit on other transactions.

These factors have to be considered, not as they have been in the past but as they are likely to be in the future, as a consequence of the decision about whether to include them in the budget. Thus, if lending transactions are excluded, and less restraint is imposed on the growth of transactions outside the budget than that of transactions inside the budget, we might expect three consequences:

1. Lending transactions would increase in an amount relative to other transactions.

2. The economic impact coefficient of lending transactions would increase because there would be a tendency for other, presumably more powerful, kinds of transactions to be disguised as loans.

3. The rate of growth of lending would tend to be systematically related to the deficit or surplus in the budget. Lending would increase when a deficit

caused a clamp to be put on budget expenditures; it would slow down when a surplus caused a relaxation of restraints on budget expenditures.

Thus, even if it were initially true that excluding loan transactions from the budget would produce better information and better policy than including them, the fact of exclusion might tend to make it untrue later.

I suppose the main point, however, is what we think is the economic impact of Federal lending. The overwhelming impression I get from Professor Break's revealing discussion of this subject is that the line between lending and not lending is just not a very good basis for classifying transactions by the size of their economic impact. Federal lending seems to be a very mixed bag of transactions whose economic impact coefficients vary substantially and overlap with the coefficients of nonlending transactions. Professor Break offers a number of reasonable explanations for differences in the economic impacts of loan transactions. Generalizing from some of his explanations, I would like to suggest a way of looking at the problem of classifying expenditures which I have found helpful. Suppose we take the view that the money national income is determined by money supply and its velocity, and that the transactions we are considering will not affect the supply of money. We are therefore interested in the effects of these transactions on velocity. Suppose we make the further judgment that the main way in which these transactions affect velocity is through their effects on interest rates, so that our concern with these transactions is with their effects on interest rates. Then we can try to classify budget transactions—not merely lending but other kinds of transactions as well—in terms of that effect.

(Five years ago this view might have seemed hopelessly old-fashioned, but apparently it has now become quite respectable even for new economists to think that monetary policy—although not necessarily money supply—determines the money national income, while budget policy influences interest rates.)

Of course this classification doesn't give us any information we didn't have before, but it does help to put lending and other transactions in one continuum. Doing this, we see that results depend not only on the kinds of paper assets that are being transferred, and their liquidity and safety, but also the kinds of real assets that are being generated, and particularly the effects on the productivity of private capital. For example, suppose the Federal Government makes a loan, as it once did, for the construction of the Pennsylvania Turnpike. I would think that the construction of the Turnpike was complementary to many private uses of capital, that it increased the productivity of private capital, thereby increasing interest rates and velocity and raising the money national income. I would think that a grant to the State of Pennsylvania for this purpose, or direct construction of the highway by the Federal Government, would have had the same effect. On the other hand, the construction of residential housing financed by

Federal loans competes with other private investment in housing, reduces the productivity of other private investment, reduces interest rates and the velocity of money and thereby reduces the money national income. (This abstracts, of course, from the way in which the Federal Government raises its money.) I would expect the effect to be similar if the Federal Government were to make a grant to states for housing construction or build the houses itself. I am suggesting that the distinction between the substance of programs—say, between houses and roads—is often more important than the distinction between forms of programs—say, between loans, grants, or direct expenditures. We have certain impressions about the economic impacts of loans because of the tendency to use the loan form for certain kinds of programs, but this association is not complete. Possibly a more reliable guide to the economic impact of transactions is their substance rather than their form.

The stabilizing or unstabilizing consequences—the macroeconomic effects—of the decision to put lending transactions above or below the line will depend on the size of the multipliers of other budget transactions, and not particularly on the multiplier of the loan transactions themselves. Thus, suppose the government's policy is budget-balancing, or tends toward budget-balancing. Then a decision to include loans in the budget will mean that revenues minus other expenditures will be larger—by an amount equal to, or approaching net lending—than if loans were excluded from the budget. The significance of this will depend on the multiplier effect of the difference in the revenues minus other expenditures. It is only fair to say that there is a wide range of opinion in the profession about the size of the relevant multipliers. A small but powerful minority thinks these multipliers are not significantly more or less than one. If the taxation and direct expenditure multipliers are small—or if the difference between those multipliers and the multipliers of Treasury borrowing and debt repayment is small—the decision to include or exclude loans in the budget will not have important macroeconomic effects unless net lending and its variations turn out to be much larger than they have been.

Probably because I think the multipliers are small, and because net lending is small—and perhaps also because I am less ambitious in my demands and expectations for stabilization—my own conclusion is different from Professor Break's. He believes that direct Federal loans are too different from Federal purchases and transfers to be placed above the line in a unitary budget, but are too important economically to be placed below the line. My conclusion is that it doesn't much matter, from the standpoint of stabilization, whether they are put above or below the line. At least, I think it matters so little, and the direction in which it matters is so uncertain, that the decision need not be made primarily in terms of stabilization effects.

The decision to include or exclude loan transactions will have a significant effect on the growth of total expenditures and particularly loan expenditures.

This is implied at several points in Professor Break's paper. I don't see how a decision can be made without taking this effect into account. In fact, it seems to me the most reliable and important effect. Also, I don't see how a 'neutral" or "scientific" decision can be made in terms of this effect. Presumably, excluding loan transactions from the budget would encourage the growth of total expenditures, and loan expenditures most of all. Do we want that? If we believe that the existing system, with what is left of the Puritan ethic, has a bias against spending and Federal lending, perhaps we want to correct that by putting lending outside the budget. This raises big questions, the essential characteristic of which is that they are not very discussable questions.

I see no reason, however, for giving a preference to those Government expenditures which in the past have been put in the form of loans or which might be put in that form in the future. I can see some reason in principle for excluding from the budget those transactions that have built-in disciplines, so that expenditures are limited by current or prospective receipts. Some loan programs might fit this category, especially if there were a clear accounting for loss reserves and for interest subsidies, as proposed in Professor Break's paper. This category would not, however, consist entirely of loans. Moreover, this policy would amount to encouraging precisely those activities which could be self-sustaining and for which Federal participation is needed least.

If there has to be one budget, my preference, obviously, would be to include the loan transactions with it. And, as I said earlier, I do think there has to be one budget.

On the assumption that it is possible to have more than one budget, however, I would like to comment on the advisability of making a distinction between lending transactions and other transactions. I find this difficult even to think about because I don't know the analytical or policy implications of the division of the budget. However, suspending this question, one must still ask whether this particular division between lending and nonlending transactions is the most helpful one. The choice of one line of division rules out others, because the total number of possible divisions, even if greater than one, cannot be many more than one. Besides, some systems of classification are incompatible with others. So the question is not simply whether the lending vs. nonlending distinction is useful but whether it is more useful than others. Professor Break was apparently not asked to evaluate other possible classifications, but I think a wise decision requires such an analysis.

One possible classification is between domestic and foreign transactions. Another, and in my opinion more interesting and important, is between current and capital transactions. We should consider which distinction we finally want to reach, and whether taking the step now to separate out lending transactions is a move in that direction or not.

Finally, I will mention one small point which I may have misunderstood. Professor Break proposes, in effect, to consolidate the accounts of the Treasury and the Federal Reserve, and to show as the increase in the net debt outstanding only that part that is held outside the trust accounts and the Federal Reserve. In that case it would seem logical to me to show as part of the increase in the net Federal debt the increase in the obligations of the Federal Reserve Banks, essentially the deposits of member banks at the Federal Reserve Banks. It would also then be necessary to show as expenditures the transactions of Federal Reserve Banks in assets other than Treasury securities, including rediscounts and gold.

PART II

Measures of the Economic Impact of the Budget

HARVEY GALPER[1]
Board of Governors of the Federal Reserve System

The Timing of Federal Expenditure Impacts

An ideal budget document should do more than provide the requisite information for congressional decision making. It should also be useful for economic analysis. The present budget is not well suited for this purpose, to some extent because expenditures are expressed on a checks-issued basis, which is inappropriate as a measure of resource use. For analyzing fiscal impacts, the Federal sector of the national income accounts (NIA) has most often been employed.

However, several observers (notably Murray Weidenbaum) have pointed out that the Federal purchases series in the national accounts is not adequate for determining the economic impacts of Federal spending. The national accounts measure purchases as the deliveries of completed goods, whereas the major direct impacts of Federal spending on gross national product (GNP) occur much earlier in the expenditure sequence, that is, at the time of actual production on Government account. This production appears in the accounts as changes in the goods-in-process inventories of private producers.

A different presentation of the timing effects of Government purchases will admittedly affect only the composition of GNP and not the total. For analysis and policy prescription, however, a knowledge of the composition of GNP as well as its total is important. During the last half of 1966, for example, inventories were accumulated at the annual rate of about $15 billion, while military prime contract awards increased from $32.6 billion in the fourth quarter of 1965 to $39.1 billion in the fourth quarter of 1966 (at seasonally adjusted annual rates). If, in fact, a significant portion of the high inventory investment of 1966 can be attributed to work-in-progress inventories arising from increased private production on defense contracts, then an analysis of the effects of defense spending in terms of NIA deliveries will not capture the complete influence of the military buildup. Furthermore, if accumulations of military goods-in-process are substantial, there need be somewhat less concern about the depressing effects on the economy generally of a large overhang of inventories.

[1] I would like to thank Edward M. Gramlich, Frank de Leeuw, Lyle E. Gramley, and Wilfred Lewis, Jr., for their helpful comments.

The subject of this paper is the determination of Federal expenditure impacts. The first part focuses on the stage in the Government spending process which is now measured by the national income accounts. In the second part, use is made of a defense forecasting equation that Edward Gramlich and I developed at the Federal Reserve Board to estimate the extent to which the national accounts fail to measure the direct economic impacts of defense spending.

THE GOVERNMENT SPENDING PROCESS

In his work on the timing impacts of Government expenditures, Weidenbaum [2] correctly asserts that the spending process must be viewed as a continuing sequence starting with congressional appropriations (or perhaps earlier with the enabling legislation) and ending with the delivery of the completed products and the final disbursement to the contractor. In between, funds are apportioned by the Bureau of the Budget, contracts are awarded, contractors initiate and then maintain full-scale production, and progress payments are made as the work proceeds. Disregarding the announcement and related anticipation effects of Government expenditure programs, the major direct (as opposed to subsequent multiplier and accelerator) impacts on the economy occur as work proceeds and income is generated under Government contracts—that is, in the stage of the expenditure process between contract award and final delivery.

For calculating these impacts, contract awards or obligations appear to be too leading a measure, and deliveries too lagging. Accordingly, NIA purchases, which essentially reflect deliveries, are likely to give a delayed representation of the impacts of Government spending.

To understand this statement fully, some discussion of Government accounting is necessary. A calculation of Federal purchases on an accrual basis would proceed as follows: to checks issued, the present basis of budgetary expenditures, add the change in Government payables to business and subtract the change in Government receivables from business. The last two adjustments would have the effect of converting expenditures that arise as cash is disbursed to expenditures that arise as liabilities are incurred.

A consistent application of this definition would imply that an accrued expenditure be recorded when private production generates an account payable on the books of the Government, even though no cash changes hands. Similarly, with respect to receivables, an advance payment to the contractor to provide him with working capital prior to his actual production would not yield an accrued expenditure even though a cash transaction has been made.

---

[2] Murray L. Weidenbaum, "The Economic Impact of the Government Spending Process," *University of Houston Business Review* (Spring 1961); and "The Timing of the Economic Impact of Government Spending," *National Tax Journal,* Vol. 12 (March 1959), pp. 79–85.

The above definition, in other words, implies a distinction between advance payments and progress payments. Advance payments are, in essence, Government loans made to defense contractors prior to the generation of an accounts payable liability. Therefore, they should be recorded as accounts receivable. Progress payments, on the other hand, are payments made to liquidate accounts payable items which arise from private production on Government account. Indeed, Bureau of the Budget Circular A–34 states explicitly that "where progress payments are made for construction or equipment, the expenditure shall be considered as accrued [that is, the liability arises] when performance is accepted as a basis for making progress payments . . ."

At least in the calculation of defense purchases, the national income accounts do not maintain the distinction between advance payments and progress payments. Both types of payment are lumped together in the Department of Defense (DOD) series used to represent Government receivables. In the application of the above definition, therefore, an increase in progress payments results in a simultaneous increase in checks issued and receivables. No immediate expenditure is shown, and none is recorded until the progress payments outstanding are liquidated at delivery time. Then, the Government's accounts receivable are reduced, and a Federal purchase is entered in the national income accounts. The effect is to convert Federal purchases to a delivery basis even though the existence of progress payments implies that production occurred earlier. In defense purchases, moreover, progress payments are quite substantial. For major procurement, they amount to about 70 percent of final costs.

In summary, the Federal purchases series of the national accounts is much closer to Federal deliveries. This statement, of course, is not news nor is it particularly worrisome to the Office of Business Economics. OBE's figures and measurements have been improved continually through the years, and, presumably, if the data were available for implementing its objective of measuring expenditures wholly on an accrual basis, they would be readily used.

THE MEASUREMENT OF DEFENSE EXPENDITURE IMPACTS

Since contract awards or obligations occur before the major direct impacts of defense spending, and NIA deliveries occur after them, one possible method of deriving the appropriate expenditure measure is to average the two *à la* Weidenbaum.[3] Another possibility is to measure the extent to which defense contracts yield goods-in-process inventories in the private sector and to add this inventory accumulation to NIA deliveries. In this paper, I have tried to obtain an indirect measure of private inventory accumulation due

---

[3] See his testimony on "Impact of Vietnam War on American Economy" in *Economic Effect of Vietnam Spending,* Hearings before the Joint Economic Committee, 90 Cong. 1 sess. (1967.), pp. 210–11.

to the Government contracting process by utilizing a defense forecasting equation developed earlier in collaboration with Edward Gramlich.[4]

The basic formulation is a distributed lag equation whereby NIA defense purchases of goods, services, and construction, DG_t, are a linear function of lagged contract awards, CA_{t-1}, CA_{t-2}, and so on.[5]

In symbols,

$$(1) \qquad\qquad DG_t = \sum_{i=0}^{n} a_i CA_{t-i},$$

where the a_i's are the weights or coefficients of lagged contract awards. Further, the a_i's are not invariant, but, following the approach of Tinsley,[6] they change in response to (1) supply bottlenecks represented by the aggregate Federal Reserve capacity utilization rate, K; (2) the urgency of military demands represented by a proxy variable A, the rate of growth of the armed forces; and (3) a composition mix variable, L, representing the proportion of total contract awards for long-lead items—aircraft, ships, missiles, and construction. Thus,

$$(2) \qquad\qquad a_i = b_i + c_i K_{t-i} + d_i A_{t-i} + e_i L_{t-i}.$$

Equation (2) was substituted into (1) for the statistical estimation.[7] Solving the resulting regression equation for the mean values of K, A, and L, yielded the a_i's or eleven weights of lagged contract awards given in Table 1.

---

[4] See Harvey Galper and Edward M. Gramlich, "A Technique for Forecasting Defense Expenditures," *Review of Economics and Statistics,* Vol. 50 (May 1968), which presents a complete derivation of the estimating equations as well as the statistical results. In the present paper, the relevant portions of this work are only summarized briefly.

[5] The contract award series used in the estimation is the one published in U.S. Bureau of the Census, *Business Cycle Developments* (various issues), as Series 92, except that the figures shown there have been converted into quarterly flows at annual rates. Defense purchases of goods, services, and construction are equal to total NIA defense purchases less defense compensation, the latter, of course, having no inventory effect.

[6] Peter A. Tinsley, "An Application of Variable Weight Distributed Lags," *Journal of the American Statistical Association,* Vol. 62 (December 1967), pp. 1277–89.

[7] Time and a constant were added to capture the coverage differences between NIA defense purchases of goods and services and the contract award series. The coverage difference arises because some spending classified as defense in the national income accounts is not preceded by contract awards in our series. Examples are Atomic Energy Commission spending, purchases from foreign firms, and purchases from educational and nonprofit institutions. The lags in the equation were estimated by the Almon technique. (See Shirley Almon, "The Distributed Lag Between Capital Appropriations and Expenditures," *Econometrica,* Vol. 33 [January 1965], pp. 178–96.) We found, after some experimentation, that aggregate contract awards, K and A, affect expenditures over an eight-quarter span, while L affects expenditures over a longer ten-quarter span.

TABLE 1.—*Weights of lagged contract awards*

Time period:	Weights [1]	Time period:	Weights [1]
0	.0787	6	.0670
1	.1249	7	.0372
2	.1443	8	.0144
3	.1426	9	.0044
4	.1253	10	.0090
5	.0983	Total, all periods	.8461

[1] The weights are for mean values of K, A, and L.

Source: Harvey Galper and Edward M. Gramlich, "A Technique for Forecasting Defense Expenditures" (mimeo., 1967), Table 1.

In our other work, we have found this approach to be quite good for forecasting defense expenditures at least two quarters into the future. The present concern, however, is to utilize it for estimating the dollar volume of partially completed defense products in private inventories. These inventories reflect production in the private sector for Government account and, thus, the extent to which NIA defense purchases fail to measure the impacts of defense spending.

The weights shown in Table 1 provide estimates of the rate at which contract awards are converted into delivered goods. Given certain assumptions about the production rate over the lag period, the delivery and production rates can be combined to obtain an estimate of work-in-process inventory changes due to defense contracting.

Two assumptions about the production rate will be examined—a rectangular production process in which production proceeds at the same rate in each period, and an "inverted V" process in which an increase in the production rate in the first half of the contract life is followed by a decline in the second half.[8] The reasoning behind the assumption of a production process such as the inverted V is that (1) some time is likely to elapse in the initial stages of a new contract before production reaches its peak, and (2) the later stages of a contract may merely involve finishing up work of fairly small dollar amounts.

Under both production assumptions, the contract awards and expenditures, as average flows over the quarter, are assumed to occur in the middle of the time period. Inventories, however, are measured as stocks at the end of the period. Therefore, inventories at the end of the quarter of the award are equal to one-half of the production rate of the first period and inventories at the end of the quarter of delivery are equal to zero. For each intervening quarter, the stock grows at a rate equal to the production of that quarter.

---

[8] For an illustration of the use of the inverted V distribution to represent a lag structure, see Frank de Leeuw, "The Demand for Capital Goods by Manufacturers: A Study of Quarterly Time Series," *Econometrica,* Vol. 30 (July 1962), pp. 407–23.

The basic distributed lag formulation of equation (1) is used to determine the production of each quarter. This equation may be interpreted in the following way: contract awards of the dollar volume of $a_0 CA_{t-0}$ have no lag between award and delivery since both events occur in the same period; contracts in the amount of $a_1 CA_{t-1}$ have a one-period award-delivery lag; $a_2 CA_{t-2}$, a two-period lag, and on so. Each award of $a_i CA_{t-i}$ thus gives rise to a total production span equal to i quarters, and the dollar volume of production in each quarter equals $p_j a_i CA_{t-i}$, where p_j equals the proportion of total awards $a_i CA_{t-i}$ produced in quarter j. P_j, then, depends on the assumptions about the production process, whether rectangular or inverted V.

Under the rectangular production assumption, $p_j = (1/2)(1/i)$ in the quarter of the award, $1/i$ in the next $i-1$ quarters and $(1/2)(1/i)$ in the quarter of the expenditure when the good is first completed and then delivered.[9]

The situation is more complex under the inverted V production assumption, which is presented in Table 2. I assume that the production rate

TABLE 2.—*Proportion of total production under inverted V production assumptions, by period*

i	Rate of production per period	Proportion of total production per period (p_j) [1]
1	1–1	$\frac{1/2(1),\ 1/2(1)}{1 \qquad 1}$
2	1–2–1	$\frac{1/2(1),\ 2,\ 1/2(1)}{3 \quad 3 \quad 3}$
3	1–2–2–1	$\frac{1/2(1),\ 2,\ 2,\ 1/2(1)}{5 \quad 5\ 5 \quad 5}$
4	1–2–3–2–1	$\frac{1/2(1),\ 2,\ 3,\ 2}{8 \quad 8\ 8\ 8}$ . . . .
5	1–2–3–3–2–1	$\frac{1/2(1),\ 2,}{11 \quad 11}$ . . . .
6	1–2–3–4–3–2–1	$\frac{1/2(1),\ 2,}{15 \quad 15}$ . . . .
7	1–2–3–4–4–3–2–1	$\frac{1/2(1),\ 2,}{19 \quad 19}$ . . . .
8	1–2–3–4–5–4–3–2–1	$\frac{1/2(1),\ 2,}{24, \quad 24}$ . . . .
9	1–2–3–4–5–5–4–3–2–1	$\frac{1/2(1),\ 2,}{29 \quad 29}$ . . . .
10	1–2–3–4–5–6–5–4–3–2–1	$\frac{1/2(1),\ 2,}{35 \quad 35}$ . . . .

[1] See text for explanation of p_j.   Source: See text for derivation.

[9] For completeness, $p_j = 1.00$ if the award and the delivery occur in the same period.

increases linearly in each period as shown in the second column. In each quarter, p_j then equals the ratio of $(1/2)\,(1), 2, 3, 4, \ldots 3, 2, (1/2)\,(1)$ to the total production throughout the entire span, itself equal to the sum of $(1/2)(1)+2+3+4+\ldots+3+2+(1/2)(1)$ or one-half of the production rate of the first and last quarters (that is, the quarters of the award and delivery) plus the production of the $i-1$ periods in between. Figure 1 shows the cumulative p_j's under both production assumptions for the two cases of $i=8$ and $i=9$.

FIGURE 1.—*Cumulative proportions of total production under rectangular and inverted V production assumptions, by period*

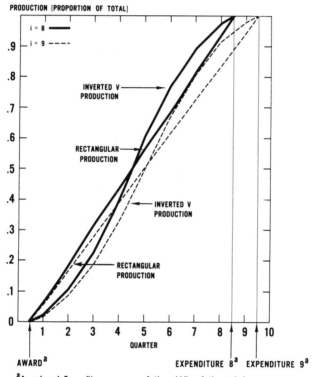

PRODUCTION (PROPORTION OF TOTAL)

$i = 8$ ——
$i = 9$ - - - -

INVERTED V PRODUCTION

RECTANGULAR PRODUCTION

INVERTED V PRODUCTION

RECTANGULAR PRODUCTION

QUARTER

AWARD [a]   EXPENDITURE 8 [a]   EXPENDITURE 9 [a]

[a]Award and Expenditures are as of the middle of the period.

Source: for inverted v production, see Table 2;
for rectangular production, see text.

It is now possible to determine the amount of goods-in-process inventory accumulation in quarter t due to CA_t, total contract awards at time t. Awards of a_0CA_t become expenditures immediately with no effect on inventories. For all other a_iCA_t, deliveries will not be made until periods $t + i$. However, production goes on throughout, and thus total inventory accumulation of

$$\sum_{i=1}^{10} p_t a_i CA_t \left(= \sum_{i=0}^{10} p_t a_i CA_t - a_0 CA_t \right)$$

occurs. The next step is finding the volume of inventory investment in time t from $CA_{t-1}, CA_{t-2}, CA_{t-3} \ldots CA_{t-10}$, that is, from all contract awards in previous periods, which still affect inventories at time t.

Summing the inventory changes in time t from all contract awards CA_t to CA_{t-10} gives the aggregate current dollar inventory investment due to the production of semi-finished goods which when completed will be delivered to the Government. Thus, in both the rectangular and inverted V cases, a time series of defense goods-in-process inventories may be derived.

Since inventory change equals production minus deliveries, the general formula is:

(3) $$\Delta Hc_t = \sum_{j=0}^{10} \sum_{i=j}^{10} p_t a_i CA_{t-j} - \sum_{i=0}^{10} a_i CA_{t-i},$$

where ΔHc_t is current dollar defense goods-in-process inventory investment and p_t is not a constant, but, as mentioned above, depends upon whether quarter t is an award, delivery, or intermediate quarter for each set of contracts $a_i CA_{t-j}$ as well as upon the particular production rate assumed. In the rectangular case, equation (3) becomes:

(4) $$\Delta Hc_t = \left(\sum_{i=1}^{10} \frac{a_i}{2i} \right) CA_t + \sum_{i=1}^{10} \frac{a_i}{2i} CA_{t-i} + \sum_{j=1}^{9} \left(\sum_{i=j+1}^{10} \frac{a_i}{i} \right) CA_{t-j} - \sum_{i=1}^{10} a_i CA_{t-i}.$$

Both the rectangular and the inverted V time series have been computed for ΔH_c using the variable weight coefficients illustrated by equation (2). These series are shown in columns (1) and (2) of Table 3 and are plotted in Figure 2.

As can be readily seen, the production assumption makes virtually no difference in the estimates.[10] This is not too surprising. Our regression equation yielded the delivery dates associated with any pattern of contract awards.[11] When these dates—and hence, the total lags—are already determined, different assumptions about production throughout the lag period would not be expected to have much of an effect on the estimates of goods-in-process inventory accumulation.

The major determinant of goods-in-process inventory investment is the rate of change of contract awards. In periods of relative stability of contract awards, such as 1955 or 1959–61, the additions to inventories flowing into the pipeline from new awards are roughly offset by the deliveries from earlier awards. This would occur regardless of the production assumption.

---

[10] The square root of the average squared differences between the two series is only $0.21 billion.

[11] See Galper and Gramlich, *op. cit.* Table 1 above presents the results for the mean values of K, A, and L.

TABLE 3.—*Defense goods-in-process inventory investment compared with total inventory investment, by quarters, 1953–66*

[In billions of current dollars]

Year and quarter	Defense goods-in-process inventory investment		Total inventory investment	Ratio: Column (1)/ column (3)
	Rectangular production assumption	Inverted V production assumption		
	(1)	(2)	(3)	(4)
1953: III............	−3. 19	−2. 85	0. 7	−4. 557
IV............	−4. 97	−4. 57	−4. 5	1. 104
1954: I.............	−5. 43	−5. 53	−2. 5	2. 172
II............	−3. 70	−4. 18	−2. 7	1. 370
III...........	−1. 54	−1. 92	−2. 2	. 700
IV...........	−. 15	−. 19	1. 3	−. 115
1955: I.............	. 28	. 37	4. 6	. 061
II............	. 08	. 08	6. 1	. 013
III...........	−. 40	−. 36	6. 0	−. 067
IV...........	. 69	. 37	7. 1	. 097
1956: I.............	1. 14	1. 22	6. 0	. 190
II............	. 74	. 88	4. 3	. 172
III...........	1. 38	1. 19	4. 1	. 337
IV...........	2. 34	2. 17	4. 3	. 544
1957: I.............	1. 59	1. 87	2. 1	. 757
II............	−. 68	−. 19	2. 3	−. 296
III...........	−1. 42	−1. 48	3. 2	−. 444
IV...........	−. 30	−. 66	−2. 2	. 136
1958: I.............	. 37	. 30	−5. 4	−. 069
II............	. 94	. 87	−5. 1	−. 184
III...........	1. 29	1. 34	. 1	12. 900
IV...........	1. 50	1. 46	4. 1	. 366
1959: I.............	. 18	. 70	3, 9	. 123
II............	−. 48	−. 39	9. 1	−. 053
III...........	−. 06	−. 23	. 4	−. 150
IV...........	. 22	. 20	6. 3	. 035
1960: I.............	−. 19	−. 09	9. 9	−. 019
II............	−. 70	−. 60	3. 9	−. 179
III...........	. 41	. 08	3. 1	. 132
IV...........	. 50	. 60	−2. 4	−. 208

Table 3.—*Defense goods-in-process inventory investment compared with total inventory investment, by quarters, 1953–66*—Continued

[In billions of current dollars]

Year and quarter	Defense goods-in-process inventory investment		Total inventory investment	Ratio: Column (1)/ column (3)
	Rectangular production assumption	Inverted V production assumption		
	(1)	(2)	(3)	(4)
1961: I	.23	.26	−3.5	−.066
II	−.07	.02	2.1	−.033
III	.42	.26	3.8	.111
IV	1.49	1.26	5.5	.271
1962: I	2.16	2.09	6.7	.322
II	1.08	1.46	6.1	.177
III	.08	.23	5.2	.015
IV	.69	.44	6.4	.108
1963: I	.63	.65	4.7	.134
II	.11	.21	4.8	.023
III	.54	.40	6.0	.090
IV	−.15	.10	8.1	−.019
1964: I	−.72	−.70	4.8	−.150
II	−.42	−.54	6.1	−.069
III	.07	−.04	4.8	.015
IV	−.47	−.27	7.7	−.061
1965: I	−1.29	−1.16	10.6	−.122
II	−.25	−.59	8.8	−.028
III	1.30	1.03	9.4	.138
IV	2.14	2.07	9.9	.216
1966: I	2.37	2.45	9.9	.239
II	3.29	3.15	14.0	.235
III	4.21	4.11	11.4	.369
IV	3.93	4.12	18.5	.212
Average, 1953–66	....	....	....	.051

Sources: Cols. (1) and (2): Computed from equation (3) in text and Galper and Gramlich, "A Technique for Forecasting Defense Expenditures" (mimeo, 1967); Col. (3): U.S. Department of Commerce, Office of Business Economics, *Survey of Current Business*, Vols. 45 and 47 (August 1965 and July 1967), pp. 24–25 and 13, respectively.

Moreover, in periods of rapidly changing contract awards, any differential effects of the two production assumptions are small relative to the common effect of the large rate of change of awards. Thus, any other reasonable assumptions about the production rate between the dates of award and delivery are not likely to yield significantly different results.

Figure 2 indicates quite clearly the large inventory investment—on the order of plus or minus $5 billion—which occurs in periods of substantial change in contract awards such as characterized the post-Korean demobilization and the Vietnam buildup. In fact, as is shown by column (4) of Table 3, in such periods, defense goods-in-process inventory investment may be a significant proportion of total inventory investment. In 1966, for example, goods-in-process inventory investment was over one-quarter of the total.

FIGURE 2.—*Estimates of defense goods-in-process inventory investment*

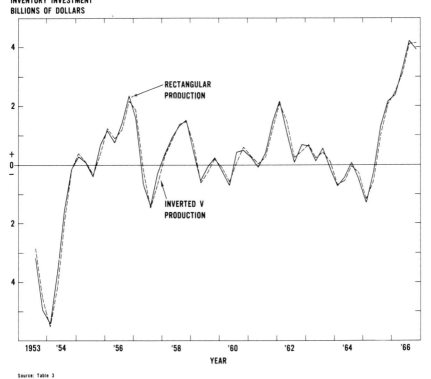

INVENTORY INVESTMENT
BILLIONS OF DOLLARS

Source: Table 3

The main significance of these time series, however, is that they represent the extent to which NIA defense purchases fail to reflect the full impact of a military buildup or cutback.[12] The estimates, then, should be added to the NIA purchase totals to derive a more meaningful aggregate as well as a more appropriate surplus or deficit figure, or to any other measures that may be used to determine fiscal stimulus or restraint.

To examine more closely the timing of the major inventory effects, equation (4) may be converted into a formulation relating current goods-in-process inventory investment to lagged contract awards by substituting in the relevant a_i's. The results are shown in Table 4 and are plotted in Figure 3 for (1) the mean values of K, A, and L (that is, the a_i's shown in Table 1), and (2) the average of the 1965–66 a_i's. The two patterns are virtually identical.

In both instances, contract awards of the current period and one period earlier have the largest positive effect on current inventory change, and contract awards three to seven periods back have the largest negative effect. The sum of the coefficients in each case is, of course, zero, indicating that an inventory accumulation will occur only when contract awards change.

It may also be useful to examine the patterns of goods-in-process inventory investment for various contract award assumptions. I have run a few simulations projecting contract awards forward and estimating the inventory accumulation which would result. Based on 1965–66 average a_i's and presenting all figures at annual rates, two of the more interesting results are:

1. Each sustained absolute increase or decrease of contract awards of $1.0 billion per quarter will, after ten quarters, cause defense goods-in-process inventories to increase or decrease by about $1.5 billion per quarter.

2. A constant percentage increase or decrease in contract awards will cause the same percentage increase or decrease in inventory investment.

---

[12] There are some reasons why our measures may not coincide perfectly with a defense goods-in-process inventory investment series which could conceivably be derived directly from defense producers. As observed in note 7, some NIA defense purchases are not preceded by contract awards, although purchases by the AEC and from educational and nonprofit institutions are largely of a research and development (R&D) nature and are not likely to have a very high inventory investment component. Offsetting this source of possible underestimation are the following: (1) inventories are normally valued at cost, whereas our measure derived from contract awards would include profits as well; (2) the lags that exist for some types of contracts such as research and development and service contracts arise from a production process which by its nature can not involve much inventory accumulation. Therefore, an estimate of inventory accumulation based on these lags may be too high. This effect is partially mitigated by the fact that rapid changes in contract awards are required to induce substantial inventory investment, and R&D and service contracts have been relatively stable as compared to major procurement. All things considered, we believe the estimates to be fairly accurate in the large.

TABLE 4.—*Weights of lagged contract awards for inventory investment*

Lagged time period	Weights based on—	
	Mean values of K, A, and L [1]	1965–66 average a_i's [1]
0	.1576	.1692
1	.1279	.1385
2	.0100	.0113
3	− .0482	− .0521
4	− .0703	− .0763
5	− .0688	− .0743
6	− .0529	− .0572
7	− .0314	− .0342
8	− .0121	− .0135
9	− .0033	− .0032
10	− .0085	− .0083
Total..................	.0000	.0000

[1] See page 98 for explanation of the symbols.

Source: Derived from equation (4) in text.

As one illustration, a 5 percent rate of growth of contract awards starting from $25.0 billion (the first half of 1965 average) would yield an inventory investment ten periods later of about $2.5 billion and growing at 5 percent per quarter.

The inventory figures may be related to an accrued expenditures measure by the use of Table 5, which presents various defense timing adjustments for recent fiscal years. Column (1) shows the estimates of goods-in-process inventory investment under conditions of rectangular production; [13] column (2) presents the Office of Business Economics' defense timing adjustments; and column (3) gives estimates by the Department of Defense of its changes in accounts payable as reported in the Treasury's *Combined Statement of Receipts, Expenditures, and Balances.*

Since accounts receivable vary little, the DOD changes in accounts payable measure the differences between accrued expenditures, which conform closely to production on Government account, and checks issued for every fiscal year. The OBE timing adjustments reflect the extent to which deliveries

---

[13] The inverted V estimates would differ only in fiscal year 1966, and then only by $0.1 billion.

exceed checks issued; and the inventory investment figures, the extent to which production exceeds NIA deliveries. The sum of these two, therefore, also provides estimates of the excess of production over checks issued, the same concept measured by the DOD changes in accounts payable.

To see if these numbers fit together, the sum of the inventory accumulation figures and the OBE adjustments, that is, column (4) of Table 5—can be compared with the changes in accounts payable of DOD. It should be noted that the latter estimates are particularly suspect in the earlier reporting years. For fiscal years 1965 and 1966, the two measures of the difference between actual production and checks issued are quite close, although earlier they diverged considerably, especially in fiscal 1962. If it is valid to be more confident of the later figures, the close correspondence seems to indicate that either an accrued expenditure measure or an adjustment such as ours to NIA deliveries is required for the analysis of defense impacts.

FIGURE 3.—*Weights of lagged contract awards for inventory investment*

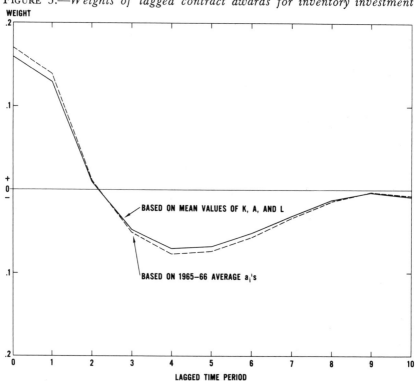

Source: Table 4.

TABLE 5.—*Defense timing adjustments, 1962–66*

[In billions of dollars]

Fiscal year	Estimated goods-in-process inventory investment with rectangular production	Office of Business Economics timing adjustment	Estimated Department of Defense change in accounts payable	Sum: Columns (1) and (2)
	(1)	(2)	(3)	(4)
1962	1.3	0.7	0.1	2.0
1963	.4	−.8	.5	−.4
1964	−.2	−1.3	−.7	−1.5
1965	−.5	.9	.2	.4
1966	2.3	−.4	2.0	1.9

Sources: Col. (1): calculated from column (1) of Table 3; col. (2): Office of Business Economics, unpublished data; col. (3): U.S. Treasury Department, *Combined Statement of Receipts, Expenditures, and Balances of the United States Government,* fiscal years 1962–66.

CONCLUSION

An expenditure concept based primarily on deliveries appears to be too lagging a measure of the impacts of defense spending, or indeed of Government purchases in general. While this measure may not be greatly inaccurate in times of stable contract awards, it can be seriously misleading when contract awards are changing rapidly. An accrued expenditure series, which reflects actual production on Government account, would largely eliminate this problem. In its absence, a useful series for fiscal analysis may be derived by adding to NIA deliveries an estimate of defense goods-in-process inventory investment.

EDWARD M. GRAMLICH[1]
Board of Governors of the Federal Reserve System

Measures of the Aggregate Demand Impact of the Federal Budget

In the last year and a half it has become apparent that better summary measures of the impact of the Federal budget on aggregate demand are needed. The crude measures that were so helpful in the early 1960's, when demand was well below its full employment potential, will no longer do now that the economy has entered a period when "fine tuning" is the word of the day.

The purpose of this paper is to contribute to a greater understanding of measures of the demand impact of the budget, with the hope that these measures can be used more effectively in the practical conduct of fiscal policy than they are at present. The paper approaches the subject both theoretically and empirically. It discusses three measures of fiscal impact which have been suggested in the literature, considers the difficulty of interpreting these measures in inflationary times, and attempts to estimate the measures for the interesting 1963–67 period.

All three of the fiscal impact measures stem from Cary Brown's pathbreaking 1956 article.[2] The first and most famous, publicized by the Council of Economic Advisers and others, is the high employment budget surplus or deficit.[3] The second is Richard Musgrave's notion of fiscal leverage.[4] The third measure follows Brown, Musgrave, and previous work that I have done in computing what is essentially a weighted high employment surplus or deficit.[5]

---

[1] I would like to thank Arthur M. Okun, James Tobin, and Robert Solomon for originally stimulating my interest in this topic, and Harvey Galper, Lyle E. Gramley, and Wilfred Lewis, Jr., for help on this paper.

[2] E. Cary Brown, "Fiscal Policy in the 'Thirties: A Reappraisal," *American Economic Review,* Vol. 46 (December 1956), pp. 857–79.

[3] See "The Annual Report of the Council of Economic Advisers," *Economic Report of the President,* 1962; Charles L. Schultze, testimony before the Joint Economic Committee, in *Current Economic Situation and Short-Run Outlook,* Hearings, 86 Cong. 2 sess. (1961), pp. 114–39; and Herbert Stein, testimony in *January 1961 Economic Report of the President and the Economic Situation and Outlook,* Hearings before the Joint Economic Committee, 87 Cong. 1 sess. (1961), pp. 209–26.

[4] See Musgrave, "On Measuring Fiscal Performance," *Review of Economics and Statistics,* Vol. 46 (May 1964), pp. 213–20.

[5] Edward M. Gramlich, "The Behavior and Adequacy of the United States Federal Budget, 1952–64," *Yale Economic Essays,* Vol. 6 (Spring 1966), pp. 99–159.

The first section of this paper reviews these three measures and presents a conceptual framework in which all have their place. It shows that the weighted high-employment deficit, though not without its drawbacks, is superior to the other measures as a general purpose tool. The second section discusses the inflation problem, specifically the uneven incidence of inflation on revenues and expenditures. An inflation adjustment is suggested to circumvent this problem. The third section uses six recently estimated econometric models to calculate the quarterly behavior of the measures. Each of these models tells a rather different story about the demand impact of the budget, pointing up the need for more reliable estimates of the structure of the economy before the effects of fiscal policy can realistically be determined. But all the models suggest that various components of the budget have quite different demand impacts, indicating that there is a need for some sort of a differential weighting scheme.

MEASURES OF FISCAL IMPACT

One can estimate the demand impact of the budget at several levels of sophistication. The most simple-minded approach would be to look only at the actual surplus or deficit. The dangers of such an approach are readily apparent. If the government were to raise tax rates by a large enough amount to cause a recession, and then, because of automatic stabilizers, the budget deficit increased, one could erroneously conclude that fiscal policy had become more expansionary. Even if the budget did not dip further into the red, such an approach would necessarily underestimate the restrictiveness of fiscal policy.

The reason for the paradox is, of course, that comparing budgets at different levels of resource utilization is not a valid exercise. To make a valid comparison one should put all budgets on a common footing by calculating them at a common level of resource utilization. For this purpose one could pick any level of utilization, but it is convenient to use the one defined as high employment and to calculate the high-employment budget surplus or deficit. In terms of the above illustration, this more refined measure would no longer lead anybody astray because now at every level of utilization the high tax rate fiscal program would be more restrictive than the corresponding low tax rate program. The question comes down to a simple matter of distinguishing a shift in a function from a movement along it.

But the high employment surplus is not the last word in budgetary analysis. For several years now even introductory students in economics have been exposed to the mysteries of the balanced budget multiplier, which demonstrates the general principle that budgetary dollars are not all alike. Chances are that purchases of goods and services have more of a demand impact than transfer payments to low income persons, which in turn have a greater per-dollar impact than taxes on high income groups. Corporate taxes, indirect taxes, government interest payments, government imports, and grants-in-aid have still different effects. To put it mildly, it would be a fantastic coincidence if all these differences were adequately reflected by a number such as the high employment (or actual) budget deficit, which makes the implicit assumption of a unitary per-dollar impact of all components of the Federal budget.

Musgrave's answer to this difficulty was to calculate what he called the "fiscal leverage" of the budget.[6] This leverage, or the net gross national product (GNP) impact of all budgetary items, is derived by calculating a hypothetical level of GNP that would obtain in the absence of the Federal budget and subtracting this from the actual level of GNP. Since fiscal leverage works in terms of the GNP effect of budgetary items, it builds in an adjustment for the differential demand impact of budgetary components.

It is helpful to use a simple income determination model to demonstrate these ideas. The model includes a consumption function, an investment function, a tax function, and four identities—all of which are specified in real terms:

(1) $C=C_o+cYD$,
(2) $T=T_o+tY$,
(3) $I=I_o+iY$,
(4) $Y=C+I+G$,
(5) $YD=Y-T$,
(6) $G=\overline{G}$ (exogenous),
(7) $GD=G-T$,

where C=consumption,
YD=disposable income,
T=taxes (withdrawals),
Y=GNP,
I=investment,
G=government purchases,
GD=government deficit.

The private spending functions in the model are extremely condensed. In both cases the intercept terms are assumed to capture all influences except that of current income. For consumption the intercept would include such things as demographic, price, and asset variables; for investment it includes the size of the capital stock, monetary influences, and price terms. The marginal propensities c and i can be thought of either as short-run impact propensities or as long-run steady-state propensities. Whatever concept is used, one must be careful to define the intercept terms accordingly.

The tax function has a negative intercept to reflect the progressivity of the tax structure. This form insures that the marginal rate·will always be above the average rate, as is consistent with the definition of progressivity.

---

[6] Musgrave, *op. cit.*

The function could also be reinterpreted to include its most important fiscal omission, government transfer payments. This reinterpretation involves thinking of taxes as net government withdrawals, the tax rate as including endogenous transfer payments, and the intercept as including exogenous transfer payments.

First, equations (1) through (5) of the model are used to calculate the reduced form expressions for GNP both with and without a government:

(7A) $$Y = \frac{1}{1-i-c(1-t)} (C_o + cT_o + I_o + G),$$

with a government, and

(7B) $$Y' = \frac{1}{1-i-c} (C_o + I_o),$$

without a government.

The GNP multipliers for budgetary components can then be derived by differentiating (7A) with respect to G and T_o:

(8) $$\frac{\delta Y}{\delta G} = \frac{1}{1-i-c(1-t)}; \frac{\delta Y}{\delta T_o} = \frac{c}{1-i-c(1-t)}.$$

Musgrave's fiscal leverage, which is denoted by L, is derived as:

(9) $$L = Y - Y' = \left(\frac{1}{1-i-c(1-t)}\right)(C_o + cT_o + I_o + G) - \left(\frac{1}{1-i-c}\right)(C_o + I_o).$$

After adding and subtracting

$$\frac{ct(C_o + cT_o + I_o + G)}{(1-i-c)(1-i-c(1-t))},$$

this reduces to

(10) $$L = \left(\frac{1}{1-i-c}\right)(G + cT_o - ctY) = \left(\frac{1}{1-i-c}\right)(G - cT).$$

Thus, fiscal leverage can be shown to equal the no-government GNP multiplier times a multiplicand term which weights actual budgetary totals according to their differential demand impact. The appropriate weights are the GNP multipliers for budgetary components relative to the GNP multiplier for purchases. These weights comprise the fundamental advantage of using fiscal leverage as an indicator of fiscal impact. One is no longer forced to treat every component of the Federal budget as if it had the same demand impact as government purchases. If there were some budgetary component which did not have much effect on demand, say transfer payments to misers, this component could be given a weight close to zero.

Yet there are still reasons why fiscal leverage is less than satisfactory as a measure of the aggregate demand impact of fiscal policy. In the first place, since fiscal leverage measures differences in real GNP due to fiscal policy, it is not applicable in times of inflation, when the economy is not able to achieve equilibrium real GNP. A country with a strongly inflationary budget policy would show a fiscal leverage that at all times exactly equalled the difference between no-government GNP and high-employment GNP— apparently a perfect fiscal policy. Since society's welfare presumably depends on stable prices as well as full employment, a measure such as this which only makes the government pass a "one-tail" test should be ruled out. The way to do this, also long-recognized in introductory economics, is to work in terms of aggregate demand functions rather than in terms of real GNP itself.[7]

A second problem with fiscal leverage, mentioned by both Brown and Musgrave, involves the questionable no-government multiplier. Both authors were eager to avoid estimating this difficult quantity, especially insofar as it required knowledge of the marginal propensity of induced investment. Such considerations might seem to be less of an issue now that several econometric models of the economy are available, but it is still a dubious exercise to decompose multipliers into their no-government components. It remains sensible to avoid working with complicated multipliers whenever possible, and to deal instead with aggregate demand functions.

A related difficulty should also be mentioned. There is a large body of business cycle literature devoted to the problem which results when $i+c>1$. In this case the no-government multiplier is infinity and the Keynesian system will not reach equilibrium by itself. The actual level of GNP must then be determined by the automatically stabilizing effect of taxes (note that $\dfrac{1}{1-i-c(1-t)}$ is always less than $\dfrac{1}{1-i-c}$, and stands a much better chance of being finite), or by such external constraints as full employment ceilings and disinvestment floors. One of the lesser tragedies of this unstable model is that fiscal leverage becomes a product of $(G-cT)$ and an infinite multiplier, an indefined quantity. This again makes it necessary to look at the underlying aggregate demand functions.

This special case should not be passed off too lightly. It is generally agreed that c is high, almost certainly over 0.5 in the long run and possibly as high as 0.95. In this context it does not take much induced investment to generate instability in the no-government system. In fact, as we shall see in the next section, in the one econometric model where the fiscal leverage computations are manageable, it turns out that the no-government multiplier is infinite, and leverage takes on this indefinable value.

---

[7] These criticisms of fiscal leverage are not meant to deprecate Musgrave's important contribution in any way. Musgrave did use fiscal leverage in his analysis to a greater extent than may have been called for in view of the defects of this concept, but he also dealt extensively with the weighted high employment deficit measure which, the author argues, is superior.

The above discussion indicates that conceptual difficulties with fiscal leverage can be avoided by working with real aggregate demand functions rather than with real GNP. Instead of deriving fiscal impact by finding the difference in real GNP with and without a government budget, one can calculate the difference in demand functions with and without the budget. As with the budget deficits, this difference could be calculated at any level of GNP, but it is convenient to use high employment as a standard. The following equations present the with- and without-government solutions of the aggregate demand (AD) function at high employment. The high employment values of endogenous variables are denoted with a star.

(11A) $$AD^* = C_0 + cT_0 + I_0 + G + (i + c(1-t))Y^*$$

with a government, and

(11B) $$AD'^* = C_0 + I_0 + (i+c)Y^*,$$

without a government.

Proceeding as before, the government's effect on the aggregate demand function, or Q, is determined by subtracting (11B) from (11A).

(12) $$Q = AD^* - AD'^* = G + cT_0 - ct\, Y^* = G - cT^*.$$

The relation between Q and the high employment budget is now apparent. Q is nothing more than the high employment deficit, with each budgetary component weighted by its GNP multiplier relative to that of purchases. The weights are also the same ones used in computing fiscal leverage.[8] The weighted deficit then combines the best of both approaches. Like the high employment deficit, it works in terms of aggregate demand functions; like fiscal leverage, it weights budgetary components. Thus the weighted high employment budget seems to be a more precise way of measuring fiscal impact.

Unfortunately, there is one flaw with even this measure. Since the weighted deficit can only be translated into a GNP figure through the after-tax multiplier, which depends on tax rates, the translation factor is not independent of the composition of the weighted deficit. Thus, the weighted deficit is not a unique and unambiguous number. It is possible for the same Q to have a different effect on GNP, or for different Q's to give the same GNP, according to the composition of Q between taxes and purchases. This is, incidentally, a problem common to the unweighted high employment surplus. Attempts to collapse that measure into a one-dimensional representation of the budget program can be foiled if the slope of the program function, which depends on tax rates, changes.

---

[8] Things do become more complicated when some high employment budgetary components affect other components, as with taxes that affect the tax base for other taxes. But even in this case the weights are readily derivable. See Gramlich, *op. cit.*, for a more rigorous discussion.

Figure 1 presents a graphic summary of the foregoing analysis. The figure plots the aggregate demand functions with and without government (AD and AD', respectively). The former has a higher intercept because of government purchases and the negative intercept of the tax function, and a lower slope due to the automatic stabilizers. The horizontal difference in equilibrium solutions is fiscal leverage; the vertical difference in demand functions at high employment is the weighted deficit. The dotted line represents an aggregate demand function with even higher government purchases and higher tax rates. It illustrates the possibility that the same Q could give different levels of GNP (Y'' as opposed to Y) depending upon the after-tax multiplier with which it is associated.

A final point worthy of mention concerns the relationship of these measures of fiscal impact to the GNP multipliers for budgetary components. The multipliers tell how much GNP would change in response to specified changes in policy variables. Such pieces of information are important in determining the optimal size of policy actions. The fiscal impact measures discussed

FIGURE 1.—*Aggregate demand impact of the budget*

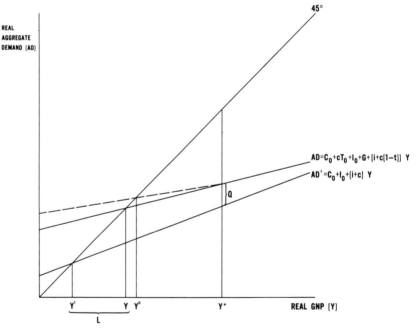

$$AD = C_0 + cT_0 + I_0 + G + (i + c(1-t))\ Y$$

$$AD' = C_0 + I_0 + (i + c)\ Y$$

Q = Government effect on aggregate demand
Y' = Real GNP without government
Y" = Alternative real GNP
Y* = Full employment real GNP
L = Fiscal leverage

Source: see equations (1) through (12) in text.

here are not appropriate for that purpose, but are instead useful for evaluating the demand impact of the entire government budget. Their usefulness hinges on the extent to which such an indicator of fiscal policy is an interesting and fruitful concept.

THE SPECIAL PROBLEM OF INFLATION

The analysis in the previous section was conducted in real terms without considering price effects. Yet because taxes and purchases behave differently when prices change, it is especially difficult to define fiscal impact in inflationary periods. This section reviews the problem of interpretation associated with inflation, and suggests a way around it.

First, we examine the behavior of progressive taxes when prices change. Tax functions are properly specified in money terms rather than in real terms. To be accurate, then, equation (2) should be rewritten as

$$(13) \qquad\qquad T^m = -T_o{}^m + t(Y)(P),$$

where P is the general price index and the m superscript refers to money terms. This equation indicates that money taxes increase more than proportionately with money income. If prices are constant and real income is increasing, it reflects the same tax progressivity as equation (2). But if real income is constant and prices are rising, as would be true in an inflation, equation (13) implies that money taxes increase more than proportionately with money income and prices—hence taxes increase in real terms.

Note that this phenomenon rests on two factors: (a) that taxes are set in money terms; and (b) that they are progressive with respect to GNP. The first factor would be true of all taxes in the United States, and probably in other countries as well. The second factor could be true either if a tax is progressive with respect to its base, such as United States personal income taxes; or if the tax base is progressive with respect to money income, such as corporate taxes. (Because of fixed costs, the short-run marginal share of income going into profits is above the average.)

With expenditures, whether purchases or transfer payments, the story is just the reverse. Generally, the budgetary process fixes expenditures in money terms, and unless price increases are provided for by government policy, real expenditures are reduced by inflation. It seems likely that this does happen in the United States, at least for nonwage expenditures. The guardians of our purse strings are not the type to be persuaded by such devious arguments for increasing money expenditures as anticipated inflation.

It thus appears that inflation would move real taxes and real expenditures in opposite directions. Real taxes would almost certainly increase, and real expenditures would almost certainly decrease. The net effect is to generate some sort of an automatic price stabilizer which takes over when the economy enters an inflationary regime, and when the real income stabilizers cease to operate. These price stabilizers have been noticed many times.[9] But what has not been noticed very often is that in calculating the impact of fiscal policy on aggregate demand, an adjustment must be made for automatic price stabilizers as well as for automatic real income stabilizers. It would be just as misleading to call an inflation-generating fiscal policy restrictive merely because of an apparent increase in the budgetary surplus (whether actual, high employment, or weighted) as it was to fail to recognize the real income stabilizers.

The appropriate inflation adjustment for expenditures is to increase real expenditures by the percentage rate of inflation not provided for by government policy. If prices were to rise 100λ percent, of which 100β percent were anticipated and provided for, real expenditures should be increased by 100 $(\lambda-\beta)$ percent to adjust for their automatic reduction due to inflation.

The adjustment for taxes depends on the parameters of the tax function. To calculate pre-inflation real taxes at high employment, post-inflation high employment real taxes are multiplied by the ratio of pre- to post-inflation real taxes. The multiplicative adjustment factor is

$$(14) \quad \frac{\dfrac{-T_o{}^m}{P}+t\dfrac{(Y)(P)}{P}}{\dfrac{-T_o{}^m}{P(1+\lambda)}+t\dfrac{(Y)(P)(1+\lambda)}{P(1+\lambda)}}=\frac{(-T_o{}^m+tYP)\,(1+\lambda)}{-T_o{}^m+tYP(1+\lambda)}=\frac{T^m(1+\lambda)}{T^m(1+\lambda)+\lambda T_o{}^m}.$$

Calculation of other inflation-adjusted fiscal impact measures follows logically. The adjusted high employment deficit is derived by applying the adjustment factor to high employment real taxes, and the weighted adjusted deficit simply weights these adjusted totals. Fiscal leverage would similarly be calculated by applying the adjustment to actual real totals.

Although the measures discussed are most meaningful in real terms, there still may be an interest in converting some of these high employment impact measures into current dollars. It is difficult to give advice on how this might be done because there are so many possible current dollar measures that might be of interest. A few possibilities are:

1. The fiscal impact number in terms of actual prices. This would be derived simply by inflating the price-adjusted real measures by actual prices.

2. The fiscal impact number in terms of prices that would obtain if the appropriate high employment target were realized. This could be calculated by inflating by hypothetical high employment prices rather than by actual prices, and then applying an additional inflation adjustment for the difference between actual and hypothetical prices.

3. A portrayal of the actual budget at high employment. One would have to undo the inflation adjustment, making this something less than the desired normative concept, and then use hypothetical high employment prices as inflators.

---

[9] See Gardner Ackley, *Macroeconomic Theory* (Macmillan, 1961), p. 425.

4. A portrayal of the actual high employment budget in actual prices. One would first undo the inflation adjustment, then multiply by actual prices. This concept loses both its normative and descriptive significance, and is the least meaningful of the four; but unfortunately it is the one most often calculated.[10]

EMPIRICAL ESTIMATES

Up to now this discussion has taken place in an empirical vacuum. In an attempt to fill this gap, six well-known econometric models are used in this section to calculate quarterly estimates of the fiscal impact measures over the 1963–67 period.

The models were chosen to give a realistic cross-section by size, degree of disaggregation, and emphasis. The largest is the Brookings model which comprises over a hundred equations estimated by specialists in different sectors.[11] The only model in this sample which uses annual data was estimated by Suits.[12] The U.S. Department of Commerce model[13] is an outgrowth of earlier work by Klein[14] and is the model probably kept best attuned for making quarterly predictions. The Ando-Goldfeld model tries to pay special attention to the impacts of Government policy, and it is the only one estimated with seasonally unadjusted data.[15] The Okun model does not purport to be a full-fledged model; the author only puts together a system of equations to investigate the effect of the 1964 tax cut.[16] It is useful here because it is the only system simple enough to permit computation of fiscal leverage. (Though Okun's basic expenditure multiplier is not unreasonably high in comparison with that of other models, it is interesting to note that even here the no-government multiplier is infinite, and the

---

[10] See Keith Carlson, "Estimates of the High Employment Budget: 1947–1967," *Federal Reserve Bank of St. Louis Review,* Vol. 49 (June 1967), and Nancy H. Teeters, "Estimates of the Full-Employment Surplus, 1955–64," *Review of Economics and Statistics,* Vol. 47 (August 1965), pp. 309–21.

[11] See James S. Duesenberry, Gary Fromm, Lawrence R. Klein, and Edwin Kuh (eds.), *The Brookings Quarterly Econometric Model of the United States* (Rand McNally, 1965); and Gary Fromm and Paul Taubman, *Policy Simulations with an Econometric Model* (Brookings Institution, 1968).

[12] Daniel B. Suits, "Forecasting and Analysis with an Econometric Model," *American Economic Review,* Vol. 52 (March 1962), pp. 104–32.

[13] Maurice Liebenberg, Albert A. Hirsch, and Joel Popkin, "A Quarterly Econometric Model of the United States: A Progress Report," *Survey of Current Business,* Vol. 46 (May 1966), pp. 13–39.

[14] Lawrence R. Klein, "A Postwar Quarterly Model: Description and Applications," in *Models of Income Determination,* National Bureau of Economic Research, Studies in Income and Wealth, Vol. 28 (Princeton University Press, 1964), pp. 11–57.

[15] Albert Ando and Stephen M. Goldfeld, "An Econometric Model for Stabilization Policies," in Albert Ando, E. Cary Brown, and Ann F. Friedlaender (eds.), *Studies in Economic Stabilization* (Brookings Institution, 1968).

[16] Arthur M. Okun, "Measuring the Impact of the 1964 Tax Reduction," paper presented to the American Statistical Association, Philadelphia, September 1965.

leverage concept breaks down.) The remaining model is one which does not yet exist in final form. It is being estimated as a joint MIT-Federal Reserve project by Albert Ando, Frank de Leeuw, Franco Modigliani, and colleagues, and is again primarily concerned with developing reliable estimates of the impact of monetary and fiscal policy on the economy.

Since fiscal leverage either does not exist or is too difficult to calculate in all cases, this paper reports results only for the weighted high employment deficit. To be perfectly consistent, one should compute the inflation-adjusted deficit for each model using the appropriate income share and tax equations. But since this paper is fundamentally concerned with the difference made by the weights, it starts instead with a common high employment deficit series, and confines the contribution of the models to the generation of appropriate budgetary weights.

The high employment deficit series was taken from recent work by Keith Carlson,[17] who brought the method of the Council of Economic Advisers up to date. This series was then converted into real terms with appropriate actual deflators, and adjusted for inflation in the manner described in the previous section. The anticipated rate of inflation was assumed to equal a four-quarter moving average of past values.

For most of the 1963–67 period the inflation adjustment was not very important. It averaged $0.4 billion for 1963, $0.5 billion for 1964, $0.4 billion for 1965, and $1.2 billion for 1966—reaching a high of $1.6 billion in the second quarter of 1966. But even though it may not have mattered much in the past, one should guard against using this as a rationalization for not adjusting for inflation in the future. After all, there is no guarantee that past moderate rates of inflation will continue.

There are no hard and fast rules about the appropriate time dimension for the weights. One has a choice of weighting budgets by the impact (one-quarter) weights, the weights that would obtain over a fixed interval of time, say one or two years, or the steady-state ultimate effect weights. The impact concept is probably the most meaningful in terms of describing the short-run pattern of movements in demand, but the steady-state concept might well be more meaningful in describing fiscal policy in some ultimate sense. It tells how much demand impact the budget would eventually generate if it stood still until the lags died out. The calculations could be made either way without a great deal of difficulty, but for better or worse this paper reports results using steady-state weights.

Many will be disappointed by the lack of disaggregation in computing the weights. Even though most respectable models these days are large enough to surpass the confines of human understanding, they still are not detailed enough to capture some of the interesting idiosyncrasies of fiscal policy. On the expenditure side, for example, only the Brookings and

---

[17] See Carlson, *op. cit.*

the MIT–FRB models make the state and local governments sector endogenous, and even the Brookings model has yet to include this sector in its simulations. Thus there is still very scanty evidence about the demand impact of Federal grants-in-aid to states, and the weighted deficit calculations for all models have used the relative multiplier derived from the MIT–FRB project. The weight for transfers to foreign countries was derived even less scientifically—by making crude estimates on the basis of work by Salant, *et al.*[18] There is also very limited information concerning differential effects of social security and unemployment benefits, interest payments, and subsidies of Government enterprises. These items never achieve more importance than supplying a missing link in some income identity, and they all are assumed by the various models to affect demand only through the aggregate marginal propensity to consume. The paper follows this convention, but there is clearly a need for further work in sharpening these distinctions.

The situation is no better on the revenue side. Again, the various kinds of taxes do little more than close up identities, and it is very seldom that one sees an attempt to investigate such things as the income distribution and price and wage effects of various kinds of taxes.[19] The much discussed question of corporate tax shifting is hardly ever considered within the context of a model. Thus for the purposes here the best that can be done is to distinguish between taxes on persons, which work through the aggregate consumption propensity, and taxes on corporations, which affect investment and dividends.

Table 1 reports these weights. It is no exaggeration to say that the differences are alarming, considering that all models are describing the same economy. If nothing else, the differences point up what econometricians have said for a long time—namely, that it is extremely important to specify equations carefully. If this is not done, one can get highly inconsistent and unreliable information.

The personal tax weights equal the steady-state propensity to consume. This propensity is very low in the Suits model because he formulates a stock adjustment model for consumer durables, such that the income response of durable goods expenditures eventually dies out. In all other models this restriction is not imposed—at least the imputed services from durable goods bear a long-run relationship to income. But there are still large differences—between .615 for the Commerce model and .949 for the Okun model—and

---

[18] Walter S. Salant, *et al., The United States Balance of Payments in 1968* (Brookings Institution, 1963). The weights are 1.063 for grants-in-aid and 0.767 for foreign transfers. The former is greater than one because of induced state and local expenditures; the latter is close to one because most foreign transfers are tied to U.S. exports.

[19] Welcome exceptions to this statement are the Brookings model and Klein's work (*op. cit.,* notes 11 and 14).

these large differences in what is supposed to be a predictable component of GNP imply quite different impacts for the budgetary items affecting consumption. (Needless to say, they also imply large differences in the multiplier through which these measures are translated into GNP.)

TABLE 1.—*Alternative high employment deficit weights, selected models, steady-state values* [1]

Model [2]	Personal taxes and transfers	Corporation taxes	Multiplier for Government purchases
Brookings model..............	0.831	0.304	2.468
Suits model [3].................	.475	.475	1.335
Department of Commerce model...................	.615	.250	[6] n.c.
Ando-Goldfeld model........	.724	.421	3.259
Okun model [4]..............	.949	1.340	3.333
MIT–FRB model [5]...........	.930	.276	[6] n.c.

[1] Steady-state weights are used. It can be shown that these weights equal the no-government relative multiplier, which implies that aside from price and distribution effects, the absolute weights for all noncorporate taxes and domestic transfers, interest, and subsidies are the same.

[2] For descriptions of the models, see pp. 119–21.

[3] Suits has effectively constrained personal and corporate taxes to have the same ultimate weight because investment does not depend on profits, and because the steady-state dividend payout propensity is constrained to equal 1.

[4] Okun has calculated the multipliers in his paper by combining the steady-state consumption propensity with the six-period dividend payout propensity. My multiplier is larger than his because I use his steady-state dividend propensity.

[5] Work on this model is still in a preliminary state and the results will not be published for some time. These weights will probably be altered when the model is presented in its final version.

[6] Not calculated.

Source: See text for derivation.

The corporate tax weights equal the propensity to consume times the marginal dividend payout ratio, plus the marginal investment effect of cash flows. The first four models have straight accelerator mechanisms for investment, implying that the steady-state marginal sensitivity of investment to cash flows or after-tax profits is constrained to equal zero.[20] The MIT–FRB

[20] The Suits model has an initial impact effect for after-tax profits, but this effect dies out in the steady state. Jorgenson has estimated investment equations for the Brookings model which do include tax-rate terms, but these equations have not been included in the most recent Brookings simulations. See Fromm and Taubman, *op. cit.*, and Dale W. Jorgenson's chapter, "Anticipations and Investment Behavior," in Duesenberry, Fromm, Klein, and Kuh (eds.), *op. cit.*, pp. 34–92.

investment sector does not make this constraint. It allows for an imputed rent effect of corporate taxes, but the cash flow effect is still rather slight.[21] Thus, in five of the models the corporate tax weights are quite low. Even the moderately high weight of the Suits model is only obtained because his steady-state dividend payout ratio is constrained to be one, which means that ultimately his corporate taxes are just like personal taxes. At the other extreme is Okun's investment function, which depends only on cash flows with no moderating stock adjustment mechanism. This form gives an extremely high weight to corporate taxes, a fact that bothered Okun and led him not to place much credence in his results for corporate taxes.

Table 2 presents the calculated series of fiscal impact, along with the unweighted deficit. As would be expected, these series are quite different in level, and they tell a very different story about the contribution of the budget to aggregate demand. The unweighted surplus and Okun's model both indicate that taxes are about as deflationary as expenditures are expansionary such that the generally positive high employment surpluses of the period meant that Government was generally reducing aggregate demand. All other models suggest that taxes are much less deflationary than expenditures are expansionary, such that the Government makes a positive contribution to demand. The obvious inference from the table is not only that estimation of the weights is important, but also that the decision whether or not to weight is crucial. The weighted deficit and the unweighted deficit tell fundamentally different stories about the impact of the budget. The consensus is that it will not do to assume, as the high employment deficit does, that all budgetary components are about alike in their effect on aggregate demand.

It may be more illuminating to look at changes in these measures of fiscal impact than at their levels. The first differences are calculated in Table 3. Here the divergences between the models are not as glaring as before, but there are still sizable differences of opinion in periods when taxes are changing. For example, in the first two quarters of 1964 the unweighted deficit increases by $10.2 billion, and the models give estimates of increases in the aggregate demand function which range from $8.9 billion for the Okun model to $4.4 billion for the Suits model. When these differences are multiplied by a GNP multiplier in the neighborhood of 3, it clearly makes a difference whether a tax cut implies an increase in the demand function of $9.0

---

[21] To be precise, this statement refers to the case where cash flows are varied by changing the corporate tax rate. If the weights were calculated under the assumption that corporate taxes were altered via the investment credit or depreciation allowances, the investment sensitivity would be much larger. (See Charles W. Bischoff, "Elasticities of Substitution, Capital Malleability, and Distributed Lag Investment Functions," presented to the Econometric Society, San Francisco, December 1966.)

billion or $4.5 billion.[22] Notice, however, that if the change in fiscal impact is inspired by purchases, as in the 1966 III–1967 I period, the variance of estimates of fiscal stimulation is greatly reduced ($9.0 billion for the unweighted deficit, and from $9.4 billion for the Okun model to $7.5 billion for the Brookings model).

---

[22] Actually the difference is even larger than this statement would indicate, because as Table 1 shows, there are large differences in the multipliers of the different models. By way of illustration, the large increase in Okun's demand function should be multiplied by 3.3, while the lesser increase in the Suits demand function should be multiplied by only 1.3.

TABLE 2.—*Levels of fiscal impact: Weighted and unweighted high employment deficits, selected models, 1963–67*

[In billions of 1958 dollars, inflation adjusted]

Year and quarter	High employment deficit (unweighted)	Brookings model	Suits model	Commerce model	Ando-Goldfeld model	Okun model	MIT–FRB model
1963: I	−9.2	18.0	32.7	31.0	20.8	−15.4	13.5
II	−13.0	14.8	30.0	28.1	17.6	−19.2	10.0
III	−12.6	14.0	29.9	27.8	17.0	−20.6	9.0
IV	−13.8	14.5	29.9	28.0	17.3	−20.0	9.6
1964: I	−10.8	17.0	31.0	29.7	19.4	−17.3	12.6
II	−3.6	21.7	34.3	33.5	23.7	−11.1	17.7
III	−5.4	21.2	33.6	32.9	23.2	−11.9	17.1
IV	−8.2	18.6	31.5	30.6	20.8	−14.6	14.6
1965: I	−8.9	18.1	31.2	30.2	20.3	−15.2	13.9
II	−8.3	18.8	32.2	31.1	21.1	−14.8	14.5
III	−2.3	24.0	35.3	35.2	25.7	−9.0	20.4
IV	−3.6	23.4	35.5	35.1	25.2	−10.2	19.6
1966: I	−3.3	24.2	37.3	36.4	26.4	−10.1	20.0
II	−5.1	23.4	37.6	36.5	25.8	−11.6	18.9
III	−2.9	25.9	40.7	39.2	28.6	−9.1	21.2
IV	.6	28.8	43.1	41.7	31.3	−6.4	24.2
1967: I	3.9	31.9	46.6	45.0	34.6	−2.2	27.2

Source: See text for explanation and derivation.

TABLE 3.—*Movements in fiscal impact: First differences of weighted and unweighted high employment deficits for selected models, 1963–67*

[In billions of 1958 dollars, inflation adjusted]

Year and quarter	High employment deficit (unweighted)	Brookings model	Suits model	Commerce model	Ando-Goldfeld model	Okun model	MIT-FRB model
1963: II	-3.8	-3.2	-2.7	-2.9	-3.2	-3.8	-3.5
III	.4	-.8	-.1	-.3	-.6	-1.4	-1.0
IV	-1.2	.5	....	.2	.3	.6	.6
1964: I	3.0	2.5	1.1	1.7	2.1	2.7	3.0
II	7.2	4.7	3.3	3.8	4.3	6.2	5.1
III	-1.8	-.5	-.7	-.6	-.5	-.8	-.6
IV	-2.8	-2.6	-2.1	-2.3	-2.4	-2.7	-2.5
1965: I	-.7	-.5	-.3	-.4	-.5	-.6	-.7
II	.6	.7	1.0	.9	.8	.4	.6
III	6.0	5.2	3.1	4.1	4.6	5.8	5.9
IV	-1.3	-.6	.2	-.1	-.5	-1.2	-.8
1966: I	.3	.8	1.8	1.3	1.2	.1	.4
II	-1.8	-.8	.3	.1	-.6	-1.5	-1.1
III	2.2	1.5	3.1	2.7	2.8	2.5	2.3
IV	3.5	2.9	2.4	2.5	2.7	2.7	3.0
1967: I	3.3	3.1	3.5	3.3	3.3	4.2	3.0

Source: Table 2.

CONCLUSION

The limited empirical investigation in the previous section leads to one very definite conclusion. Clearly, more reliable information about the structure of the economy is needed before it is possible to estimate the fiscal impact of the budget. The most obvious difficulties pertain to the basic structural parameters such as the marginal propensity to consume and the tax sensitivity of investment. But even after these difficulties are solved, or at least the variance of the estimates reduced, there remain such additional problems as the implications for income distribution and consumption, and the price and wage effects of different governmental activities. As a final step not even discussed in this paper, this fiscal analysis must eventually be integrated with an analysis of the demand impact of the monetary and credit policies of the Government.

But it will be a long time before these events come to pass. In the meantime policy makers will have to go on making decisions, and one indispensable factor in their decisions will be the impact of the budget. The decisions will be very delicate ones, and it is incumbent on policy makers to use the most refined procedures that are available. Hopefully, these procedures will begin to include such considerations as adjustments for the automatic price stabilizers and for the differential demand impact of various budgetary components. There may still be considerable uncertainty about how these adjustments should be made, but surely trying to adjust for known problems on the basis of reasonable assumptions is better than doing nothing at all.

COMMENTS BY DISCUSSANTS

E. Cary Brown

Department of Economics, Massachusetts Institute of Technology

I will first take up Gramlich's paper on measuring the fiscal impact of the Federal budget. I am in complete agreement with the purpose of his exercise—to attempt to quantify discretionary fiscal policy—and with his conclusion that such measurement depends heavily on the values that are set for spending coefficients of economic units, a matter about which present models differ. My commentary should be thought of as a qualification or amplification of a fine paper.

1. We must bear in mind that the total fiscal impact of the budget is necessarily composed of its discretionary components and its automatic components. If, for policy purposes, we wish to focus on the discretionary components, as does Gramlich, we must be careful not to call what we are measuring *the* fiscal impact, but rather the fiscal impact shorn of its automatic elements.

2. With the first section of his paper, which develops his measure of the fiscal impact of discretionary budget policy at less than full employment, I

am in complete agreement, along with his criticism of the fiscal-leverage concept. I would make the obvious caution that the impact of two budgets on aggregate demand at different levels of real income may differ not only in amount but also in sign because of differing slopes in the tax-transfer schedules. This is, of course, familiar ground.

3. Gramlich's important and interesting contribution is in the second section, where he adjusts the full-employment budget impact for the automatic effects of inflation on spending. On the expenditure side, his concept of real Government purchases desired by the Government is the actual expenditure in the light of some expected price level. The expected price level may be either greater or less than the price level that actually turns out. Say the Government has spent 100 real units one period and, expecting prices to increase by 50 percent, budgets 150 money units for the next period. If instead prices double, the actual real units spent drop to 75. The budget was more contractive than planned by some 25 real units, and since these arose automatically, in some sense, they are eliminated from the discretionary budget impact.

When applied to the far side of full employment, this notion raises difficulties which do not arise on the near side of full employment. The measured shift in full-employment demand brought about by discretionary budget policy when the economy is at less than full employment has a use that is lacking in the inflationary situation. If all other things remain the same and the policy is to maintain the less than full-employment level of income, discretionary action need only repeat itself. Or if aggregate demand is to be expanded, the impact of the budget on full-employment demand will be equal to the previous full-employment budget impact plus the change instituted under the new policy. In other words, this full-employment budget impact concept has workable implications for policy making.

To return to my earlier example, again assume all other things are equal, and an equilibrium situation after prices have doubled. Assume further a desire to maintain the new, doubled price level. If the previous full-employment budget impact is maintained, expenditures can be increased to 200 money units—or 100 real units; but to do this would be inflationary since the unplanned decrease of 25 real units has not been taken into account. Stable policy requires an increase in this measured concept by these 25 real units. Although I can appreciate what Gramlich is trying to get at, this seems awkward.

There is also, of course, considerable ambiguity in that price expectations are virtually impossible to ascertain. Moreover, I am not at all sure but that the use of actual prices can be defended on the grounds that the Government can always keep up with the price level by supplemental appropriations or new legislation on tax-transfer payments, but implicitly chooses not to. In other words, we get into the subtle point made by Samuelson years ago— that even automatic policy is discretionary if we choose to accept its results.

4. For reasons not entirely obvious, Gramlich treats taxes differently from expenditures. Since some taxes are progressive with respect to money GNP, they can rise in real terms as prices rise. (One should note, however, that some large taxes, like tobacco, liquor, and gasoline are specific excises and hence *fall* in real terms as prices rise.) Gramlich then wishes to estimate the real taxes that would have been collected had prices not risen, attributing the real increment to automatic rather than discretionary policy.

If taxes were to be treated like expenditures, I suppose that the tax function should be estimated by the use of the *expected* price change, rather than the actual price change. We would then have similar problems to those faced on the expenditure side, but at least there would be a kind of symmetry. But Gramlich has used actual prices in estimating the portion of real taxes attributable to automatic budget policy. Parenthetically, I was startled to see that an estimate of pre-inflation taxes was made by multiplying post-inflation taxes by the ratio of pre- to post-inflation taxes! Since pre-inflation taxes had to be estimated to get this ratio, this is rather a roundabout process. Actually, if tax schedules get to be more complicated than the simple ones Gramlich uses, then a direct estimate of pre- and post-inflation taxes would be the best procedure. The same cautions that were mentioned earlier apply here—the measured fiscal impact will change even though no action is taken.

5. My tentative view of all this, then, is that the adjustment of effective demand for changes in price level are interesting and important numbers. But I would want to base my fiscal decisions on the actual demand impact of the budget at full employment, including the so-called automatic effects from unforeseen price changes.

I turn now to Galper's paper on the timing of the impact of federal expenditures on the economy. I have virtually nothing to report here. This paper, like Gramlich's, is a careful piece of work. The model used seems a reasonable one; the variables make sense; and the finding of the relationship between orders and defense goods-in-process an important and useful one.

Warren L. Smith

Department of Economics, University of Michigan

If we are to implement effectively what has come to be called a "finely-tuned" economic policy, it seems to me that greater use must be made of flexible fiscal policy. While both monetary and fiscal policies have important roles to play in economic stabilization, monetary policy has frequently been saddled with a disproportionate share of the stabilization burden. If fiscal policy is to be relied upon to a greater extent, we need (1) improved budget concepts and data, (2) better economic analysis of the magnitude and timing of the effects of fiscal policy, and (3) greater administrative flexibility in adjusting fiscal policy to changing conditions.

Presumably, the President's Commission on Budget Concepts is concerned primarily with the first of these three needs. On the other hand, the papers by Edward Gramlich and Harvey Galper contribute primarily to the second—that is, the analysis of the effects of fiscal policy. For that reason, their direct relevance to the work of the Commission does not appear to be very great.

Gramlich's effort to estimate a weighted full-employment surplus is a valuable contribution to the literature of fiscal policy. The only serious question of a technical nature that I have about the paper relates to the adjustment for inflation that Gramlich introduces. This adjustment appears to be based on a model in which expanding aggregate demand raises real output with no increase in the price level up to some point called "full employment," beyond which further increases in demand cause prices to rise with no increase in real output. In a world of this kind, it would seem to make sense to adjust the full-employment surplus to eliminate the automatic reduction that would result from rising prices. In fact, however, it appears that there is a more or less continuous relation of the Phillips-curve type between inflation and unemployment so that rising aggregate demand normally has an effect on both real output and the rate of change of the price level.

Suppose the authorities pick 4 percent unemployment as a target, fully expecting 2 percent inflation as a cost that must be paid to achieve their employment objective. Suppose further that with a full-employment surplus of $2 billion, private demand is just sufficient to achieve 4 percent unemployment, with prices in fact rising at the acceptable 2 percent rate. If underlying conditions remain unchanged (in some rather complex sense), the rise in prices will reduce real Government expenditures and increase real taxes. The increase in the real full-employment surplus will depress the economy below the target of 4 percent unemployment; indeed, if the target position is to be maintained, Government expenditures in money terms will have to be increased and/or tax rates reduced to make up for the effects of inflation on the full-employment surplus.

It would seem to me improper in these circumstances to correct for inflation along the lines suggested by Gramlich, thereby making it appear that the full-employment surplus was not changing. In principle, a correction for inflation in excess of the rate judged acceptable by the authorities might be appropriate, but such an adjustment would be impracticable, because there is no way of knowing what rate of inflation is in fact judged acceptable. In short, it seems to me that Gramlich's inflation adjustment is inappropriate and should be eliminated.

The purpose of the Gramlich paper is to construct a measure of the impact of fiscal policy. As a basis for judging the usefulness of his results, it may be helpful to review the three major purposes to which measures of fiscal impact may be put.

1. *Public education about fiscal policy.* The problem here is to counteract the gross misunderstanding that arises from the two-way relation between the budget and GNP—the fact that a fall in GNP resulting from a weakening of private demand will move the budget toward a deficit, but a discretionary change in fiscal policy that moves the budget toward a deficit at a given level of GNP will cause GNP to rise. What we have in this case is the classic economic problem of getting people to understand the difference between movements along a given schedule and shifts in the schedule itself.

For this purpose, I believe the full-employment surplus concept, as expounded, for example, in the 1962 *Annual Report of the Council of Economic Advisers* has proved to be extremely useful. It permits one to draw the distinction between the active and passive elements of fiscal policy in a very simple and fundamental way. Indeed, it may well have made a substantial contribution to the improved public understanding of fiscal policy which I believe has occurred in the last few years.

The only disadvantage I can see in the full-employment surplus for this purpose is that it focuses too much attention on the deficit or surplus itself— about which people are more concerned than they should be to begin with— rather than on changes in expenditures and taxes, the true prime movers of fiscal policy. But this is not an unduly high price to pay for the substantial improvement in understanding which has occurred. While an adjusted full-employment budget deficit or surplus with taxes and transfer payments weighted with the appropriate propensities to spend might yield a more accurate estimate of the impact of fiscal policy, it would be of little use for purposes of educating the man in the street, because it would simply be too difficult for him to understand.

2. *Evaluation of past fiscal policy.* The classic example of historical analysis and critique of fiscal policy is Cary Brown's study of fiscal policy in the 1930's.[23] This study served the valuable purpose of showing that, in spite of the large deficits that were incurred, fiscal policy was not very expansionary during this period. Indeed, it shifted in a perverse way at certain critical points during the decade. Brown invented the weighted full-employment deficit (or surplus) concept for use in this study, attaching a weight of unity to Government purchases and using a crude estimate of the marginal propensity to spend out of income as the weight attaching to taxes and transfer payments. This was a useful technique, although his conclusion would probably have been altered very little if he had simply used an unweighted full-employment deficit.

---

[23] E. Cary Brown, "Fiscal Policy in the 'Thirties: A Reappraisal," *American Economic Review,* Vol. 46 (December 1956), pp. 857–79.

In his careful study of fiscal policy in postwar recessions, Wilfred Lewis, Jr., made extensive and very effective use of the unweighted high-employment surplus as a means of separating the discretionary and automatic elements of fiscal policy.[24] Richard Musgrave used the concept of fiscal leverage as the basis of his analysis of fiscal policy during the period 1957–63.[25] However, fiscal leverage seems a less attractive technique than the weighted or unweighted full-employment surplus, not only for the reasons given in Gramlich's paper but also because it does not make any distinction between the automatic and discretionary elements in fiscal policy.

3. *Current analysis and policy prescription.* While the weighted or unweighted full-employment surplus is a useful device for organizing and presenting information in connection with historical studies, it is not evident to me that this kind of analysis is of much value as an aid in the actual formulation of policy. Here the unweighted full-employment surplus is not a very satisfactory tool, because (1) the multipliers attaching to different components of the surplus are different in both magnitude and timing; and (2) changes in legislation governing taxes and transfers will commonly change the slope as well as the level of the budget line. This means that the injection or withdrawal of purchasing power resulting from a change in fiscal policy at the current income level may be different from the change in the full-employment surplus and, furthermore, that the multiplier itself may be changed by the fiscal action. The use of weights, along the lines attempted in Gramlich's paper, is a way of dealing in part with the first of these problems, but it does not solve the second. But even with respect to the first problem there is the question of timing. What time period should be used in computing the weights? Gramlich uses steady-state weights, which seems to me to be an especially bad choice, but any other choice would also be open to objection.

In arriving at decisions concerning fiscal policy, I can see no alternative to a continuing careful review of the economic outlook and a consideration of alternative actions that might be taken to head off or counteract inflation or deflation. Some kind of model must inevitably be used to arrive at judgments concerning (1) the magnitude, and (2) the time profile of the effects of alternative policies not only on aggregate demand but on the composition of demand.

Of course, monetary and other policies need to be considered along with fiscal policy. This points to another difficulty with Gramlich's paper: the impact of fiscal policy will surely differ according to the nature of the accompanying monetary policy. Gramlich says nothing about monetary policy, the implication being, I suppose, that the Federal Reserve follows an

---

[24] Wilfred Lewis, Jr., *Federal Fiscal Policy in the Postwar Recessions* (Brookings Institution, 1962).

[25] R. A. Musgrave, "On Measuring Fiscal Performance," *Review of Economics and Statistics,* Vol. 46 (May 1964), pp. 213–20.

"accommodating" monetary policy. But it is by no means clear what this means; indeed, the definition of an accommodating monetary policy would differ from one to another of the six alternative econometric models with which Gramlich experiments.

I suppose the only question the Gramlich paper poses for the Commission on Budget Concepts is whether the Commission should recommend regular publication of information concerning the full-employment surplus. Clearly, the uncertainty about weights is so great that no official publication of a weighted surplus could be recommended at this time. It was pointed out in the course of the conference discussion that it is the change in the surplus from one period to the next that is most significant and that Gramlich's Table 3 shows that, on the average over the period covered, the first differences of the various weighted surpluses are quite similar to those of the unweighted series. This might suggest the desirability of publishing the unweighted full-employment surplus or its first differences. It should be noted, however, as Gramlich himself points out, in some periods such as the first half of 1964, there is a considerable range of variation in the first differences shown in Table 3. Moreover, there are substantial differences in the multipliers generated by the models used by Gramlich.

It should also be noted that, even assuming that the change in the full-employment surplus were a good measure of the impact of fiscal policy, it would have little significance unless interpreted in the light of other governmental policies—notably monetary policy—and developments in the private economy. The truth is that it is not possible to boil fiscal policy down to a single number and, even if it were, the significance of that number would not be apparent except in the context of a careful analysis of other developments affecting the economy. For this reason, I think it would be unwise for the Commission to make any hard and fast recommendations concerning official publication of the full-employment surplus.

The second paper I have been asked to discuss, by Harvey Galper on the timing of Federal defense purchase impacts, is a very good piece of work— as is also the earlier paper on which it is based prepared by Galper and Gramlich on forecasting defense expenditures. The estimating equation for NIA defense purchases of goods, services, and construction, using past contract awards as explanatory variables with a flexible distributed lag, yields excellent results. By making assumptions about the time profile of the production process, Galper is able to use the lags between contract awards and deliveries to deduce the rate of production of defense goods in each period. Then, by deducting deliveries from production, he is able to estimate the change in inventories.

The crucial result is his ability to estimate the current rate of production of defense goods from present and past data on contract awards. The one difficulty I can see is that there is no really satisfactory independent check on his estimates of production and the derived series on inventory investment. The main evidence to indicate that the results are probably quite accurate is the highly satisfactory performance of the underlying equation in forecasting defense expenditures, together with the fact that the estimates of production and inventories are very similar for the two alternative assumptions that are made about the time profile of the production process.

Galper's results make it possible to remove changes in defense inventories from the inventory series. One advantage of this is that in a period such as the latter half of 1966 when a rapid buildup in defense spending leads to a rise in inventories of defense goods, the availability of a reasonably accurate estimate of this inventory buildup makes possible a more satisfactory diagnosis of the economic situation. A buildup of this kind in inventories in the defense pipeline does not have the same economic implications as the appearance of an overhang of private finished-goods inventories in relation to sales. Indeed, if the defense-connected inventory changes can be estimated and removed from the inventory series, it may be possible to clean up the whole inventory area considerably. Of course, as Galper and Gramlich point out in their earlier paper, the same difficulties that exist in the national income accounts with respect to defense purchases are also present with respect to other goods produced under order. However, defense orders and expenditures are especially prone to rapid expansions and contractions, which give inventories in the defense sector a special importance. Moreover, it is possible that a technique similar to that employed in this paper may be capable of application in the estimation of goods-in-process inventories in areas other than the defense sector.

Good as Galper's results are, their relevance to the work of the Commission seems quite limited. Although his model can be used to estimate accrued defense expenditures, which would be an improvement over the deliveries basis on which such expenditures are now recorded in the national income accounts, it would hardly be practicable to use results derived from such an econometric model to generate official entries in the accounts. Perhaps the only lesson for the Commission is that if defense—and other—Government purchases could be recorded on an accrual basis, the value of budget data for fiscal analysis would be improved, and the kind of laborious econometric estimation that Galper has so ingeniously contrived could be dispensed with except for purposes of forecasting.

Paul J. Taubman

Department of Economics, University of Pennsylvania

There can be no question that a government should supply reliable information on what it is doing to meet society's goals. In the U.S. economic arena, these goals are legislated to be full employment, reasonable price stability and maximum growth and, as a further goal, or an important constraint, a satisfactory balance of payments. We have now reached the point where only a monotonic transformation is needed to turn the phrase "these goals are often contradictory" into a cliché. The triteness of the phrase, however, does not detract from the importance of its meaning. If these goals are contradictory, how do we assign a score to Government policy and how do we quantify these policies? To simplify matters, I will ignore the growth goal because I do not think we as economists have the slightest idea of such matters as the quantitative relationship of growth to Government expenditures and taxes. I am also not considering balance of payments, because I am not interested in the problem.

This leaves full employment and prices. The present Administration *tentatively* believes that the shape of the Phillips curve is such that a 4 percent unemployment rate gives the maximum welfare in terms of both employment and prices.

Given these goals, how should we keep score? For full employment Gramlich, in his useful and worthwhile paper, suggests and analyzes three measures—the high employment deficit, fiscal leverage, and the weighted high employment deficit. Gramlich argues that the weighted deficit is the most appropriate. I find all his arguments convincing, except the one on inflation. In principle I would agree with using some sort of weighted method, although in practice the uncertainty about the weights gives me cause for concern. It is encouraging in any case that the different models seem to agree fairly closely when first differences are examined. While I think that a weighted method is the best, I want to raise some serious questions about the theoretical proposition of computing the deficit at high employment, about the empirical proposition of using long-run coefficients or weights, and about using all rather than discretionary Government action in the leverage and weighted deficit calculations.

The first problem is, why should we calculate weighted or unweighted deficits at the high employment level? Other than convention, the only reason that I know is that we want to know if the current Government fiscal structure is consistent with full employment. It is very easy to construct examples where by starting from less than full employment the Government could stimulate the economy towards full employment while not changing the weighted or unweighted high employment deficit. In fact, Gramlich does give one example. Another example can be constructed merely by shifting from a progressive to a proportional tax system. This would yield the same high employment revenue, as shown in Figure 1. At less than full employment, the action is stimulative, and the Government deserves some credit for stabilization.

Gramlich constructed his example to illustrate the one flaw in his weighted method; I think the flaw exists because we haven't specified what we want to measure. My feeling is that we should concentrate not on the high employment deficit, but on the deficit based on the employment level if no Government discretionary policy were undertaken. My major reasons for this are: I want to know what the employment level will be and how much more Government action is needed. Unfortunately, there is no magic number for the right amount of high employment surplus, but the appropriate number varies over time and will depend on the strength of private aggregate demand. I want, therefore, a deficit measure related to how much of any goal the Government deficit is eliminating.

FIGURE 1.—*Revenue from progressive and proportional tax systems*

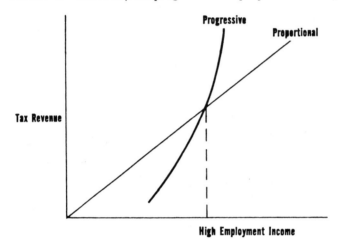

In order to get this, I cannot use long-run coefficients as Gramlich does and Musgrave did in his leverage paper. Other than in India, where in the long run we are never dead, the entire rationale for fiscal and monetary policy is that the Government should intervene if it can, through its normal activities, eliminate unemployment more quickly than the private economy. In order to know where the economy is and how well the Government is doing, fiscal leverage or weighted deficits must use impact or short-run coefficients. By the way, in the short run, it is not even clear that the Government expenditure multiplier is greater than the tax multiplier. Examples can be constructed where the opposite is true.

I also think that only discretionary policy counts because this shows what the Government is doing and how well it can forecast and evaluate the policy. Notice that this means that if the user chooses bad forecasters, it is given a bad score. I think this is fair. This suggests that in the leverage and weighted average concepts, the "no-Government case" should mean not to exclude normal expenditures and taxes. Some expenditures and taxes must be in his formula in (7B) anyway because the Federal Government is not responsible for the State and local governments, who of course do have taxes.

Next let us take a look at prices. Gramlich's paper in this instance is terribly out of date. He uses the old textbook concept that until high employment is reached, prices are constant and then at high employment, prices rise but output is constant. Any price-unemployment curve says that the first part of the statement is certainly wrong and the last part only true if high employment means the point where all resources are employed. If the only impact of Government fiscal actions on prices is via unemployment, then given the optimum unemployment rate, for example, 4 percent, the weighted deficit measure (calculated at the pre-discretionary income level) will contain all the information needed for judging Government impact on prices or prices and unemployment combined.

But Government fiscal actions can influence prices in other ways. For example, if there are sectoral imbalances—say the investment goods industries are operating at peak capacity and still not meeting demand, while other areas have excess capacity but the power to maintain prices—aggregate prices will rise. The Government could avoid some price increases by redistributing demand from investment to other areas, by using the investment tax credit, and so on. Similarly, the Government can alter prices through changes in excises or agricultural policies.

In these cases, we can set up price equations which depend directly or indirectly on Government actions, and then compute prices with and without Government policies. Once again a weighted deficit will result. This deficit will have different weights than for GNP, but the two can be combined using the same welfare function the Administration used to select its 4 percent goal.

These points cover my general comments on Gramlich's piece. I have some more specific ones. First, Gramlich argues for an inflation adjustment since prices affect Government revenues but not expenditures. While he has a good point, I think he has overstated his case. Not only are specific excises set in real terms, but many Government expenditure programs are set in real terms. Certainly many military expenditures will go on at their planned level regardless of price changes, and in other durable goods areas estimates incorporate expected inflation. In mid-1966, when the Administration was keeping its careful watch on the situation, I was supposed to show what would be the impact of a tax increase on prices. For this purpose I asked the Bureau of the Budget about the impact of price changes on spending and was told that half the purchases would be in real terms and half in money terms. So on these grounds I think the inflation adjustment should be recalculated.

Finally, I think that the author has erred in both his theoretical and empirical work. He talks consistently about marginal propensities to consume out of GNP less taxes, but uses marginal propensities to consume out of personal disposable income. I do not find any recognition of the role of corporate saving. Also, I really do not understand the statement that fiscal leverage values could not be calculated because of the inability to get "no-Government" multipliers. For any complete model, get rid of all Government policies (or in my case discretionary policies), solve the model, and resolve with more exogenous investment and we have the multiplier.

In the brief space left, I turn to Galper's piece. This paper, which is really very good, starts from the hypothesis that the direct impact of Government expenditures should be measured in terms of productive resources tied up, and not shipments of completed items. In periods when the production line is being sharply changed, the two measures are different since the goods-in-process are counted as private inventories. I might note in passing that a similar problem exists for equipment investment since here work-in-process inventories rise until production is over. In some years the problem will disappear if we look at work-in-process and raw and finished materials. Unanticipated inventory accumulation only takes place in raw and finished materials. To correct this "misclassification" the author starts with a function which gives the time profile of shipments from prime military contracts. Using the length of the production process (computed from the first equation) and some simple but reasonable assumptions on production lags, the work-in-process inventory can be found.

The accuracy of this method depends on the equation explaining shipments. First let me say that the equation developed by Galper and Gramlich is better than the one following the much earlier work that Murray Brown and I did. Compared with our approach, the prime contract data are better, the Almon lag is a better technique, and the supply constraint is included. But I am not sure how accurate their answer is, partly because there is a deficiency in the prime contract data. My understanding is that this series does not standardize for time. A contract for 100 planes this year would be half as much as a 200-plane contract with 100 delivered this year and 100 next year. This makes it very difficult to get or interpret a time profile.

Finally, the authors have overlooked one other method of getting the work-in-progress inventories. Information is available on progress payments made by the Department of Defense. These payments are about 70 percent of costs incurred on work-in-progress and are made on a fairly regular basis soon after the work is done. Dividing the change in progress payments by 0.7 yields another estimate of these work-in-progress inventories, which should be compared with the estimates given in this paper.

REPLY
Edward M. Gramlich

The most fundamental criticism of "Measures of the Aggregate Demand Impact of the Federal Budget" pertains to the value of having a summary description of fiscal impact. Warren Smith holds that it is not worthwhile to isolate the performance of fiscal policy. One should only be interested in the total impact of Government policy, as reflected in deviations of actual values of policy objectives from their targets.

It is my position that while one should be fundamentally interested in deviations of objectives and targets, it is also very useful to have guidelines for evaluating the contributions of different policies towards the achievement of different objectives. These guidelines are fruitful both for historical evaluation and for decisions about optimal doses of other policies. It is here that an examination of the aggregate demand impact of fiscal policy has its value.

At the same time, I hasten to emphasize that these measures are definitely a lower-order species than the policy utility indexes developed by Fromm and Taubman. My measures calculate the impact of fiscal policy on only the aggregate demand objective—they say nothing about the balance of payments, income distribution, growth, and price stability objectives. In principle, the Fromm-Taubman indexes are superior in this regard because these indexes can be extended to include the multi-objectives which actually bear on fiscal policy. But even though the Fromm-Taubman analysis is intellectually more satisfying, operationally it is still quite impractical. It is rather unrealistic to calculate policy utility indexes when we have very little idea about (a) the appropriate mathematical form for the policymakers' utility function; (b) the arguments of the utility function; (c) the utility weights for these arguments. These issues will no doubt be settled some day, but until they are, it does not seem wise to ignore devices which attempt to measure the budgetary contribution to aggregate demand.

Turning now to technical questions raised by the discussants, I did not mean to imply that I view the economy as being dichotomous with respect to inflation. I recognize that prices can rise at all levels of resource utilization, and I am of the opinion that an adjustment for automatic price stabilizers should be made whenever prices rise. In fact, I did make such an adjustment both in 1963 and 1964, years which certainly would not be thought of as inflationary.

A general point raised in the discussion of Tables 1 and 2 of my original paper was that weighting the high employment deficit was of rather limited empirical value. On the one hand, the weights are very uncertain; on the other hand, they do not seem to matter much. The best answer to this criticism is to redo the calculations using the shorter time horizon weights suggested by Taubman. Though I do not share Taubman's implied lack of concern with the long-run properties of models, he may well be right in that it is more meaningful to analyze fiscal policy using short-run weights.

Table A1 presents the appropriate weights using time horizons of one quarter and one year. The one-quarter weights were used to calculate the weighted deficit series for the different models in Table A2. Here both the weighted and unweighted deficit series have been computed using the accrued expenditure concept of the Galper paper (the change in real goods-in-process inventories for defense producers was added to actual NIA purchases).

The one-quarter weights accentuate the difference between purchases and taxes, and computations using them suggest that the unweighted deficit is even more biased as an indication of the level of fiscal impact than it was with steady-state weights. At the same time, it is noteworthy that the various models are much more in agreement about the level of fiscal impact than they were with steady-state weights.

Table A3 gives the first differences for Table A2. Again the models are quite close in their appraisal of changes in fiscal impact, and again their consensus differs from the unweighted deficit more than in the original paper. The expansionary fiscal stimulus in the first half of 1964 is now rated at $9.9 billion by the unweighted deficit, and from $4.0 billion (Brookings) to $2.4 billion (Ando-Goldfeld) by the models.

Table A4 demonstrates a computation suggested by Joseph Pechman. It compares first differences in the unweighted deficit with the average of the models' estimate of first differences in the weighted deficit. Results are presented both for one-quarter and steady-state weights. In most periods the one-quarter average change differs appreciably more from the unweighted deficit change than does the steady-state average change. This again indicates that using a one-quarter time horizon noticeably increases the importance of weighting.

Thus the time horizon does make a difference in comparing weighted with unweighted deficits. Not only does using a short time horizon increase the importance of weighting; it also seems to reduce the variance of estimates of the weights. This means that we can simultaneously be more confident that our weighting scheme is important, and more confident that we are doing it correctly.

TABLE A1.—*Alternative high employment deficit weights, selected models, one-quarter and one-year values*

Model	One quarter		One year	
	Personal taxes and transfers	Corpo-ration taxes	Personal taxes and transfers	Corpo-ration taxes
Brookings model..........	0.512	0.049	0.534	0.127
Suits model.............	(1)	(1)	.668	.758
Department of Commerce model................	.485	.020	.518	.074
Ando-Goldfeld model......	.311	.053	.636	.276
Okun model.............	.371	.019	.819	.791
MIT–FRB model........	.400	.024	.657	.135

[1] Because the Suits model has been estimated with annual data, one-quarter weights cannot be calculated.   Source: See text.

TABLE A2.—*Levels of fiscal impact: Weighted and unweighted high employment deficits using one-quarter weights, selected models, 1963–67* [1]

[Billions of 1958 dollars, adjusted for inflation and accrued expenditures]

Year and quarter	High employment deficit (unweighted) [2]	Brookings model	Commerce model	Ando-Goldfeld model	Okun model	MIT-FRB model
1963: I	−8.6	42.4	44.7	53.1	50.8	49.1
II	−12.9	39.2	41.5	50.3	47.8	46.1
III	−12.1	39.7	42.0	51.1	48.6	46.8
IV	−13.9	39.2	41.4	50.4	47.9	46.2
1964: I	−11.4	40.1	42.2	50.5	48.3	46.5
II	−4.0	43.2	45.3	52.8	50.8	49.3
III	−5.3	43.2	45.3	52.7	50.7	49.2
IV	−8.6	40.6	42.7	50.3	48.3	46.8
1965: I	−10.0	39.5	41.6	49.3	47.2	45.7
II	−8.5	41.5	43.7	51.5	49.4	47.8
III	−1.2	46.3	48.3	55.1	53.4	52.0
IV	−1.8	47.2	49.2	56.5	54.6	53.0
1966: I	−1.3	49.2	51.2	59.0	57.0	55.3
II	−3.3	50.3	52.5	60.9	58.7	56.9
III	.6	54.0	56.2	64.8	62.5	60.7
IV	3.9	56.0	58.1	66.6	64.3	62.7
1967: I	6.2	58.2	60.5	69.0	66.7	65.0

[1] One-quarter totals cannot be calculated for Suits model, shown in Table 2 of original paper.

[2] This series differs from the one presented in the original paper because of adjustment for accrued expenditures.

Source: Table A1.

TABLE A3.—*Movements in fiscal impact: First differences of weighted and unweighted deficits using one-quarter weights, selected models, 1963–67*

[Billions of 1958 dollars, adjusted for inflation and accrued expenditures]

Year and quarter	High employ-ment deficit (unweighted)	Brookings model	Commerce model	Ando-Goldfeld model	Okun model	MIT-FRB model
1963: II	-4.3	-3.2	-3.2	-2.8	-3.0	-3.0
III	.8	.5	.5	.8	.8	.7
IV	-1.8	-.5	-.6	-.7	-.7	-.6
1964: I	2.5	.9	.8	.1	.4	.3
II	7.4	3.1	3.1	2.3	2.5	2.8
III	-1.3	....	....	-.1	-.1	-.1
IV	-3.3	-2.6	-2.6	-2.4	-2.4	-2.4
1965: I	-1.4	-1.1	-1.1	-1.0	-1.1	-1.1
II	1.5	2.0	2.1	2.2	2.2	2.1
III	7.3	4.8	4.6	3.6	4.0	4.2
IV	-.6	.9	.9	1.4	1.2	1.0
1966: I	.5	2.0	2.0	2.5	2.4	2.3
II	-2.0	1.1	1.3	1.9	1.7	1.6
III	3.9	3.7	3.7	3.9	3.8	3.8
IV	3.3	2.0	1.9	1.8	1.8	2.0
1967: I	2.3	2.2	2.4	2.4	2.4	2.3

Source: Table A2.

TABLE A4.—*Divergence between weighted and unweighted change in fiscal impact using one-quarter and steady-state weights, 1963–67*

[Billions of 1958 dollars, adjusted for inflation and accrued expenditures]

Year and quarter	Change in unweighted high employment deficit [1]	Average change in weighted deficit, one-quarter weights	Average change in weighted deficit, steady-state weights [1] [2]
1963: II	−4. 3	−3. 0	−3. 8
III	. 8	. 7	−. 4
IV	−1. 8	−. 6	−. 1
1964: I	2. 5	. 5	1. 9
II	7. 4	2. 8	5. 0
III	−1. 3	−. 1	. . . .
IV	−3. 3	−2. 5	−3. 0
1965: I	−1. 4	−1. 1	−1. 2
II	1. 5	2. 1	1. 6
III	7. 3	4. 2	6. 4
IV	−. 6	1. 1	. . . .
1966: I	. 5	2. 2	1. 0
II	−2. 0	1. 5	−1. 0
III	3. 9	3. 8	4. 1
IV	3. 3	1. 9	2. 6
1967: I	2. 3	2. 3	2. 4

[1] Different than the average of values calculated from original paper because of the adjustment for accrued expenditures.

[2] Excludes Suits model in order to give an average comparable to that for one-quarter weighted deficit.

Source: Table A3.

PART III

Comments by Participants and Observers

Comments by Participants and Observers

GLENN E. BURRESS AND CHARLS E. WALKER [1]

American Bankers Association

The role of the Federal budget

Let us first state our complete agreement with the notion that there is no single set of budget totals equally satisfactory for all the various purposes the budget serves. Four sets of figures seem to be needed to answer the following questions: (1) What is the over-all size of Federal fiscal activities, in either absolute or relative terms? (2) What is the economic impact of Federal fiscal activities on income and production in the private sector? (3) What is the economic impact of Federal fiscal activities on liquidity in the private sector? (4) What is the best guidance to give the Executive and Congress on Federal programs which require their annual approval and appropriations?

Although there is no doubt widespread interest in budget totals that answer all of these questions, it would seem that the public is most interested in the first question, economic analysts and Congress in the second and third questions, and that Congress is most interested in the fourth question. Indeed, of all the messages sent to Congress by the President, public interest in the Budget Message is probably second only to that in the State of the Union Message. We recommend that the set of figures that reveals the size of Federal activities—that is, which answers the first question—should be given primary attention in the annual January presentation; only intermediate attention should be given to the budgets that answer the second and third questions; and there should be a deliberate attempt to play down public interest in the administrative budget, which answers the fourth question. It is unfortunate that so much attention, especially in the press and therefore among the public, is directed towards the administrative budget.

To answer the first question, we recommend that the Commission use gross Federal spending and its logical counterpart, gross Federal receipts, *as defined below*, to determine the over-all size of Federal financial activities. Neither of the three popular budgets—the administrative, the consolidated cash, or the national income and products accounts (NIA)—offers a spending total that measures the size of Government. There are three

---

[1] See addendum at end of paper. The views expressed here are those of the authors and do not purport to represent those of the Association.

primary reasons: (1) the accounting treatment of the sale of participation certificates (PC's); (2) the extensive netting of spending against receipts so that only the difference is entered into these budgets; and (3) the accounting treatment of spending and receipts of Government-owned and Government-sponsored enterprises. Each of these is commented on below in order to arrive at an appropriate measure of gross Federal spending.

For any economic unit—be it the consumer, the firm, the Government, or one of its agencies—the sale of an asset is a balance sheet transaction, namely the exchange of that asset for another asset, cash. As Budget Director Charles L. Schultze stated (during a February 1967 closed meeting, but nevertheless "on the record"), "There is no significant difference between the flotation of General Treasury obligations and PC's—except for the small difference in interest rates." And in reply to a question from one of the authors, he emphatically declared, "The method selected for financing government spending is completely independent of decisions regarding the level of government's spending." Against this background, it is difficult to conceive of an acceptable rationale for subtracting the amount of PC's sold from total budget spending.

On the other hand, however unreasonable, the procedure *may* be explained in the history of the Federal lending programs. Furthermore, a brief review of that history may provide some guidelines for the Commission in its recommendations to the President. The first truly major Federal lending program was the Commodity Credit Corporation (CCC). Under this program there was little reason to expect the farmer to repay the loan. From this it would seem most reasonable to treat the acquisition of loans as Federal spending. The logical counterpart to treating acquisition of loans as spending is, of course, to treat the sale of loans as reduced spending. But this makes sense only under the assumption that the loan will not be repaid. It is suggested that, as a guiding principle, when such an assumption is reasonable, "lending" should be considered Government spending; otherwise, lending should be treated as the acquisition of an asset.

The logic of this approach is so compelling that loans made by the Commodity Credit Corporation are already included in the NIA budget as spending, despite the common assumption that one of the most important distinctions between the cash budget and the NIA budget is that the latter excludes loans. Apparently this same logic leads to the exclusion of CCC loans from the portfolios from which the PC's are sold.

This, in turn, suggests another principle. If a loan qualifies for inclusion in the portfolio from which PC's are sold, it should be considered a Government asset, and the sale of the PC should be viewed merely as a conversion of that asset to cash. The amount of such conversion, however, should not be deducted from the spending total otherwise reported in the cash budget. Such transactions are independent of Federal spending; their accounting treatment will be considered below in the analysis of the fiscal impact of Federal fiscal activities on liquidity.

Given this first approximation of gross Federal spending, the total would then be adjusted for the process of netting that is built into the three traditional budgets. To illustrate: under present legislation, it is estimated that in fiscal year 1968 expenditures of the Post Office Department will run $6.7 billion, and receipts $5.2 billion. This will leave a net deficit of $1.4 billion. In the three conventional budgets, only the $1.4 billion deficit is recorded, and, of course, as an expenditure. But this clearly understates postal expenditures by $5.3 billion. It is estimated that such netting throughout the Government will total $21.4 billion in fiscal 1968. This, then, must be added to the first approximation of cash budget spending.

Finally, one must add expenditures of Government-sponsored and Government-owned enterprises—such as the Federal Deposit Insurance Corporation, the Milk Marketing Administration, and Comptroller of the Currency—which have not, for various reasons, been included in the cash budget. For fiscal 1968 this is estimated at $9.9 billion. Hence, for fiscal 1968 gross Federal spending would be estimated at $210.2 billion.

Before turning to the question of economic impact, a few brief notes on timing seem to be appropriate. The difference between accrual and cash collection is becoming insignificant due to the acceleration of corporate tax collections and the monthly, rather than quarterly, deposit of wages withheld from employees. However, "loans" made by the CCC are considered spending at the date of "default" rather than when the "loan" is made. This is no small matter, since it is estimated to be $1.4 billion for fiscal 1968. We recommend to the Commission that such loans be considered spending when the loan is made. This is obviously significant if the budget totals are to be used to estimate the short-run impact on the economy.

The second question, namely, the economic impact of Federal programs, calls for careful definitions. We use the term "economic impact," rather than "fiscal impact," because the latter is typically interpreted as referring solely to the impact on production and income. We urge the Commission to interpret fiscal impact broadly, including both the income and liquidity effects of a proposed budget. Estimation of the full economic impact of a proposed Federal budget would therefore require two separate accounting statements. Before turning to the difference between these statements, we will first comment on a problem common to both.

Under the widely accepted assumption that the Federal budget should be used as a tool to foster high employment, price stability, and growth, it is clear that economic impact may not be determined by netting the difference between proposed gross spending and receipts. Given expected *levels* of private demand and concomitant monetary policy, an alternative to mere netting is required if the economic impact of a proposed budget is to be estimated. Two possible procedures are available. One procedure has been developed by the Federal Reserve Bank of New York. One of its merits is that it simply provides an estimate of the initial fiscal impact, in half-year periods, compared to the preceding half year, and requires no estimate of a hypothetical full-employment GNP. This, however, is also one of its weaknesses: It fails to yield an estimate of the adequacy of a proposed fiscal policy in attaining full employment; nor does it provide an estimate of the effect on the economy of growth of Federal revenues that result from growth of the economy. In short, it is a "clean" but narrow estimate of the *initial* effect of changes in either spending or tax rates on aggregate spending. It should be added that the appropriate time period for the *initial* effect is also open to question.

An alternative is to estimate how a proposed budget would affect the economy if it were at full employment, that is, the full-employment budget (FEB). This budget has been so widely discussed in recent years it hardly needs definition here. However, as a final comment on the common denominator underlying both income and liquidity effects, it should be emphasized that these effects cannot be estimated in the absence of assumptions, hopefully made explicit in the budget presentation, about expected private demand, monetary policy, and conditions in the financial markets.

To estimate the economic impact of a proposed budget on income and production, it may appear that the obvious candidate for budgetary figures is the NIA budget, using either the New York Federal approach or the FEB, or both. Given assumptions about the private sector and monetary policy, and so on, the Executive can clearly make estimates into the future regarding the effect of a proposed NIA budget on income and production. Indeed, this was illustrated in the President's January 1967 budget message. Given the present state of NIA accounting, however, the economic analyst will encounter serious difficulties in his attempt to determine *current* fiscal impact on income and production. The NIA figures are available only on a quarterly basis, and then with considerable lag. For example, in early March 1967, some NIA information was available through December 1966, but total spending and receipts of the Federal Government were available only through September 1966.

Needless to say, this is an extremely serious time lag. In view of the fact that the 1968 budget message was based on the national income accounts, the NIA budget seems to be a front-runner as the basic budget document to be presented to the public. If the Commission should recommend the NIA budget as the basic document, it should urge the executive branch to expend whatever effort is necessary to improve the NIA budget's usefulness for analyzing current fiscal impact. Figures should be available on a monthly basis, like the cash and administrative budgets.

It is for these and other reasons that we stated in our *Comments on the President's 1967 Economic Report*, "In view of the President's decision to seek . . . advice, we deem it unfortunate that the Administration has, starting this year, adopted the national income accounts budget as the basic instrument for presentation of the Federal program." [2]

To estimate the effect of a proposed budget on liquidity in the private sector, we suggest a separate statement consolidating all expected loans and repayments. There are now about a hundred programs of direct, insured, and guaranteed loans, the exact number being a matter of definition. At the end of fiscal 1967, it is estimated that direct loans outstanding will amount to $33.8 billion, guaranteed and insured loans $105.5 billion, and outstanding loans of Government-owned and sponsored enterprises $23.8 billion.

As indicated above, a consolidated statement of expected loans should not include those where there is no expectation of repayment, for example, the loans by CCC. Those so-called loans, and only those, should be considered Government spending. What we are suggesting is a statement of *all* expected loans and repayments by the Government and its agencies which are implied in a full-employment budget. Additional details would be desirable. For example, it would be extremely important to know whether the Government and its agencies are intending to borrow, and in what amounts, from the public, the commercial banks, the Federal Reserve, or the Treasury.

It is obvious that the budget we propose includes spending and receipts of many programs, the management of which has been delegated by Congress to others. Examples are trust funds and programs that are either Government-sponsored or owned. Hence, to assist both Executive and congressional decision making, it is clear that still another budget is required. We see no reason why the administrative budget, which deals exclusively with fiscal operations for which Congress alone has operating responsibility, is not satisfactory. Because it is a tool for congressional decision making and of little interest to those concerned with the over-all size and impact of Federal fiscal operations, every attempt should be made to reduce its relative importance in public discussion and educate the public about its limitations.

Specific issues

Federal accounting procedures. Where the Government has an up-to-date census on a given flow, such as personal income tax collections, the only rationale for a statistical estimate based on a carefully designed sample would be a cross-check. On the other hand, where a census of a flow would be too time-consuming—as, for example, in many flows of national income accounts—statistical estimates are mandatory, especially if data are to be up to date. It should be pointed out that accountants have long used statistical estimates, based on samples, where a census would be too time-consuming. This is more usual, however, for stocks rather than flows.

---

[2] American Bankers Association (1967), p. 12.

Checks issued vs. checks cleared in Federal accounting. There has been some debate over whether gross Federal activity should be measured on checks-issued or checks-cleared basis. It is our view that the issue is generally insignificant, especially in the short run.

Treasury deposits vs. checks cleared. In the past, the difference between accrued taxes and Treasury deposits has received wide attention from specialists. Due to the present acceleration of corporate tax payments, increased withholding from wages, and the acceleration of deposit of wages withheld, however, the importance of this issue is rapidly fading.

Transactions between Federal funds. These transactions would cancel out in the global budget we proposed above.

Treatment of trust funds, revolving funds, and other activities not included in the general funds of receipts and expenditures. The answer to this issue should be determined by whether Congress wants a long-run program with occasional (or even annual) review. For example, it would be undesirable to have the Social Security program subject to the political process required for annual appropriation and taxation. Inasmuch as the Social Security program is designed to replace only a fraction of income upon retirement, the public confidence provided by a stable, long-range program is highly desirable in order to encourage supplemental private plans. For different reasons, such as the time required to build a new Federal highway program, a trust fund—avoiding annual appropriations and concomitant logrolling—has considerable merit.

On the other hand, it appears that even long-established programs (such as the farm program) or relatively new programs (such as the National Aeronautics and Space Administration) are logical candidates for annual or biannual review and revision through the established political process.

In summary, the criterion governing establishment of trust funds, revolving funds, and other accounting entities, is whether it is desirable to have financing of Federal activities dependent on the fluctuations and instability that are built into the process of annual appropriations.

The capital budget. We are against the development of a separate budget for capital items, such as is used abroad and here in the United States by many states and their subdivisions. Our reasons fall broadly into three categories:

> 1. Capital budgeting usually implies that expenditures on capital items are financed by borrowing with repayment over at least some part of the expected lifetime of the asset. Both borrowing and repayments under such a program may be inconsistent with the appropriate short-run employment when, for short-run stabilization policy, the capital item should be financed through taxation. On the other hand, repayment on the loan might take place when resources are underutilized, with the result that repayments depress the economy even more.

2. There would be an inevitable debate over just what should be considered a capital item and the appropriate rate of depreciation. Problems of this nature abound. For example, a given outlay may be an investment for society, but an expenditure for a firm. If a firm undertakes the training or retraining of a worker, for example, it would properly view this as an expense; an expenditure of the same type, however, is an investment for society.

On the other hand, it would indeed be unfortunate if a supplemental accounting or breakdown of the budgets between current expenses vs. capital and development items were not provided. The Bureau of the Budget is to be applauded for providing such a breakdown in Special Analysis D in the 1968 Budget. This section might be improved, however, by excluding military hardware as assets and including the assets of Government-owned and sponsored enterprises.

3. Finally, some observers argue that adoption of a capital budget would facilitate Government ownership and construction of more capital assets, presumably because the cost would be amortized rather than covered out of current receipts. We do not personally believe this argument is very strong, but think the Commission should consider it.

The need for a Federal balance sheet. In recent years considerable progress has been made towards developing a balance sheet for the private sector. It is difficult to conceive of a good reason why the same program should not be developed for the public sector—the Federal as well as state and local governments. Needless to say, many of the same problems outlined in the section on capital budgeting would arise here. Certainly accrued taxes should be included as a Federal asset. On the other hand, we can find no convincing reason for including *total* contingent liabilities of Government loan and insurance programs as liabilities in a Federal balance sheet. Sufficient data are available to estimate accurately the probable loss under such programs.

There seems to us to be an implicit error in any statement that treats unfunded retirement and similar social insurance programs, especially Social Security, as liabilities. In reality, these are not insurance programs, but programs of transfer of income from producers to nonproducers. If fully funded, such programs would require roughly $400 billion. The adverse effects of full funding on the economy hardly need to be spelled out. We might add that following those principles, we see no reason why expenditures and receipt totals should not be tied into the balance sheet.

Defining the public debt. This is an exceedingly difficult question to resolve. From a purely intellectual standpoint, and perhaps implicit in answers above, Treasury debt held by trust funds should not be viewed as part of the public debt—that is, they do not reflect the results of past Federal deficits—and agency obligations should be so considered. In view of the fact that adequate breakdowns are not available, however, we would not recommend any such radical change in definition at this time.

We strongly believe that participation certificates should be viewed as part of the public debt, especially in view of the Attorney General's ruling last year relating to such certificates.

The need for more frequent reviews of the Federal budget. We consider the midyear budget review to be very important. Moreover, there is much to be said for budget presentation providing semiannual or half-year estimates of both spending and receipts on the four bases discussed at the beginning of this paper. We would hope that once semiannual estimates are developed, they would be quickly followed by quarterly estimates and reviews.

Three- to five-year estimates of spending implicit in existing legislative programs would be most useful, especially when compared to full-employment receipts. In the early 1960's, David Lusher of the Council of Economic Advisers developed such an estimate for 1970, dramatically showing the need for a massive tax cut—such as that provided in the Revenue Act of 1964. Three- to five-year estimates of Federal spending and full-employment receipts would provide the necessary framework for the analysis of fiscal policy that is required for full employment without inflation.

Concluding Comment. We should like to emphasize the important fact of *ex ante* analysis of economic impact on both income and liquidity. Finally, we should like to emphasize that in this era when tax increases and payments are unmatched in their timing—such as Social Security changes in recent years—semiannual or quarterly estimates of the future, as well as monthly reports on current Federal finance, are becoming extremely important.

ADDENDUM

This paper was submitted to the President's Commission on Budget Concepts in advance of the Brookings Conference. The discussion at the Conference—especially the strong preference for a "unitary" budget concept—requires some additional comments.

We believe strongly that Federal lending operations must be included in any unitary budget. Otherwise, the over-all size of Federal financial operations will be greatly understated and, more importantly, the economic impact of Federal lending operations—which can be of considerable influence—may be underemphasized.

The experience of the first half of calendar year 1967 demonstrates that trends in the surplus or deficit of any budget can be strongly misleading and should not be accepted without further analysis. For example, the sharp decline in the estimated deficit in the consolidated cash budget—as opposed to an opposite movement in the estimated NIA deficit—was inevitably confusing for those attempting to analyze the economic impact of the

Federal Government. The decline in the cash deficit was clearly a contractionary influence, and was *not* reflected in the NIA budget. Here we refer to the large payoff of loans by savings and loan associations to the Federal Home Loan Bank. To the extent that such liquidation occurred, mortgage loans of savings and loan associations (as well as the volume of home building) were less than they would otherwise have been.

The question we raise is whether the 1967 experience has general applicability or was simply a special case. If the former is true, *ex ante* analysis of shifts in the surplus or deficit in the consolidated cash budget—rather than the alternatives—makes it clearly the superior indicator of the economic impact of Federal financial operations.

We strongly suggest that the Budget Commission and its staff examine this matter further.

SAMUEL B. CHASE, JR.

The Brookings Institution

Analysis of the economic impact of Federal policies requires, among other things, an accurate statement of the financial operations of the Government. The economic impact of the Federal Government derives, to be sure, from numerous other causes in addition to financial activities, but a properly constructed comprehensive budget statement is uniquely capable of providing information necessary for assessing the economic impact of Federal finances. Within the constraint that it does this job, the budget should be designed to convey information pertinent to the analysis of other classes of economic impacts of Federal activities. Much of this other information can best be displayed in special analyses. But these other objectives should not be allowed to interfere with a coherent presentation of the financial accounts.

The format of the budget should be immune to the vagaries of changing patterns of economic relationships, and to the vagaries of economic analysis as well. Economists are not unanimous in their appraisal of the impact of the budget and its components, and the weight of opinion on matters of detail is constantly shifting. This is not necessarily an indictment of economics or of economists. It is, however, reason to resist efforts such as Professor Break's to categorize budgetary items according to their "impact coefficients," and to list these items in the official budget document in descending order of the coefficients attached to them. Not only does the present state of knowledge preclude responsible assignment of such rankings; there is good reason to believe that the coefficients, even if known with tolerable accuracy, change, perhaps drastically, over time. Constant review and reclassification would be required, and the obvious need for a more timeless format would remain.

Considerably different from Professor Break's proposal is the present consolidated cash budget, which some consider the ideal budget format. In principle, the cash budget is not comparable to an income statement as accountants normally conceive such a statement for two reasons. First, measurement is, for the most part, based on cash flow. Both accounting theory and economic theory employ accrual concepts of income. If the budget, or part of it, is to serve as an income statement, or something analogous to it, Government expenditures and revenues having their counterparts in private income and taxes ought to be reported on an accrual basis. Lack of adequate data presently precludes, or partially precludes, preparation of such a statement. This in no way affects the need for such figures, and the Commission on Budget Concepts should not pass up the opportunity to urge that accrual data be used when available and that further development of accrual accounting be undertaken.

The second reason that the cash budget is not analogous to an income statement is that it separates neither loan programs from other expenditures, nor loan repayments by borrowers from current receipts such as taxes. The impacts of these two kinds of expenditures and receipts differ in principle.

On the one hand, expenditures on goods and services, subsidies, and transfer payments *are* private income, and tax receipts *are* reductions of private income. This is not a matter of cause and effect but a fact. Loans, and loan repayments, are different. The accounting counterpart of a Government loan is private (or foreign) debt. The private "receipt" that corresponds to the Government's "expenditure" in this case is matched by a liability for repayment. If the loan has no subsidy element, there is no concurrent net financial gain of income or net wealth to be shown in the private (or foreign) sector account as a counterpart of the "expenditure." Although the loan may have consequences for subsequent private expenditure just as important as those of a transfer payment, it is, analytically, a very different kind of transaction and ought to be kept separate in the Government accounts.

This is abundantly clear if "deficit" and "surplus" are to be measures of the net increase or decrease in the Government debt. Private and foreign net claims on the Government are equal to Federal debt instruments held by these sectors less their debt to the Federal sector. The deficit or surplus in the present cash budget is calculated on the basis of an expenditure figure that includes net lending by the Government. Since Government loans have grown rapidly in the last two decades, it is not surprising to find that the cumulated cash deficit approximates the increase in gross Federal debt outstanding during this period, while the increase in *net* debt of the Federal Government is vastly overstated. Between 1946 and 1964, the last year for which I have been able to make the calculation, the net debt of the Federal Government has declined. I am sure that at least ninety-nine out of a hundred people believe the opposite. If so, past budget accounting has surely been misleading, and the cash budget deserves much of the blame.

A proper budget statement, in my view, would require consolidated flow statements of:

(1) Federal expenditures that enter directly into the calculations of private income, on an accrual basis, subdivided into purchases of goods and services, subsidies and other transfer payments (including interest);

(2) Federal receipts that are deducted in calculating disposable private income, on an accrual basis, subdivided into proceeds of sales of goods and services and transfer receipts (including interest payments);

and consolidated stock (asset and liability) statements of:

(3) Federal holdings of claims on the private and foreign sectors, including accrued unpaid tax liabilities, Federal holdings of private debt instruments, and so on;

(4) Federal liabilities to the private and foreign sectors, including unpaid obligations of all sorts.

The first two items are the "income" account, and the second two are the asset-liability account.[3]

Ideally, all Federal agencies, including the Federal Reserve System, would be included in the consolidated accounts.

Conceptually, the current account is the so-called national income accounts budget, amended to put all transactions on an accrual basis and to include the subsidy element of loan programs. The asset-liability account is a consolidated statement of Federal claims and debts of all forms, with subsidy elements written off.

The net of (1) and (2), which measures the current account deficit or surplus, will show up as a change in the net of (3) and (4), which measures the net debt of Government. This figure measures the historically cumulated) net deficit of Government. The change over a year or other accounting period equals the current account deficit or surplus for that period.

The major items in the asset and liability account of the Federal Government would be:

Assets	Liabilities
Accrued tax liabilities	Guaranteed interest-bearing debt held outside Government, including accrued interest
Prepayments	
Treasury bank deposits	
Private and foreign debt (including Federal Reserve loans outstanding and Federal Reserve discounts and advances)	Participation certificates
	Accrued liabilities on purchases of goods and services
Foreign currency	Currency
Gold and silver	Bank reserves

---

[3] This is *not* a capital budget. It does not capitalize Government expenditures for assets other than those that are legal claims for future payments.

There would be others, of course, but these are sufficient to give the general idea. If the Federal Reserve were not included, Treasury deposits at, or debt to, the Federal Reserve Banks would have to be added, while Federal Reserve discounts and advances, and Federal Reserve currency and bank reserve liabilities, would be eliminated.

In subsidiary analyses, any items could be disaggregated as far as seemed desirable, and year-by-year changes in the individual asset-liabilities accounts presented in detail. Subsidiary or underlying tables might be "grossed up," to reflect inter-agency transactions, but the goal should be to keep the end product completely consolidated. In the detailed analyses, separate consolidated statements (both in current and asset-liability accounts) of Federal transactions with the domestic private and foreign sectors could be shown.

This approach has the advantage of making more sense, in terms of accounting and economic principles, than the cash budget. Some observers contend that the cash budget has the advantage of reporting, as the deficit or surplus, the gross borrowing requirements of the Federal Government. There is nothing in the scheme outlined above to preclude deriving and presenting this figure in the budget document. It is simply the sum of the deficit or surplus plus the net increase in Federal loans. But neither economic analysis nor informed public discussion will be served by using this figure as if it represents the amount the Government goes into the red, or the black, in a given year.

GARY FROMM

The Brookings Institution

Given the complexity of today's social and economic objectives, it is dubious whether any single budget statement can satisfy the Government's policy-making needs. The national income accounts (NIA) budget, the favorite of the unit budgeters, cannot simultaneously mirror stabilization and growth goals, equity and income distribution considerations, program evaluation criteria, cash and accrual accounting, and managerial and administrative requirements. To aver that this is the budget that should be publicized and that its deficit, especially on a nonaccrual basis, is of paramount importance, would do more to mislead the public than today's practice of giving prominence to three concepts—the national income accounts, administrative, and cash budgets. Certainly current budgeting practices can be improved. But a unitary budget is not the answer.[4]

---

[4] It is well known that in a system with n simultaneous equations (for example, consumption, investment, and production functions), with m targets (unemployment rates, balance of payments positions, growth rates, income distribution, and so forth), at least m instruments are required to achieve desired goals. Of course, this does not mean that we need m budgets. But, neither is it likely that a single budget would suffice.

George Break's proposal for a multibudget *concept* is far preferable. Nevertheless, his specific proposal suffers in some details. For example, the separation of loan from guarantee programs might be questioned. But what is most debatable is the segregation of items on the basis of estimated economic impact coefficients. Break does not indicate the exact nature of these parameters, but, presumably, they are much the same as Gramlich's weighted multipliers.

Both Break's and Gramlich's sets of coefficients present a distorted view of the structure of the economy. They assume, implicitly, that the world is:

1. *Static.* No cognizance is taken that the parameters may change over time due to technological, institutional, demographic, legislative, or economic factors. More importantly, there is no recognition that changes in different budget or monetary items involve different time response paths of the economy. For example, an increase in Government employment results in a far more rapid change in national product than an increase in Government durables purchases; but, the ultimate impact of the durables outlays is significantly greater than that of employment. Therefore, if nondynamic impact coefficients are to be used, at a minimum they should be stated on a discounted, rather than on a final equilibrium or static basis. Elsewhere, such impact coefficients have been termed discounted multipliers.[5]

2. *Linear.* A related point is that multipliers may change with cyclical conditions in the economy as a whole, in individual industries, or in international financial or trade markets. For example, the impact of Government orders for military hardware is likely to be far different per dollar of expenditure at high levels of capacity utilization in the steel and machine tool industries than at low levels.[6] Moreover, it cannot be assumed that the amount of the order will not affect the size of the multiplier.

3. *Additive.* Along the same lines, aside from the linear effects for any individual budget item, it cannot be assumed that impacts of contemplated policy actions can simply be added. This is invalid when they directly or indirectly compete for the same factors of production or where there is lumpiness or economies of scale in augmenting capacity. For example, a new steel rolling mill built to satisfy military needs for

---

[5] Gary Fromm and Paul Taubman, *Policy Simulations with an Econometric Model* (Brookings Institution, 1968).

[6] In this area Gramlich's treatment is misleading. He assumes that constant dollar multipliers are fixed until full employment output is reached, and then suddenly drop to zero. In fact, the variation in multipliers is likely to be continuous. Additionally, at any arbitrarily selected full employment level, whether 6, or 4, or 0 percent, more real output can always be produced via the route of increasing average weekly hours of labor and capital utilization, attracting more entrants into the labor force (including by immigration), and capital-labor substitutions.

armor plate can also fabricate structural shapes for Government construction programs.

4. *Independent.* Another, related way of stating this is that consideration must be given to complementary policies or possible substitutions of policies. For example, the effectiveness of an income tax cut, like that of 1964, depends on the concurrent pursuit of an accommodating monetary policy that prevents interest rates from rising and restraining the tax cut stimulus to demand.

For all these reasons, Gramlich's concept of a multiplier-weighted full employment deficit has limited value. A preferable approach, which satisfies the same ends, is to assess the impact of Government policy actions within the framework of a complete systems analysis.

To state this in another way, a slightly more sophisticated "back-of-the-envelope" calculation of fiscal impact is better than a less sophisticated computation or a "seat-of-the-pants" guess. But, it is no substitute for a comprehensive analysis.

The same observation can be made on the Galper paper. While it is an interesting extension of earlier work by Murray Brown and Paul Taubman, the prediction of payout streams for defense contract awards seems far too aggregative to be very useful. For the past few years, the Department of Defense has been compiling records on contract performance in terms of employment, inventories, and expenditures. Information is calculated monthly, by type of item, by class of item, by contract. Subcontracting information has also been gathered. It is possible to use these records to make predictions of time-phased employment and expenditure impacts. Moreover, since this can be done by item, and specific contract terms such as target delivery dates and production schedules can be taken into account, the results should be more accurate than an arbitrary set of polynomial distributed lags at the aggregative level.

It is true that the data are still not of a quality that would permit incorporating accrual estimates of defense outlays in the national income and product accounts. Since these data are used by the Council of Economic Advisers, the Budget Bureau, and the Treasury Department for forecasting purposes, however, they must have some value.

MICHAEL E. LEVY [7]

National Industrial Conference Board

My suggestions for increasing the usefulness of the Federal budget document for economic analysis are presented below.

---

[7] Opinions expressed are my own and do not purport to represent the views of the National Industrial Conference Board.

FISCAL EFFECT AND LIQUIDITY EFFECT

The Federal budget exerts both fiscal and liquidity effects on the national economy. The fiscal effect arises from Government activities that impinge directly on the nation's income and output. The liquidity effect results from Government operations that affect the composition or size of assets and liabilities within the private sector, thereby modifying its overall liquidity.

The fiscal effect of the budget operates through two channels: (1) Purchases of goods and services by the Federal Government represent a direct claim on gross national product; (2) taxes and transfer payments affect the private sector's buying power directly (both personal disposable income and corporate profits after tax liabilities) and, through it, private spending for consumption and investment at one level removed.

The budget's liquidity effect is a result of purely financial transactions which do not enter directly into the national income accounts but rather affect income and output indirectly. These financial transactions by the Government or its agencies consist mainly of borrowing and lending, purchases and sales of such financial assets as mortgages and the recently issued participation certificates (PC's), and accelerated tax collections. They affect either (1) the total size of both assets and liabilities within the private sector, or (2) the composition of privately held assets and/or liabilities.

The fiscal effect of the budget directly modifies total GNP and its major components, whereas the liquidity effect directly affects demand and supply conditions in the money and capital markets and the level and/or structure of interest rates. Hence, two separate budget accounts should be specifically designed to measure, on the one hand, the fiscal effect of the budget, and on the other, its liquidity effect.

Among the currently available budget data, the national income accounts budget is the best measure of the *fiscal effect*. By itself, however, this budget is not entirely satisfactory for fiscal analysis, because it records Government purchases of goods and services on a "delivery" basis. Most capital goods, especially in defense, have a long lead-time in production. By the time these items are delivered, the direct fiscal impact on output and income (and most of its multiplier and accelerator effect) is past history. In order to improve the analysis of the fiscal impact of Government purchases of major "hardware," two steps are necessary. First, at least one of the following two sets of data is required on a regular basis: (1) information on that part of business inventories which represents the flow of Government purchases through the production pipelines, or (2) detailed and matching data on Government ordering and contract awards, obligations incurred, and delivery of the finished products (that is, national income accounts expenditures) by major product category.[8] Second, from these data, estimates of the average production time for each major category of Government hardware have to be undertaken.

Among the currently available budget data, the consolidated cash budget comes closest to measuring the *liquidity effect* of the budget. It could be modified and expanded into a "financial budget" that would provide a more satisfactory measure of the liquidity effect. In contrast to the present cash budget, such a financial budget would cover all Government borrowing and lending, or buying and selling of financial assets, on a gross rather than a net basis. Thus, sales to the public of such "financial assets" as participation certificates would be treated as a Government *source* of funds similar to the sale of Government debt instruments, rather than being treated as a "negative use of funds " (that is, an offset to Government spending) as is done in the present cash budget.

The financial budget may be viewed as consisting of three parts: (1) Government receipts and expenditures as shown in the national income accounts, but restated on a cash rather than an "accrual" basis. These give rise to a surplus or deficit on "income and product account" which affects Government borrowing or cash balances. (2) Transactions involving the exchange of assets and/or liabilities between the Federal Government or its agencies on the one hand, and the private sector on the other. These usually flow directly through the money or capital market and may also give rise to a surplus or deficit on "asset account." (3) "Equilibrating transactions." In this accounting system, these are changes in Government cash balances and/or in the publicly held Federal debt required to balance total Government sources and uses of funds.[9] A blueprint for this financial budget is provided in Table 1.

---

[8] The first set of inventory data presents extremely difficult identification and collection problems. The statistical framework which would cast the second set of data in the form of an interlocking system of accounts was outlined in testimony by Michael E. Levy before the Joint Economic Committee's Subcommittee on Economic Statistics at its Hearing on *The Federal Budget as an Economic Document,* April 30, 1963; 88 Cong. 1 sess. (1963). (The basic tables were included also in the Joint Economic Committee's final *Report,* August 14, 1963, pp. 21–22.)

[9] Conceptually, this financial budget represents an elaboration of the basic approach for analyzing the liquidity effect which had been outlined earlier by Michael E. Levy in "Federal Budget: Deficit or Surplus?," *Business Record* (February 1962), and in *Fiscal Policy, Cycles and Growth* (National Industrial Conference Board, 1963), Chap. 7.

Table 1.—Financial budget

Income and product account [1]

<table>
<tr><td>Receipts:</td><td>Expenditures:</td></tr>
<tr><td>Income tax liabilities</td><td>Government purchases of goods and services</td></tr>
<tr><td>Excise taxes and other revenues</td><td></td></tr>
<tr><td>Revenues of trust funds</td><td>Transfer payments, including trust funds</td></tr>
</table>

Asset account [2]

<table>
<tr><td>Sources:</td><td>Uses:</td></tr>
<tr><td>Revenue from accelerated tax payments and similar liquidity changes</td><td>Gross lending by the Government and its agencies</td></tr>
<tr><td>Gross borrowing by Government agencies and enterprises</td><td>Purchases of mortgages and other financial and nonfinancial assets by the Government and its agencies</td></tr>
<tr><td>Revenue from sales of PC's and other financial and nonfinancial assets</td><td></td></tr>
</table>

Financial budget balance

<table>
<tr><td>Balance on "Income and Product Account" (surplus or deficit)</td><td>Change in Federal debt held by the public (reduction or increase)</td></tr>
<tr><td>Balance on "Asset Account" (surplus or deficit)</td><td>Change in Treasury cash balances (increase or reduction)</td></tr>
<tr><td>Equals: Total financial budget balance</td><td>Equals: Total equilibratory transactions</td></tr>
</table>

[1] All entries are recorded on a cash accounting basis; entries exclude all borrowing, lending, or transactions in existing assets. For most entries, subcomponents should be shown in considerable detail.

[2] All entries are recorded on a cash accounting basis; entries include borrowing, lending, or transactions in existing assets, but exclude income-and-product-account transactions. Subcomponents should be shown in considerable detail.

QUARTERLY AND LONGER-TERM BUDGET ESTIMATES

It would be advisable to have the estimates for the two basic budgets outlined above presented and revised on a quarterly basis. For maximum usefulness, quarterly revisions would best be broken down into (1) revisions due to unforeseen changes in economic activity and the availability of later data; and (2) revisions due to modifications of the original budget proposals by the Administration and/or the Congress.

It would also be desirable to develop and publish five- and ten-year projections of the basic budget data on a regular and continuing basis in order to facilitate the longer-term evaluation of Government operations and to improve the quality of economic projections. Despite the intrinsically contingent nature of such projections, the record of a few intermittent attempts is encouraging and would probably improve once such projections were updated and revised from year to year.[10]

---

[10] For a comparison and evaluation of five major budget projections—one each by the Bureau of the Budget and Murray Weidenbaum, one by Gerhard Colm and Manuel Helzner (jointly), and two by Otto Eckstein—see Michael E. Levy, assisted by Juan de Torres, "Federal Budget: Trends and Projections," *The Conference Board Record,* Vol. 1 (March 1964).

Estimating Government Revenues

The Federal budget revenue estimates are prepared by the Treasury Department in consultation with the Bureau of the Budget and the Council of Economic Advisers (CEA). They are based on the CEA's forecast of GNP and its components which is published every year shortly after the new budget is presented to the Congress. But the Treasury Department does not make available to outsiders details of its general revenue forecasting procedures.

These Federal revenue estimates may be viewed as consisting of two basic components: (1) Revenue changes under the existing tax structure which arise mainly from changes in income and output (GNP, personal income, corporate profits, and so on). Well-established statistical procedures incorporating a set of past empirical observations can be used to relate such revenue changes to the economic changes. (2) Revenue changes which result from *statutory changes* in tax rates or tax bases in contrast. These must usually be estimated without the benefit of an adequate body of relevant past data. The first of these two revenue components has to be estimated every year according to a fairly systematic procedure. This is not true in the same way for the second component.

It would be useful if the Treasury spelled out the relationships employed in estimating the first of the above revenue components, by major tax source (that is, the process by which projected changes in income and output are translated into estimates of changes in revenue). Not only could these relationships be used in order to estimate Government revenues at levels of economic activity other than the one projected by CEA (for example, at the "full employment" level), but, more importantly, the estimating procedure could be studied and tested by a wider body of specialists who might be of assistance in refining and improving the state of the art.

Carl H. Madden
Chamber of Commerce of the United States

The country needs a single Federal budget, a single financial plan showing the President's financial program for Government operations. The budget should be comprehensive, understandable, and beyond reproach in its integrity. As a document of vital significance to the nation, the budget is used by Congress, by policy makers and economists, by the Treasury, by monetary authorities and financial analysts, and by foreign observers of United States actions. Therefore, from the many possible logical concepts of a budget, the President's Commission on Budget Concepts should choose a single budget concept to predominate in the President's annual budget report.

I believe that major emphasis should be on the consolidated cash budget, which has the most comprehensive coverage. But some modifications should be made. The cash budget should include direct lending by Federal Government. It should also include a memorandum account, giving a special analysis of the capital market requirements of the Federal Government for related agencies. The memorandum account should set forth actual results and projections for changes in the public debt, financing through trust funds, financing through financial asset sales or sales of participation certificates, and financing of Federal agencies which is in addition to direct Federal financing.

The Federal budget is essentially a financial plan showing the money flows of the Government and reflecting the President's financial program for the year. The Federal budget has uses that are much broader than the uses of economists in tracing the economic impact of Government transactions. Even so, the needs of economists for evaluating Government operations justify a special analysis in the budget document—not labeled as a budget—of the economic impact of Government operations to the extent that such an analysis can depict the Government's economic impact. Currently, the requirements of such an analysis would be met by the type of calculation of Government purchases and transfers which appears in the national income accounts (NIA) budget.

The NIA budget should not be chosen by the Commission as the central budget concept in the annual budget document. In neglecting financial transactions, it not only falls short of the consolidated cash budget in meeting the test of comprehensiveness, but is conceptually weaker since it ignores both the operational and economic impact roles of such transactions.

The Brookings Conference has discussed many important logical elements involved in considering budgetary concepts at a high level of economic sophistication. Valid technical objections have been raised with respect to each budgetary concept including the notion of a matrix of budgets with coefficients of economic impact given for each classification of Government expenditures and receipts. The judgments reflected in this statement in support of the predominance of the consolidated cash concept are made in awareness of the technical limitations of any budgetary concept. On balance, however, it is my judgment that the needs of economists to analyze economic impact are less important than the needs of other budgetary users to grasp with some comprehensiveness the scope of a Federal fiscal and financial operation. In this, as in other areas of modern life, it may well be that the needs of experts should be subordinated to the broader public interest; after all, in considering budgetary transactions, the technically sophisticated should be able to adapt special analyses to their own purposes.

Murray L. Weidenbaum
Department of Economics, Washington University

Several key questions need to be answered in any fundamental rethinking of Federal budgetary concepts:

1. Should there be one or more central budget concepts?

2. What should be the rationale of the budget concept?

3. What should be the scope of the budget concept?

4. How net or gross should budgetary transactions be reported?

5. At what stage of the expenditure and revenue processes should the transactions be measured?

Suggested summary answers to these questions follow.

The number of budget concepts

No single budget concept will satisfactorily meet the needs of the various users. The budget is, alternatively and simultaneously, a basic document of public policy, a mechanism for congressional review of the executive branch, a tool for executive management of governmental resources, and a means of governmental communication to the public.

Because so many of these uses involve either political forces or persons not expert in budgetary concepts and terminology, it is essential that a single, capstone budgetary statement be the common meeting ground for all of the users, thus reducing both confusion and lack of confidence in the entire budgetary process.

This factor of budgetary unity should be considered sufficiently important to merit whatever sacrifices are needed to achieve agreement on one concept. Of course, subsidiary budgetary statements can and should continue to be prepared and presented in the document. This supplementary information, including below-the-line items, should not be so directly linked to the unitary budget statement that it defeats the central aim of simplicity and clarity.

One possible future shortcoming of a unitary budget concept needs to be acknowledged. In a sense, any budget concept tends to become eroded over time, as more ways are found to abuse it. For example, the administrative budget lost favor with the growing use of the trust fund device, especially the one created for the highway program. The consolidated cash budget lost much support with the growing use of subterfuges such as the participation certificates, which are debt instruments rather than the program receipts currently shown in the cash budget. Perhaps the current interest in the so-called national income accounts (NIA) budget mainly reflects the relative newness of the concept (or at least of its use) and the little if any effort to date to degrade the concept. Were the NIA basis to be adopted as the central budget concept, we might find that in time it too had succumbed. Perhaps another Commission on Budget Concepts would then be in order!

The rationale

There are numerous logical bases for selecting budget concepts. The fact that the budget is the most all-encompassing report and evaluation of Federal governmental operations leads to the desire for a central budget concept of great comprehensiveness. The traditional coverage of fiscal policy can usefully be followed here: the revenues and expenditures of the Government. The coverage would approximate that of the existing consolidated cash budget, if borrowing and repayment of borrowing were to continue to be excluded.

The scope of the budget

Proceeding from the above rationale, the scope of the budget transactions can be determined: (1) by identifying the agencies which are to be treated as part of the Federal Government, (2) by estimating their expenditures and revenues, and then (3) by eliminating debt operations. Clearly, the Cabinet departments and agencies and wholly Federal-owned enterprises are to be included. The problem of coverage arises with the relatively small fringe of agencies which are owned in whole or in part by non-Federal organizations or individuals (as in the case of the Federal Intermediate Credit Banks) or in which the original Federal investment has been repaid (Federal Deposit Insurance Corporation).

Some guidelines are needed about which, if any, of these fringe agencies are to be included. At the minimum, it is suggested that those agencies— such as the Federal Reserve System and the Federal Land Banks—which are privately owned should be excluded from the budget. In addition, the other financial intermediaries, notably the Federal Home Loan Banks, perhaps also should be excluded; an added reason is the nature and volatility of their transactions, which are mainly purchases and sales of Federal securities reflecting the borrowing needs of their member banks.

Budgetary revenues would include tax receipts as well as fees, surplus property sales, and other existing sources of miscellaneous receipts. The expenditures would include purchases, transfer and interest payments, subsidies, and loans. All debt transactions, even those backed by collateral such as the participation certificates, would be excluded.

Net versus gross

The question of how net or gross Government expenditures should be reported (for example, whether postal revenues should be shown under receipts and total postal payments on the expenditure side or the net postal deficit on the expenditure side only) is a matter more of judgment than of correctness. The major point to be made is the overriding need for consistency of treatment over time.

It is highly desirable to avoid in the future the experience of recent decades where the budget total for a given fiscal period is redefined frequently at successively lower levels. Adoption of an extremely net concept would tend to eliminate future incentives for altering the budget totals merely to show that the Federal Government is keeping within a $100 billion (or $200 billion) limit.

Timing of transactions

There are many stages in the governmental revenue and expenditure processes. The most important point to note here is the need for selecting comparable stages for both revenues and expenditures. The present cash budget generally meets this criterion, measuring transactions at the point that cash flows into or out of the Treasury. The NIA budget, were it adopted, would need to be modified to an accrual basis on both the income and outgo sides. This would eliminate the present defect whereby receipts are either recorded when the cash is received by the Government or earlier (as in the case of corporate profits tax accruals), and expenditures are recorded on a cash paid basis or later (as in the case of delivery of military equipment).

PART IV

Summary of Conference Proceedings

DAVID J. OTT

Department of Economics, Southern Methodist University

Summary of Conference Proceedings

The conference discussion centered on several important issues, most of which were raised in the three background papers by Messrs. Break, Gramlich, and Galper; by the formal discussants of these papers; or in two staff papers on Federal credit programs prepared earlier for the President's Commission on Budget Concepts and distributed to conference participants.

The most pervasive issue was the criterion (or criteria) upon which to base the choice of budget concepts. This problem persistently emerged as the basis for most of the specific differences among the conferees over the proper budget concept or concepts. If the conference produced agreement on anything, it was that the "proper" budget depends on the purposes it is intended to serve.

The specific issues discussed can be summarized as follows:

(1) Should the budget be a "unibudget," with a single surplus or deficit figure, or a "multibudget," with several parts and several surpluses or deficits?

(2) If a "multibudget" is used:

(a) How should the budget be organized and how much detail should be presented in each category?

(b) Should the transactions of the Federal Reserve System be integrated into the budget?

(3) If, instead, a "unibudget," with a single surplus or deficit figure is deemed desirable (ignoring problems of timing and internal consistency):

(a) Should Federal lending be counted as a budget expenditure as in the present consolidated cash budget? Or should it be excluded as in the present national income accounts (NIA) budget, but with a provision for counting as expenditures the subsidy elements in lending programs (which is not now done in the NIA budget)?

(b) If the "adjusted" NIA budget is used, how should the subsidy elements in Federal loans be calculated?

(c) How should federally guaranteed and insured loans be treated in the budget, whether cash or NIA?

(4) Is there a relatively simple measure of the fiscal impact of the budget? If so, should it be included as a part of the budget message,

left to the President's annual economic report, or should no recommendation about its use be made?

(5) How far should accrual accounting, as opposed to cash accounting, be carried in the budget?

The discussion of each of these issues is summarized below.

Unibudget vs. Multibudget

Break's paper advocates a "multibudget," with different categories of receipts and expenditures grouped together at least roughly according to their economic impacts. In effect, Break argues that since the economic impacts of different types of Federal fiscal actions may differ considerably, they should not be presented as simple totals. Rather, they should be subdivided. The formal discussants of his paper all took issue with the idea of a "multibudget" and argued for a single budget, with Richard Goode and Herbert Stein arguing for essentially the consolidated cash budget and Okun arguing for an adjusted NIA budget. All the discussants of Break's paper felt that a multibudget with several categories of receipts and expenditures and a surplus or deficit for each category might make sense in providing information for the specialist, but that the public requires a single budget with a single surplus or deficit figure, not a complete sources-and-uses-of-funds statement. People want to know the size of "the budget" and "the deficit" and they must be given figures to gauge these, even though they may not know exactly what the figures mean. A unitary budget, it was held, is important for a "meaningful dialogue between the Administration, Congress and the public."

Little direct argument was presented in support of the multibudget position during the first day and a half of the conference. Since it appeared to be fairly widely agreed that a unibudget was essential, the discussion centered mostly on what unibudget concept should be used. However, as the discussion progressed, it became clear that the proper unibudget concept would depend on the purpose the budget should serve. A number of purposes were suggested: (1) to measure the economic impact of the budget; (2) to measure the "size" of government; (3) to specify the financing needs of the Government; (4) to enforce some concept of "fiscal responsibility," and (5) to serve as an instrument of management over programs by the Executive and Congress. The subsequent discussion of the multiple purposes the budget serves led to something of a shift in favor of the multibudget position The argument was strongly advanced that just as multiple economic objectives require multiple policy tools to achieve them, multiple objectives in presenting budget information require multiple budgets. Since budget information is needed for all these purposes, it was argued, it is fruitless and perhaps even misleading, to try to find *one* budget concept that serves all these ends.

At one point near the end of the conference, there seemed to be a substantial number of conferees in favor of a Break-like "multibudget" (modified to include both the assets *and* liabilities of the Federal Reserve System and to exclude the net change in Government-guaranteed or -insured loans). However, there was considerable debate over the meaning of the terms "unibudget" and "multibudget," and a majority also indicated satisfaction with an NIA budget (adjusted for loan subsidies) supplemented with interlocking data on changes in Government assets, liabilities, and financing requirements.

In any event, there seemed to be a consensus that the information contained in a comprehensive sources-and-uses-of-funds statement for the Federal sector was vital for many types of economic analysis and is not currently readily available in the budget document. Whether this should be presented in one place in the budget document as *the* budget of the Federal Government, or whether the adjusted NIA budget should be presented as *the* budget, with supplementary data on Federal financing, lending, and other transactions in assets reconcilable to the NIA deficit or surplus, was left unresolved.

If a multibudget were used, how should the receipts and expenditures of the Federal Government be categorized? The group agreed that, given the present state of knowledge, economic impact could not be used (as proposed by Break) to arrange receipt and expenditure items into subbudgets. Fairly general agreement was reached that the only meaningful criterion for sub-budgeting would be the economic distinction between transactions by the Federal Government which tie in directly with the private sector's *income* (the NIA budget items) and those which affect the composition or amount of financial assets held by the private sector (lending and borrowing activity of the Federal sector). There was disagreement over whether the net change in Federal Government assets and liabilities should be reconciled with the (adjusted) NIA surplus or deficit. Some held that this was the purview of monetary analysis, and too much detail in the budget document would only be confusing. Others felt that a reconciliation was vital (see, for example, the comment by Samuel Chase). Some participants maintained, as they had during the first day's discussion, that the present cash budget (with some modification) which does not distinguish between NIA budget items and loan programs, is superior to any of the alternatives.

Particular attention centered on the treatment in the budget (or supplementary tables, as the case might be) of the Federal Reserve System. In the Break paper, the Federal Reserve was partially reflected in the "Monetary Transactions" sub-budget—Federal debt held by the Federal Reserve was netted against liabilities of the Federal Government. There was fairly general agreement, however, that if the transactions of the Federal Reserve were to be actually included in the budget, consistency would require its liabilities (mainly bank reserves and Federal reserve notes) to be counted as part of the total liabilities of the Federal sector.

However, a number of participants were skeptical about including Federal Reserve transactions in the budget at all. It was noted that the budget must present proposed budget totals for the future, not just summarize past fiscal activities of the Federal sector. This being so, Federal Reserve inclusion was opposed by some because of the difficulty—both political and practical—of having the executive branch attempt to forecast Federal Reserve transactions. As noted above, others felt that fiscal and monetary policy should be kept apart, and attempts to reflect actions by the monetary authority in the budget would create problems of accountability and division of responsibility.

On the other hand, the proponents of including Federal Reserve transactions in the budget argued: (1) forecasting Federal Reserve transactions is not likely to be less successful than forecasting other Federal receipts and expenditures was in the past; (2) putting the "Fed" into the budget might encourage more coordination of fiscal and monetary policy; and (3) the Federal Reserve *is* part of the Federal sector economically regardless of legal considerations, and not putting it in distorts greatly data on the amount of net interest-bearing debt of the Federal sector and the composition of claims on the Federal sector and its claims on others.

Several other interesting questions were raised about the treatment of Federal transactions in a multibudget:

(1) On purely accounting principles alone, the net change in federally-insured or guaranteed loans could not be included in the budget, since no receipts or expenditures are involved. Yet their impact is not unlike that of direct Federal lending. How are they to be accounted for in the budget?

(2) Should Federal Government employee retirement and life insurance plans and the various social security funds be treated as a liability of the Federal sector as they now are in the flow-of-funds accounts?

(3) Do foreign loans by the Federal Government have such a different impact from domestic loans that they should be shown separately and given prominence in the budget?

No resolution of these problems emerged from the discussion.

In summary, the conference produced no clear consensus on the "unibudget vs. multibudget" issue. In part this may have been the result of semantic tangles over the meaning of the terms and a difference in emphasis on the need for providing a simple, understandable budget for public consumption as opposed to the complexity involved in providing budget information suitable for sophisticated economic analysis. While there was agreement that no budget with a single deficit or surplus figure would be adequate for all purposes of economic analysis, there was disagreement over whether to publish and give prominence to such a budget (supplemented with the information necessary for other types of analysis) or whether to provide a set of interlocking sub-budgets.

If a Unibudget: What Type?

Most of the discussion on the first day of the conference centered around the issue of what unibudget concept, if one has to be chosen, is "best." On this, the conferees generally took one of two positions:

(1) The best unibudget would be a cash consolidated budget "cleaned-up" to remove some of the timing and definitional inconsistencies that exist in the present cash budget. In particular, those favoring the cash budget favored treating sales of participation certificates as the equivalent of the sale of Federal securities rather than as negative expenditures (as they are currently treated).

(2) The best unibudget concept would be essentially the national income accounts budget concept, modified to include in expenditures an imputed measure of the subsidy element in Federal loan programs.

It is useful to begin first with a summary of the initial arguments advanced for each position, and then to summarize the points of agreement and disagreement which developed in the ensuing discussion.

Arguments for the cash budget

The arguments initially put forth for using the cash budget as *the* unibudget centered around its comprehensiveness—particularly the inclusion of net Federal lending as an expenditure. Advocates of the cash budget felt that the inclusion of net loans in expenditures was essential to provide "political accountability" and "allocative rationality." Leaving out loans could encourage the practice of making loans that are in effect grants (in the sense of being virtually interest-free or with little expectation or provision for repayment) to finance governmental programs and thus keeping reported expenditures down. The cash budget, they felt, would be better than NIA for measuring the "size" of the Government in that it roughly measures that part of total output whose use the Federal Government influences. It would encourage fiscal responsibility by providing a deficit or surplus equal to the financing needs of the Government.

The argument was also advanced that net lending should be "above the line" (counted as an expenditure) in the Federal budget because not doing so ignores the important economic impact of the budget in the money and credit markets. The cash deficit or surplus indicates the Government's withdrawal from or injection of funds into the credit markets, and the NIA budget, by excluding net lending, would neglect the monetary and financial aspects of budget policy. Leaving lending out of the budget comes close, as one participant put it, to saying "money doesn't matter."

In short, many advocates of the cash budget felt that even in terms of measuring the economic impact of the budget, the cash concept is superior to the NIA budget. If not better, at least it was not significantly worse. If net lending is small relative to the NIA surplus or deficit, there is no real

difference in the measurement of fiscal impact, and the view was expressed that comparison of the cash and NIA surplus or deficit would
not have led to wrong fiscal policy decisions at critical junctures in the
business cycle, such as in 1958 and the middle of 1965. Another consideration noted is the extent to which lending substitutes for Government purchases, transfers, or taxes. Finally, if an increase in lending causes Government purchases to fall or taxes to rise, then lending will have at least a
derivative importance and should be reflected in the budget.

Arguments for the NIA budget (modified to account for loan subsidies)

Another group of participants argued that the NIA budget is the best
single available measure of Federal receipts and expenditures, both for
analytical purposes and for public consumption as well. Several reasons
were given for this view.

One argument was that the NIA budget focuses on the *fiscal* impact of
Government receipts and expenditures—their effects on the income stream
of the private sector. This is what fiscal policy—as distinct from monetary
and credit policy—is all about. The fact that it ignores financial asset
transactions is not a relevant criticism—these can be provided in below-
the-line supplementary statements. As one participant put it, no one suggests that the budget should provide measures of the economic impacts of
Government regulatory activities, wage-price policies or foreign policy—
why should it necessarily have to say anything about the impact of Federal
credit market intervention?

It was also noted that any tendency to shift to lending programs to keep
expenditures and the deficit down under an NIA budget can be counter-
acted by counting as part of expenditures under NIA the subsidy component
of Federal lending—both the interest subsidy and the subsidy involved
in losses when loans are not repaid.

To the argument that the cash budget is a fuller measure of economic
impact, it was replied that the cash budget can give a seriously misleading
and incomplete picture. For example, the final outcome for the NIA and
cash budget deficits for fiscal year 1967 were compared with the January
1967 predictions. The cash deficit was estimated at $6.2 billion in January
and turned out to be about $1.8 billion, some $4.5 billion less than predicted. At the same time the NIA deficit swung from a predicted $3.8 billion
deficit to a $7.5 billion deficit. The swing in cash deficit figures for this
period is highly misleading in that it gives the impression that the budget became more restrictive than estimated earlier. The turnaround in the cash
budget largely reflected unanticipated repayments of Federal Home Loan
Bank advances by savings and loan associations. This enabled the Home Loan
Bank Board to retire its own debt, which is included in the public debt. The
Federal Government simply acts as a financial intermediary buying risky
assets and selling safe ones.

In essence then, the Federal sector supplied $4.5 billion less credit to the private sector and borrowed $4.5 billion less; there was no appreciable net effect on credit markets.

More generally, critics of the cash budget pointed out that Federal lending programs financed by Federal debt are similar to lending by private financial intermediaries. By the same reasoning, direct lending is quite similar in economic impact to Federal loan insurance and guarantee programs. In both cases the Federal Government, in effect, turns a risky demand for private credit into a safe demand for private credit. Why put direct lending in (as the cash budget does) and leave insured and guaranteed loans out, especially with Federal guaranteed and insured loans three times as large as direct Federal lending? More generally, the similarity suggests that the line between included and excluded items must be drawn so that direct loans and loan guarantees are on a comparable footing. Otherwise there will be incentives to shift from loans (if included) to guarantees (if excluded).

Advocates of an NIA budget (adjusted to include subsidy elements of Federal credit programs) pointed out that excluding financial asset transactions from the calculation of surplus or deficit does not necessarily imply they are unimportant. By analogy, changes in the gold stock are below the line in the balance-of-payments accounts, yet no one has suggested they are unimportant. The issue is not whether the information in the cash budget ought to be suppressed, but whether differences between the NIA and cash budgets are something of importance. All kinds of supplementary information can be provided for those wanting to analyze the asset transactions of the Government.

Open discussion of the arguments for the cash and NIA budgets

After the initial agreements for the NIA and cash budgets were presented, the conferees discussed the two approaches more generally.

A great deal of time was spent discussing the criteria relevant to the choice of a budget concept. The discussion first centered on whether economic impact could be used as the basis for choosing a budget. A number of participants noted that present knowledge of the "multipliers" appropriate for different components of the budget is so uncertain that they cannot serve as the basis for choice of a budget concept. Furthermore, even if the multipliers were known with certainty, they would not provide a conclusive basis for choice. To take an extreme case, suppose, as some economists have argued, the fiscal multipliers are zero. Does this then imply no budget at all? Or that the choice of a budget concept is of no importance? As the discussion progressed, substantial agreement was reached on this point—impact multipliers cannot, at present, be a definite basis for choice of a budget concept.

If, then, Government purchases, transfers, grants-in-aid on the one hand, and financial transactions—direct loans, loan guarantees and insurance—on the other, cannot be distinguished from one another by different quantitative estimates of economic impact, on what grounds can they be separated?

One basis for distinction is the accounting distinction between transactions on income account of the private sector and transactions on capital account. In their view, the traditions of accounting suggest fundamental differences between operations entering directly into private income flows and those affecting the composition or amount of private assets and liabilities. Federal loans have two components—the first increases private assets and liabilities and the second is a current income flow representing the subsidy involved in the loan, either in the form of lower interest rates than the borrower could otherwise obtain or in the form of expected losses.

The income-asset transactions dichotomy was supported by the argument that the *type* of economic impact (not its magnitude) of income and asset transactions is a meaningful reason for distinguishing between them. To analyze the impact of Government actions affecting assets and liabilities, different approaches are required because the effects occur in a different way.

Several participants found fault with this criterion as the basis for deciding on a budget concept. One criticism was that the cash and even the administrative budget meet accounting standards of a sort—why should one particular accounting standard be picked as the one to satisfy? Another comment was that this distinction between transactions on current account and capital account leads logically not to the adjusted NIA budget but to a capital budgeting system for the Federal Government. If loans are to be capitalized, why not all durable assets owned by the Federal Government as well?

Some proponents of the cash budget argued that it is a good measure of the "size" of the Federal Government. Others contended that no single budget or budget number could serve as a measure of the "size" of the Government, and that consequently this was not a basis on which a choice could be made. The "size" of the Federal Government, according to this view, is an ambiguous concept at best; in any case it has more than one dimension. No budget could measure the "size" of Federal regulatory activity, or the influence over state and local government activities through special purpose grants-in-aid. It was also pointed out that the "size" of the Federal Government is usually measured in *relative* terms, by comparing Government purchases of goods and services with GNP, Federal employment with total employment, and so on. What would one compare expenditures in the cash budget with? Total transactions?

There was, however, general agreement that the budget should give an indication of the total financing needs of the Government. It was pointed out that this could be provided in a "below-the-line" reconciliation of the adjusted NIA deficit (or surplus) and a statement of net Federal lending. Several participants emphasized that *net* financing (that is, the financial counterpart of the NIA budget) is just as important—some said more important—than *gross* Federal borrowing (that is, the financial counterpart of the consolidated cash budget). A minority felt, however, that the need for emphasis on gross borrowing requirements constitutes a strong argument for the cash budget.

Several other points brought up in the cash vs. NIA budget discussion also deserve mention.

It was pointed out that the distinction between income and asset transactions favored by NIA advocates refers to *private,* not governmental, assets, and does not lead to a capital budget for the Federal sector. The possibility was also raised that, rather than putting Federal lending all in or all out of the budget, it might be proper to put some lending in the budget while leaving other lending out. Federal loans vary widely in their "softness" as well as in the interest subsidy involved, and while setting up loss reserves and including them in the adjusted NIA budget as expenditures along with the interest subsidy seem promising conceptually, considerable difficulty might be experienced in practice. Congress might balk, for example, when a "soft" loan it particularly favored was counted as an expenditure (like a grant or subsidy) in the budget.

In a summing up, the conferees did unanimously recommend that the administrative budget be discarded completely. A substantial majority, when asked if they were forced to select a single budget, indicated they would choose the "adjusted NIA," that is, with the subsidy element in loans "in" and net lending "out." As noted above, however, it was not clear the following day that a majority of the conferees would, of their own volition, choose a single budget concept.

It is noteworthy that very few of the NIA advocates based their main support for the adjusted NIA budget heavily on the 'economic impact" criterion.

The Calculation of the Subsidy Element in Federal Loan Programs

Among the background papers for the conference discussion was a staff paper of the President's Commission on Budget Concepts, entitled "Problems in Implementing a Capital Budget for Loans." This paper, reprinted in this volume, explores the idea of putting Federal lending "below the line" and calculating a subsidy component of Federal lending and including *this* in expenditures "*above* the line"—essentially the adjusted NIA budget debated so extensively at this conference.

The major problem with this approach is calculating the subsidy component of Federal lending programs. There are three subsidy elements that have to be identified and computed to make the expenditure imputation:

(1) The difference between the lending rate and the Treasury borrowing rate on securities of comparable maturity. For example, the present value of a 35-year 2 percent loan discounted at $4\frac{1}{2}$ percent is

approximately 70 percent of face value. In this case the borrower in effect receives an asset worth $100 and a liability worth only $70, and the $30 difference is an expenditure just like any ordinary grant, subsidy, or transfer payment.

(2) A further subsidy element is reflected in the difference in risk between a Treasury security and the loan extended by the Government. Treasury securities are free of default risk; many Federal loans carry a high probability of default on payments of interest and principal. This subsidy could theoretically be computed by comparing Treasury borrowing costs and the terms on which borrowers could obtain *private* credit; alternatively they could be estimated by setting up loss reserves for different types of Federal loans.

(3) The final subsidy element in Federal lending programs is the agency costs of administering the loan programs. The obvious problem here is separating such costs from other agency costs and allocating them by loan program.

The staff paper proposed two alternatives for treating the interest-subsidy component [(1) above]; the subsidy amount might be charged annually over the life of the loan or given recognition at once to the extent of the discounted present value of the difference at the time the loan is initially made. The latter alternative was favored. The paper recommended accounting for the risk differential subsidy component by setting up loss reserves, charges to which would be included in expenditures when the loans are extended. While the administrative costs are already included in the budget totals, a change in budget accounting may be appropriate to make the amounts more explicit and noticeable.

A number of comments were made at the conference on this problem of accounting for loan subsidies. One participant observed that while he found no conceptual objection to the loan subsidy imputation in the budget, there is the problem of consistency—tariffs, price supports and the tax structure, for example, all involve implicit subsidies. If a subsidy is to be imputed for loan programs, how can one avoid applying the same logic to all other Government programs containing subsidy elements? Where shall the line be drawn on subsidy imputations in the budget? This participant favored separating the loan and subsidy elements of Federal lending programs *"below the line,"* *not* counting the subsidy as expenditures in the budget.

It was also noted that setting up loss reserves for the risk differential component of Federal loans might pose delicate diplomatic problems within the Administration and between it and Congress. Extremely "soft" loans might show up in the budget as a complete subsidy or grant, which in essence might involve implying that the lending agency and/or Congress had misnamed the program in calling it "lending." For this reason, it was argued, the imputation for the risk differential would be kept to a minimum.

Other participants felt that ways might be found to separate the diplomatic problems from the analytical problems, and to avoid the problems of diplomacy, perhaps by finding a "neutral" agency to determine the subsidy element in each loan program.

One participant expressed the view that the Government had no business making "hard" loans in any case, and that the risk differential subsidy might in fact prove to be more important than the interest differential subsidy. Another participant disagreed with the contention that the Government should make only "soft" loans. In his view, the tax structure discriminates against saving, and loan programs, even of the "hard" variety, are an offset to the tax disincentives to saving and thus desirable.

All in all, there was no strong opposition to the proposal to estimate the subsidy element in loan programs and put it in expenditures. On the contrary, a substantial majority favored treating the interest differential subsidy as discussed in the Commission's staff paper, namely, capitalizing the subsidy and charging it to expenditures when the loan is made.

Budget Treatment of Guaranteed and Insured Loans

In the debate over the cash vs. adjusted NIA budget and in the discussion of the sub-budget categories of a multibudget, the treatment of federally insured and guaranteed loans was a recurring issue. The conferees agreed that the amount of outstanding federally insured and guaranteed loans and the likelihood of further extensions of this approach make the problem one deserving careful study. Yet on this issue the Conference produced no consensus, although some interesting comments were made.

It was noted that insured and guaranteed loans involve no cash outlay, and hence in an accounting sense the net change in this item cannot appear in the budget, either "above the line" or "below the line" (in an integrated system of accounts). They are *contingent* liabilities of the Federal Government and whether they are converted into an *actual* liability depends partly on policies to preserve full employment, which cannot be quantified for accounting consistency. Yet at the same time, the point was made and generally accepted that the *type* of economic effect (if not the magnitude) of such loans is basically similar to direct loans. It would thus seem that on accounting grounds, guaranteed and insured loans cannot be in the budget, or even in a reconcilable "below the line" account, while on economic grounds they must be treated similarly to direct lending. Otherwise, incentives are set up to shift from direct loans to loans and guarantees.

There was some discussion about imputing a subsidy expenditure for guaranteed and insured loans just as for direct loans. One participant noted that if, for example, the Federal Government buys $1 billion of, for example, mortgages and sells $1 billion of Federal debt, there is basically no difference from guaranteeing the mortgages themselves. Conceptually, therefore, the same subsidy calculation made for the direct loan (the purchases of mortgages) would be relevant if instead the Government guaranteed the mortgages; imputing the subsidy involved in guaranteeing and insuring loans would avoid bias towards using these techniques were the direct loan subsidy to be imputed to expenditures. There would still be a question, however, whether even the subsidy amounts could be properly included in the budget, since Federal taxpayers and/or Federal creditors would not be financing the outlays as in the case of direct loans.

MEASURES OF DISCRETIONARY FISCAL POLICY AND THEIR INCLUSION IN THE BUDGET DOCUMENT

In the paper by Gramlich, three relatively simple summary measures of fiscal impact were compared: (1) the full-employment surplus (FS); (2) Musgrave's fiscal leverage"; and (3) a *weighted* full-employment surplus (WFS). The first was rejected because it implicitly gives all budget items equal "multiplier effects"; the second was rejected because it is meaningless under conditions of full employment and inflation, it is difficult to calculate for large-scale econometric models, because it requires a precise notion of the "accelerator" effects on investment, and finally because it does not discriminate between discretionary and induced fiscal effects. Gramlich argued that a weighted full-employment surplus could provide a useful summary measure of fiscal impact by avoiding the major weaknesses of the two alternative measures. The WFS measures the impact of the budget on aggregate demand at full-employment output (or some other standard level) with the various Federal tax and expenditure components weighted according to the relative relevant private spending reaction. Gramlich stressed the WFS is not intended primarily as a measure of the need for current fiscal actions, but as a device for studying fiscal impact in past periods.

The novel analytical feature of Gramlich's paper was the argument that the WFS must be adjusted when inflation occurs because rising prices have automatic effects on federal expenditures and taxes that must be taken out of this measure of discretionary fiscal impact just as the effects of the so-called automatic stabilizers are (by measuring taxes and expenditures at full employment output). In brief, Gramlich argued that rising prices affect real expenditures and real taxes differently; real expenditures fall when prices rise, while real taxes rise (because taxes are collected on money income and the tax system is progressive). Thus during a period of rising prices expenditures must be adjusted upward, and taxes downward, if these automatic effects of price changes are to be "washed out."

A novel empirical feature of the paper was a comparison of the WFS's using weights obtained from the "steady-state" multipliers implied by six econometric models. The absolute values of the WFS differed considerably from one model to the next and from the unweighted full-employment surplus.

However, in first difference form, measuring changes in fiscal impact from one period to the next, there were much smaller differences between the various models.

The discussants of Gramlich's paper focused their critical comments on three topics covered in the paper: (a) the adjustment to the WFS for price changes; (b) the method of calculating the WFS from the six models; and (c) the uses to which the WFS might be put.

The inflation adjustment was recognized by the discussants as a needed modification of the WFS. Criticisms related mostly to the technique used by Gramlich. It was argued that the adjustment was not symmetrical for taxes and expenditures; an "unanticipated price change" (the actual price level change minus the expected price level change) was used for expenditures while the actual price change was used in the adjustment of taxes. Since price expectations are generally hard to ascertain, actual prices might well be used in adjusting expenditures because the Government can always "keep up" with inflation if it wants to. It was also noted that the effects of price changes in Federal expenditures and receipts might not be so different as Gramlich argues—for example, excise taxes fall in real terms as prices rise, and many spending programs are fixed in real terms.

The potential usefulness of the WFS concept was also discussed. One discussant pointed to three uses for summary measures of fiscal impact. One is to help the public understand the two-way relation between the budget and GNP—a fall in GNP caused by a weakening of private demand moves the budget toward a deficit, but a discretionary change in fiscal policy that moves the budget toward a deficit (at a given level of GNP) will cause GNP to rise. The unweighted FS might communicate the critical relationship to the public; a weighted FS, on the other hand, might provide a more accurate measure of fiscal impact, but would be of little use for this purpose.

A second use of fiscal impact measures is to study the fiscal policies of past periods; for this the WFS is useful. The third (and most important) use of a summary measure of fiscal impact is to formulate appropriate policies to deal with the current economic situation as it unfolds, a use Gramlich specifically denies.

It was also commented that the difference in weights for budget components obtained from the six models was not surprising, given the variety in the structure and resulting "fiscal multipliers" of these models. On the inflation adjustment, it was argued that Gramlich was implying an economy where the "Phillips curve problem" (the tradeoff between unemployment and price changes) is ignored, and that this was just not realistic. The relation of Gramlich's work to the problems facing the President's Commission on Budget Concepts was also questioned; an unweighted FS might be included in the budget document, but the WFS seemed too complex for use in public education, whatever its analytical value to economists.

Two major criticisms were raised about the weights used in Gramlich's calculations of the WFS and the use of full-employment GNP as the base for the calculations. One discussant believed that the long-run or "steady-state" multipliers of econometric models should not be used to calculate a WFS, since in measuring the fiscal contributions to stabilization policy we are interested in the short-run, or "impact" multipliers. He could not see why the WFS had to be calculated at full employment, other than by convention; and he argued that in measuring the contribution of *discretionary* fiscal policy to aggregate demand, certain "normal" expenditures and tax receipts should not be taken out in arriving at the "no-government" GNP. The discussants believed also that Gramlich overstated the differential impact of prices on expenditures and tax receipts, and that his inflation adjustment presumed an economy where prices did not rise until full employment was reached.

Gramlich replied at some length to some of the criticisms (see his written reply in this volume). He disagreed with the contention that the WFS is not suitable for public education about the two-way relation between the budget and GNP; for years sophomore economics courses have discussed the unequal GNP impacts of Government purchases and taxes. The WFS is no more difficult a concept than the "balanced-budget multiplier." Gramlich also stated that he did *not* assume prices rise only when full employment is reached—the inflation adjustment was made (and should be made) for years where unemployment existed and prices were rising; that corporate savings were not ignored in obtaining the weights (although the paper did not make this clear) ; that the WFS could be computed at other GNP levels; and that perhaps it would be better to use the impact multipliers in computing the WFS.

In the general discussion, the WFS came under severe attack. It was argued that this measure is derived from a model which is linear, static, and additive, and where policies are independent of one another, whereas fiscal impact can only be properly measured within the framework of an econometric model with many interdependent equations incorporating lags, nonlinearities, and the time-path of the relevant variables. As an example, results of simulations of various fiscal and monetary actions from the Brookings model were presented for 1960–62 in the form of (1) the real input and fiscal multipliers for each policy action at the end of 1, 4, 7, and 10 quarters, and (2) the average quarterly *discounted* input and fiscal multipliers (average per quarter of the sum of multipliers discounted quarterly at annual rate of 6 percent).

It was also argued that alternative actions could not be chosen on the basis of demand impact alone; as the logical followup to the simulation of alternative policy actions a utility function had to be postulated for the policymakers and each alternative action then ranked according to the resulting effect on the utility function. This was also done for illustrative purposes for the policy actions simulated with the Brookings model where four alternative forms were assumed for the utility function of policymakers. In short, the argument was that the administration and Congress would be interested in many variables other than aggregate demand, output, or employment—for example, the consumption-investment mix, the balance-of-payments deficit or surplus, and the price level. No one-dimensional measure of aggregate demand effects alone would be adequate in policy formulation.

In the discussion that followed about the use of simulations and the use of utility functions postulated for policymakers, it was stated that a ranking of fiscal policy actions obtained with this analysis would be more arbitrary than the WFS because the arguments contained in the utility function and the weights attached to them would be completely arbitrary. Therefore, until more is known about the utility function of policymakers, it may still be useful to have a summary measure of the effect of fiscal policy on one objective—aggregate demand. In reply, it was argued that even though we do not now have enough information to decide on the utility function for policymakers, the conceptual point still holds that in evaluating policies we must think in terms of multiple goals, and the proper weight to attach to each, rather than in terms of a single goal.

Another argument advanced against formulating policy by calculating discounted multipliers and other effects of fiscal actions from econometric models was that the variety of models with different structures might yield different results, leaving the ranking as ambiguous as before. In reply, it was stated that more research admittedly would be needed, but that now not too much difference exists among the major models in terms of simulation results.

The discussion then turned from the issue of whether multiple goals should be considered in measuring fiscal impact to a discussion of how well the weighted or unweighted FS measures the aggregate-demand impact of fiscal policy, aside from the effects of fiscal policy on other goals. It was argued that what really matters in judging the weighted or unweighted FS in this respect are *changes* in the magnitude of the FS or WFS, not the absolute *level*. One participant noted that a comparison of the average of the first differences of the six weighted FS's and the unweighted FS in Gramlich's Table 3 showed only small differences. On this basis he suggested that perhaps the unweighted FS is not bad as a measure of the aggregate demand impact of fiscal policy; it may be a useful device until there are models on which most economists can agree.

The question was then raised: Should the President's Commission on Budget Concepts endorse the use of the unweighted FES and its publication in the budget? Three general views emerged from the ensuing discussion:

(1) One group believed that the (unweighted) FS was a crude but nevertheless informative summary of fiscal impact (if adjusted for in-

flation) and should be put somewhere in the budget presentation, perhaps in a special analysis.

(2) Another group believed that the unweighted FS was too ambiguous a measure of fiscal impact, and that the Commission might therefore recommend against its use. At the same time, this group argued that perhaps a weighted FS (modified by the use of weights obtained from the "impact multipliers" of econometric models, the inflation adjustment suggested by Gramlich, and expenditures on an accrual rather than delivery basis) would be a more useful measure of fiscal impact and that the Commission might recommend that this be studied for possible inclusion in a future budget presentation.

(3) A third group felt that no summary measure of fiscal impact on aggregate demand should be recommended for use in the budget documents. In their view, econometric models should be used to estimate the impact of various fiscal actions on a multiplicity of goals and to formulate a fiscal program. It would be a mistake, they believed, to tie future administrations to an analytical concept which might prove faulty; they would prefer the budget to focus on economic goals and the contribution of the fiscal program toward their achievement, using whatever analytical apparatus was appropriate.

No consensus was reached on these specifics. However, a majority seemed to feel that, in one form or another, at least the *idea* embodied in the full-employment surplus—that is, a distinction between induced and autonomous budget effects—was useful to stress in order to increase public understanding of the budget.

Accrual Accounting in the Budget

The final subject discussed at the conference was the question of accrual accounting in the budget.

The paper by Galper provided the starting point for the discussion. The purpose of his paper, as he put it, was

> . . . to assist the Commission in deciding upon the appropriate (timing) basis for expressing budgetary expenditures . . . by providing quantitative estimates of the differences involved in using one timing basis as opposed to another timing basis.

Specifically, Galper sought to estimate the adjustment needed to put a large component of Federal expenditures—defense expenditures—on an accrual rather than a delivery basis as they are carried in the NIA budget.

He did this by use of a model for estimating defense *purchases* (deliveries) as a lagged function of contract awards (the lags varying with several other variables—the rate of capacity utilization, changes in the rate of growth of the armed forces, and the proportion of "long-lead" items in defense expenditures). Then, by making alternative assumptions about the rate at which awards are converted into production, an estimate of the change in defense goods-in-process inventories is obtained (since production less deliveries equals the change in inventories).

The principal conclusions reached by Galper were: (1) the main determinant of changes in defense goods-in-process inventories is the rate of change of contract awards—rapid changes in contract awards can lead to substantial changes in defense goods inventories and a consequent substantial misstatement of fiscal impact in the NIA accounts. For example, in the last half of 1966, some $4 billion (annual rate) should be added to NIA deliveries to get a true measure of the fiscal impact of defense purchases during the period; (2) a consistent set of accounts payable would show accrued defense expenditures and their impact, but these are not available; (3) cash defense expenditures come somewhat closer than deliveries to capturing the impact of defense purchases since progress payments amount to some 70 percent of contracts.

His general conclusion was that if economic impact is adopted as a criterion for measuring Federal Government purchases of goods and services, then an accrual expenditure measure would be most appropriate. The accounting system of the Government does not now provide this data directly in summary form; hence, the effort to obtain an adjustment item indirectly, at least for defense spending.

Although there were virtually no criticisms of Galper's paper by the discussants, a surprising amount of discussion was generated among the conferees over what had seemed to be a rather noncontroversial issue.

This was perhaps stimulated by the first comment "from the floor" on Galper's conclusions. A participant observed that the national income accounts in general are on a "goods-delivered" basis in measuring expenditures; this is true for consumption, business fixed investment, and exports as well as for Government purchases. In his view, it could hardly be otherwise, and if the accounts were consistently on an accrual basis throughout, it would involve liquidation of much of the inventory change component of GNP. Inventory change would be allocated instead to the various components of final demands. This, he argued, is objectionable because (1) it is pragmatically impossible; and (2) it would not be analytically desirable in view of the importance of the inventory component of GNP to business cycle theory. There is, in short, fuzziness in the accrual concept of Government expenditures and perhaps a better case for a deliveries basis than is usually recognized. At the same time, he recognized that the national income accounts are partially on an accrual basis already, particularly in the area of construction expenditures. The object should be to estimate the inventory adjustment and leave users with the option of putting it in the Federal sector or leaving it in the private sector, and he would favor direct estimates using Census Bureau data rather than indirect estimates such as Galper's.

Another participant argued that the most glaring inconsistency in the present NIA budget is between the timing basis for the receipt and expenditure sides of the budget, with taxes already partially on an accrual basis and expenditures largely on a delivery basis. He argued that accrual accounting should be used on both sides, and that Galper's paper was thus a step in the right direction. He also noted that defense expenditures are not as invariably timed on a delivery basis even now: under "cost-plus" contracts, expenditures are recorded promptly as a purchase while under "fixed price" or "fixed price incentive" contracts, expenditures are recorded only when delivery actually occurs. When it is considered that defense construction outlays are on an accrual basis, then the lead in the impact of Federal defense expenditures varies both with product mix and type of contract. Finally, expressing a lack of confidence in the accounting system, he indicated a lack of enthusiasm for seeking to measure accrued expenditures through the accounts rather than by statistical estimation. There was further discussion of this question, with some participants favoring hard, accounting data on contract payments and others favoring indirect statistical estimation such as Galper's.

A conceptual issue was then raised about the meaning of accrued expenditures. To at least one participant this concept meant the acquisition (change in ownership) of the good as far as the private sector is concerned, and should mean the same thing for the Federal Government. In reply, it was pointed out that relatively few defense goods were produced for inventory—most are produced to order, so that acquisition accrues as production occurs, not when the goods are actually delivered.

With only a few dissents, a clear preference was expressed by the participants for placing the budget conceptually on an accrual basis, although there seemed to be considerable doubt about whether the Government's accounting system could any time soon record accruals as accurately as it now records cash payments.

LIST OF CONFERENCE PARTICIPANTS

George F. Break, University of California (Berkeley).

E. Cary Brown, Massachusetts Institute of Technology.

Samuel B. Chase, Jr., The Brookings Institution.

Samuel M. Cohn, U.S. Bureau of the Budget.

Gerhard Colm, National Planning Association.

James S. Duesenberry, Council of Economic Advisers.

Gary Fromm, The Brookings Institution.

Harvey Galper, Board of Governors of the Federal Reserve System.

Raymond W. Goldsmith, Council of Economic Advisers.

Richard Goode, International Monetary Fund.

Kermit Gordon, The Brookings Institution.

Edward M. Gramlich, Board of Governors of the Federal Reserve System.

Arnold C. Harberger, University of Chicago.

Walter W. Heller, University of Minnesota.

George Jaszi, U.S. Office of Business Economics.

Michael E. Levy, National Industrial Conference Board.

Wilfred Lewis, Jr., The Brookings Institution.

Carl H. Madden, Chamber of Commerce of the United States.

Robert P. Mayo, Continental Illinois National Bank and Trust Company.

Arthur M. Okun, Council of Economic Advisers.

David J. Ott, Southern Methodist University.

Camille B. Pantuliano, Federal Reserve Bank (New York).

Joseph A. Pechman, The Brookings Institution.

Joseph E. Reeve, U.S. Bureau of the Budget.

Earl R. Rolph, University of California (Berkeley).

William B. Ross, U.S. Department of Housing and Urban Development.

Charles L. Schultze, U.S. Bureau of the Budget.

Carl S. Shoup, Columbia University.

Warren L. Smith, University of Michigan.

Beryl W. Sprinkel, Harris Trust and Savings Bank.

Elmer B. Staats, Comptroller General of the United States.

Herbert Stein, The Brookings Institution (formerly Committee for Economic Development

Paul J. Taubman, University of Pennsylvania.

Stephen Taylor, Board of Governors of the Federal Reserve System.

Charls E. Walker, American Bankers Association.

Murray L. Weidenbaum, Washington University.

Index